# Poverty and Antitheatricality

# Poverty and Antitheatricality

## Form and Formlessness in Latin American Literature, Art, and Theory

STEPHEN BUTTES

**Rutgers University Press**
New Brunswick, Camden, and Newark, New Jersey
London and Oxford

Rutgers University Press is a department of Rutgers, The State University of New Jersey, one of the leading public research universities in the nation. By publishing worldwide, it furthers the University's mission of dedication to excellence in teaching, scholarship, research, and clinical care.

Library of Congress Cataloging-in-Publication Data

Names: Buttes, Stephen, author.
Title: Poverty and antitheatricality : form and formlessness in Latin American literature, art, and theory / Stephen Buttes.
Description: New Brunswick : Rutgers University Press, [2025] | Includes bibliographical references and index.
Identifiers: LCCN 2024046341 | ISBN 9781978844612 (paperback) | ISBN 9781978844629 (hardcover) | ISBN 9781978844636 (epub)
Subjects: LCSH: Arts, Latin American—20th century—Themes, motives. | Poverty—Latin America—History—20th century. | Form (Aesthetics)—History—20th century.
Classification: LCC NX501.5 .B88 2025 | DDC 700/.4526942098—dc23/eng/20250122
LC record available at https://lccn.loc.gov/2024046341

A British Cataloging-in-Publication record for this book is available from the British Library.



∞ The paper used in this publication meets the requirements of the American National Standard for Information Sciences—Permanence of Paper for Printed Library Materials, ANSI Z39.48-1992.

rutgersuniversitypress.org

For my parents, Tony and Connie Buttes

# Contents


Introduction 1

1 Managing to Get By: Lizardi, Cantinflas, and the Problem of Horizontalism 30

2 Icons of the Everyday: Calculating Poverty in Pablo Neruda's *Odas elementales* 69

3 The Afterlife of Mexico, 1968: Posthegemony and Its Antitheatrical Alternatives 89

4 Photography and Borges's Landscapes of Poverty 118

Conclusion 148

Acknowledgments 161

Notes 167

Works Cited 175

Index 185

Poverty and Antitheatricality

# Introduction

This book begins with the premise that poverty is the result of economic exploitation and dispossession.[1] Many people and maybe even most people today would claim to accept, at least in part, this commonsense and possibly banal statement. However, a cursory survey of some of the best known and most widely implemented antipoverty solutions demonstrates that understandings of poverty today generally do not have notions of economic exploitation and dispossession as their starting premise. Indeed, antipoverty programs today often bring into focus a variety of other kinds of factors: cultural factors (such as family structures or specific daily practices that enable poverty to persist or to be overcome), social factors (such as gender or gender identity, race or racial identity, ethnicity, language, ability status, and many other identity-based social factors that are often the organizing focus of antipoverty initiatives), political factors (such as corruption, clientelism, and cronyism), and, increasingly, even psychological and psychobiological factors (such as mindset or the shaping of brain chemistry by environmental factors).[2] In these models, poverty is not an *objective relational aspect* of a historically particular and specific structure of economic organization but instead a subjective and negative social, cultural, political, or even psychobiological *experience* of *any* economic system, an experience that is transhistorical in nature, can appear anywhere, and does appear everywhere in each and every economic system. In this way, poverty is articulated as being "with us always" because it is an unavoidable part of every economic system. This, in turn, makes the amelioration of the negative experiences of an economic system—whether it be capitalist, socialist, or something else—the most any antipoverty initiative could hope to achieve.

When expressed in its simplest formulation, the model (with its many variants) that I critique can generally be summarized as follows: An actual end to poverty can never be achieved because someone somewhere will always experience social relations negatively. Because one group or another will always be pushed to society's margins and experience society negatively, an end to poverty only ever exists as a dream or a fiction. If marginality (the negative experience of having one's needs unseen and unmet) is an inevitable part of *every* system, the ultimate goal of antipoverty initiatives can only ever be to have no one *experience* the exploitation and dispossession they actually live.[3] In other words, the goal would be that this negative experience of existing forms of social organization not *feel like* exploitation and dispossession, which are taken as unavoidable, seminatural experiential phenomena. What this requires is the transformation of the negative experience that poverty is understood to be into the positive experience of the process of equality instead. When this "mindset" conversion takes place (often through poverty amelioration measures that lead individuals to transform collective and structural problems into internalized examinations of individual behaviors and practices), the material structures of exploitation and dispossession that produce the problem of poverty and inequality do not need to be changed and, perhaps worse, can actually be welcomed: the experience of being outside or on the margins of normalized social structures can be utilized as a resource for producing the positive experience of rejecting or reforming those norms in a kind of equality-in-process.

The primary goal of this book is to draw attention to this paradoxical logic in which exploitation can be experienced positively as part of the *process* of equality, which becomes an end in itself. In addition to demonstrating the ways that this widely held experiential view of poverty has manifested throughout the twentieth century in Latin America, the book explains the reasons why this conceptualization of poverty is mistaken. It examines its effects in Latin America and, ultimately, posits alternatives to the experiential understanding of poverty. Thus, throughout this study, the target of my critique and the primary focus of my analysis is the mistaken conviction that poverty is, at its core, an experience of being outside or on the margins of normalized social structures, which is to say, the mistaken conviction that poverty can be understood as an experience of what I call formlessness. I use this formulation—"formlessness" or "poverty as an experience of formlessness"—to signal the conceptual thread that runs through the political and economic sequences I study throughout this book. These sequences—Mexico's Partido Revolucionario Institucional (PRI) and its postrevolutionary conceptualization of Mexican identity (Mexicanism, *la mexicanidad*), Argentina's experience with Peronism, Chile's experience of a coalitional left built from various parties and movements—are unique in their details and material circumstances.[4] But as we will see, the conceptualization of poverty dominant in each these contexts was inflected with a commitment to formlessness, which is synonymous with a commitment to the experiential account of poverty that is my object of critique.[5]

This account of poverty—the experience of formlessness—can generally be described as having two key characteristics. First, it sets aside objective accounts of the global economic system and the unequal social relations it organizes. It establishes poverty as a subjectively experienced phenomenon characterized by the negative encounters associated with having no part in existing social, cultural, or political orders. In other words, poverty is understood as the experience of having no pathway (or having no social form) that could make one's needs, desires, values, or claims understandable to others living in the same society. Second, that subjective and negative experience of having no part in the existing social distribution—that is, formlessness—is understood to operate as a resource. Formlessness can function as a way of making visible needed correctives to the ways of being, seeing, doing, and knowing that structure existing unequal ways of organizing society. Alternatively, formlessness can also serve to demonstrate that each and every form of social organization contains a group who inevitably experiences or will experience the subjective and negative effects of having no part in existing forms of social order and organization: someone is always excluded, someone always marginal. In conceiving of poverty as first and foremost the experience of not being seen or not being heard or being heard only as noise, the problem that comes into view is not the concrete political, economic, and social forms of material exploitation and dispossession that transcend any individual experience of poverty. Instead, poverty, problematically, comes to be understood as a localized problem that contains its own solution: the negative experience emerges as an episode that is compatible with ever-evolving processes that produce equality.

Now, it is important to say that poverty, of course, *is* experienced: unwanted hunger feels like something; it feels like something to have a bill coming due with not enough money in your pocket to pay it; it feels like something when it seems like you'll never get ahead no matter how hard you work.[6] But when poverty is reduced to those feelings—the experience of not having enough and the experience of no one seeing or caring that you do not have enough—the focus shifts away from the need for a structural change in the economic system. In other words, in that model, it doesn't matter *why* someone doesn't have enough money, doesn't have enough stability from working, or doesn't have enough to eat. What matters is that, from the margins, they produce experiences that reorder and disrupt, however episodically or temporarily, the existing social order, no matter its order.

This is because every social order is assumed to inevitably contain some form of "poverty," which is understood to be a transhistorical negative subjective experience inherent to all economic systems (e.g., hunger for this group here, unemployment or lack of land ownership for that group there, etc.). Thus, poverty is conceived as an unavoidable, seminatural phenomenon of subjective human experience. As a result, the goal is transformed from eliminating poverty into recognizing the poor's ability to make available new and multiple experiences of equality through their disruption of the existing system. The problem, however, is that this model ultimately presumes and *requires* that *poverty remain a continually existing phenomenon*. This, ultimately, is the paradox of understanding poverty as an experience of formlessness: poverty must always exist—it must be understood as an inherent, seminatural part of economic systems—so as to produce the necessary conditions for the negative experiences of those systems to be transformed into the positive experience of equality-in-process. This position, of course, misses the point that poverty is *not* a natural, unavoidable phenomenon but instead a social relation created by human systems and behaviors: it is an objective relational aspect of a historically particular and specific structure of economic organization.[7]

There are both logical and historical reasons that explain the rise to dominance of understandings of poverty as an experience of formlessness. While those reasons are explained and elaborated in the pages that follow, it is important to note that this book is not only interested in how this paradoxical model emerged and established itself in practice but also committed to describing and analyzing alternative, competing understandings of poverty. This book argues that the clearest path to recognizing the problems embedded in the experiential understanding of poverty as well as to seeing alternatives to that understanding is not by interrogating it head-on but instead by approaching it indirectly through an analysis of art and literature.

At first glance, this may not seem like an obvious approach. One reason is that art, by design, does not possess the tools of sociology, economics, and political science to provide datasets useful for making policy. Another reason is that this kind of claim may appear to falsely aggrandize artistic creation as if it provides a "truer truth" than other modes of knowing the world. This book does not seek to diminish the knowledge made available by the social sciences nor to place art in a privileged position. Instead, the claim is more practical. The problem this book is interrogating is the difference between understanding poverty as an objective relational aspect of a specific structure of economic organization—poverty as a problem of concrete, historical *forms* of social organization that are, of course, experienced—and understanding poverty as first and foremost an unavoidable, seminatural phenomenon of subjective human experience: poverty as the experience of *formlessness*. The relevant categories for analyzing the problem of poverty in twentieth-century Latin America—form and formlessness—dovetail with the fact that form and formlessness are also central categories in the history of twentieth-century art and literature. The hinge on which the relationship between poverty and art hangs, then, is the paired terms form-formlessness.

That relationship functions through the development of, on the one hand, projects for modernity—which included many antipoverty projects that achieved or failed to achieve making the nation and its inhabitants identical to the idealized promise of certain economic or political or social models of organization—and, on the other hand, projects for modernism, which were premised on achieving or failing to achieve certain values within an artwork that could make it "hold" as an artwork within a given historical sequence.[8] One of the central arguments of this book, then, is that by understanding debates about what art is and how to approach it, we can also reveal underexamined debates about what poverty is and how to approach it. Or to put this same point differently, understanding debates about what kind of problem art is can provide a pathway for understanding what kind of problem poverty is. To understand just why this kind of analysis is not only possible but, I am arguing, necessary, it is important to examine first the historical circumstances that gave rise to the problematic conceptualization of poverty I aim to critique.

## Modernity: From Formlessness to Form

The simplest way to explain the rise to dominance of the conceptual linking of poverty and formlessness is to begin by highlighting Latin America's role in the twentieth century as a kind of regional laboratory for antipoverty initiatives from across the ideological spectrum. On the capitalist side, the region saw everything from the legacy of the hacienda's paternalistic relations (expressed in monopoly capitalism's philanthropy) to programs seeking to address the so-called culture of poverty emerging in growing cities to the neoliberal reforms of the 1980s and 1990s.[9] On the left, strategies ranged from armed revolutionary struggle to worker, peasant, and indigenous collectivist activity to parties implementing socialist policies. Despite the stark ideological differences between the competing models of modernity (capitalism and socialism) that played a significant role in twentieth-century Latin America, both are operationalized through the appeal to predetermined formulas for social intelligibility. In other words, poverty was understood as a problem to be solved by realizing and putting into practice the particular modes of social intelligibility that enabled one to be seen and heard within those systems, the particular "structures of feeling" that underscored them, and so on.[10]

To the extent that establishing and maintaining specific forms of social structures and social practices was the central goal of modernization, the solution to poverty was understood as having the poor more fully and more closely hew to the norms, conventions, and commonsense behavioral patterns associated with one model of modernity or the other. In this way, the primary problem modernization set out to solve, whether in its capitalist or socialist iteration, would be the problem of formlessness. Those whose behaviors and experiences fall outside the forms that produce and sustain modern sociality (i.e., those who are "formless") were understood as needing interventions that would reshape them in the model of the generally accepted norms and conventions that constituted modern societies. This model of poverty reduction or elimination would be summarized as something like: the formless must be formed.

As Ericka Beckman shows in her study of the literature and cultural production of Latin America's "Export Age" (roughly 1870–1930), the forms of sociality that developed and organized Latin American republics (and therefore also their understandings of poverty) largely emerged from the ideas held by an educated ruling class (the lettered elite, or *los letrados*) that had "reached consensus regarding the desirability of 'progress' and 'civilization' by way of economic liberalization" (ix), which is to say, by way of the commonsense understandings of nineteenth-century capitalism. This largely took shape through the implementation of economic development projects rooted in ideas like the "generalized acceptance of Ricardian [i.e., comparative] advantage" (xxiii) or the supposed "'universal law' . . . that lasting prosperity can be created only through . . . free exchange [of goods in the market]" or free trade (12–13). As Beckman shows, elites pursued these ideas despite evidence—such as "the frequent disasters resulting from market integration and liberalization" (x)—that suggested that poverty-ending prosperity in a "perfect future . . . [created by] the market" (7) could not be made a reality.

Nevertheless, these elites were able "to believe . . . that integration into" and prosperity within "the world order of capital . . . [was] not only desirable, but inevitable" (ix) because, Beckman argues, they developed what she calls "capital fictions": the convergence of "ideology and imagination in governing economic life" (xi) through the melding of "political economy, civic rhetoric, and aesthetics" (6–7). These "capital fictions," which emerged in both literary works and other cultural forms, operated as a kind of "ideological therapy" (xxv) during historical sequences in which there was the expansion, acceleration, and exaggeration of acts of dispossession. They enabled the effects of those historical sequences to be "domesticated" (xxv) and converted from a negative experience of the "impoverished [realities] of the present" (19) that must "*for now* . . . [be accepted as] limitations" (13) into a positive experience of the operation of the "universal laws" of capitalist economic development with its "desirable and inevitable" outcomes of a world made free of poverty through the modernity of markets and trade, even in the face of crisis.

While capitalist writers, artists, and political and business leaders developed numerous strategies for "ideological therapy" that would elide the "conditions under which commodity production for the global market would take place" (22), the left developed its own alternative model of modernity, which became increasingly formalized after the founding of the Comintern in 1919. The state and the working-class party's visions for economic prosperity—the party's promised "great and glorious future" (Clark 421)—were not persistently or uninterruptedly realized, and as such its projects for modernity also required strategies for managing crisis. This was represented, perhaps most famously, in the rise of socialist realism, which is sometimes called Zhdanovism due to its association with the Soviet politician Andrei Zhdanov in the 1930s and 1940s. While "capital fictions" sought to install the market as the "desirable and inevitable" form of equality and freedom, socialist realism's "didactic aim" was to instruct "the masses" with "people's heroes inspired and guided by the Communist party" (Boterbloem 116). Katerina Clark explains that the socialist realist writer was viewed as an "engineer of human souls" (Stalin's term) and came to be "expected to adhere to a particular code of construction" that was "both aesthetically and thematically . . . conservative and even somewhat puritanical" (420): a model hero, through loyalty to the party and through the careful tutelage of a party elder who serves as a "moral/political mentor" (426), is able to acquire the necessary "public values" (426) to overcome obstacles to modernization, ranging from the "natural world" (427) to "enemies (national or class) . . . [in] the hero's bureaucratic administration" (427). While there were various experiments with socialist realism in Mexico, Chile, and other Latin American countries, its most famous practitioner was Brazilian novelist Jorge Amado, who abandoned it as an aesthetic practice after Khrushchev's famous 1956 repudiation of Stalin, which produced a kind of global crisis within models of socialist modernity and forced a reckoning with that modernity's underlying premises.[11]

I will return to the case of Amado in a moment, but what is important to note first is that both capitalist and socialist modernities required the work of writers and artists in order to develop the necessary "ideological therapy" that could transform impoverishment from an objective, relational and, in fact, conflictual and constituent component of historically particular structures of economic organization into, more simply, a negative experience of those systems, an experience that was based in the deviation from the proper forms of social relations necessary to bring about the desired form of modernity. While claims for insufficient freedom in the market and claims of bureaucratic corruption or "antirevolutionary" disloyalty to the party prompted the creation of works that, without a doubt, differed from each other and were based on starkly different premises, they both locate the origin of poverty in a kind of nonnormativity: the deviation from the norms and conventions thought necessary to bring about the realization of modernity. What we see in works of art that remediate the underlying convictions of a capitalist or socialist modernity, then, is both the articulation of what poverty is and the elaboration of its solutions. These works of art imagine what shape formlessness must take so that the material world (the "impoverished present") is consonant with the "laws" of capitalist prosperity or the "values" of socialist plenty. That imagination is premised on the notion that there are desirable, necessary, and inevitable norms and conventions that organize both social life and literary/artistic production. The challenge, of course, emerges when there is skepticism regarding the notion of desirable or necessary or inevitable norms and conventions. Or to put the point a little differently, a significant challenge emerges when, within a specific historical sequence, no amount of "ideological therapy" can plausibly restore "free enterprise" or "party loyalty" to the position of *necessary* norms or conventions.

As Neil Larsen explains, the modernist novel in Latin America (better known as the Boom novel) is best understood as a response to precisely such a crisis.

In the 1940s and 1950s, when politicians and artists alike became convinced that neither the wholesale adoption of the forms (the norms and conventions) that structured the operation of U.S. capitalist imperialism nor the hewing to the orthodoxies and party discipline of the Soviet model would provide stable, plausible, or implementable norms and conventions for the region, the desire for a "third position" emerged. While in the political realm this took shape in various forms of populism, such as Juan Domingo Perón's Justicialist political movement in Argentina, Larsen argues that the modernist novel in Latin America is also a response to the crisis of norms and conventions that produced populism (i.e., a response to the absence of *necessary* norms and conventions). Key in his analysis is Jorge Amado's modernist novel *Gabriela, cravo e canela* (1958), which, in the wake of the post-1956 crisis in international socialism, breaks with Amado's previous socialist realist literary production. As Larsen explains, *Gabriela* was almost instantly accepted "by the Brazilian bourgeois establishment" (*Reading North by South* 76) as well as by critics and artists from across the ideological spectrum as "the expression of a Latin American *essence*" (78).

The notion that the midcentury modernist novel was the expression of Latin American cultural "essence" was part and parcel of "mythical" accounts of the Boom, which interpreted those novels as giving voice to the deeply embedded cultural realities of hybridity, *mestizaje*, and transculturation, phenomena that were then packaged in the promotion of these novels as "magical realist" or "neo-baroque" fictions. As Larsen notes, interpretations focused on cultural essence enabled critics to analyze the Boom as a capitalist phenomenon—such as Ángel Rama's thesis that the Boom novel operated as a literary commodity filling preexisting market demand on the part of an upwardly mobile "reading public" in urbanizing and modernizing Latin American societies—and as a socialist phenomenon—such as arguments by Jaime Mejía-Duque and Gerald Martin that read the Boom as the literary expression of a "new political consciousness generated in Latin America by the Cuban Revolution" (*Reading North by South* 60) and the "anti-imperialist and socialist objectives of peasants and workers" (72). But as Larsen points out, these analyses remain insufficient given that they do not account for what Tulio Halperín Donghi argues is the Boom authors' need to take as given "the neocolonial [intelligentsia's] . . . deep-seated pessimism regarding the capacity of the masses to overcome their purportedly pathological 'backwardness' and usher Latin America onto the threshold of modern civilization" (72). In other words, if Boom novels are concerned with producing "utopias of form and language" (72), those utopias must premise themselves on rejecting the imposition of existing ("imperialist") social forms on the unavoidable, seminatural cultural phenomena—the hybrid cultural "essence" of the region or nation—from which Latin American modernity should be constructed.

What that rejection also entailed was accepting the formulation of Latin America's central social problem as the experience of formlessness, but in a newly inverted way. Whereas "capital fictions" and socialist realism sought to impose orthodox economic and social forms (i.e., "market orthodoxy" or "party orthodoxy") as solutions to poverty, the Boom's "utopias of form and language" (72) assigned to itself the task of exploring a Latin American "essence," thus turning to the poor's nonnormative experience of formlessness—that is, their being outside or on the margins of imperialist forms of modernity—as a readily available resource for that project. Poverty was reconceptualized and transformed into a dynamic of cultural essence. Poverty was a problem that could be addressed not by imposing predetermined, "imported" forms on the formless but instead by turning to the poor and their lifeways as the essential cultural resource for producing modernity itself (i.e., a "third position"). No longer a negative experience that must be endured "for the time being" as part of the positive experience of inevitably becoming modern, poverty—as an experience of formlessness or nonnormativity repackaged as "cultural essence"—came to be understood as productive of its own alternative modernities emergent from local cultural particularities.

In this framework, there emerges a commitment to formlessness within the crisis of form. Rather than a problem to be solved, poverty is transformed into the necessary resource for the production of a needed nonnormativity (or "cultural essence") that, in its multiplicity, could operate in place of the *absent, necessary* norms and conventions that would produce modernity. For this reason, Larsen argues, the "'boom' modernist is an anti-*yanqui* nationalist before he or she is an anticommunist" (77), and as such, the Boom's modernist novel can "just as easily support a Perón or an Omar Torrijos as it does a Fidel" (77).[12] In this way, the poor emerge as the producers of at least two paths to modernity: (1) the creators of new, culturally specific norms and conventions (alternative modernities); or (2) the producers of a rejection of all norms and conventions in favor of the experience of formlessness or nonnormativity itself. In the next section, I examine each of these in turn.

## The "Crisis in Representation" and the "Balcony Effect"

On their face, these two pathways seem to be in opposition to each other. In the first variant, the void left by the absence of evident and necessary norms and conventions that would promise a lasting solution to the problem of poverty is filled by norms and conventions derived from the lifeways and cultural practices of those who are marginalized, unseen, or unheard (i.e., those who are poor). The first variant, in other words, is identified with the search for norms that are *culturally* appropriate for "us," which cannot be discovered in "foreign" models of modernity like capitalism and socialism.[13] In the second variant, the challenge presented by the crisis of form is understood not as how to fill the void left by the absence of necessary social norms but instead as how to recognize that the effort to establish *any* norm (be it foreign, national, regional, ideological, or something else) necessarily entails creating experiences of feeling marginalized, unseen, or unheard. The second variant, in other words, sees the creation of poverty as resulting from all efforts to establish norms (e.g., "laws," "public values"), be they aspirationally egalitarian or not.

Obviously, there are clear disagreements between these two pathways. It can perhaps go without saying that arguments to reject *all* norms regardless of their origin or ideological content are decidedly at odds with arguments to reject U.S., European, and Soviet norms in favor of the norms created by Latin American workers, peasants, and shantytown dwellers or by indigenous, Afro-descendant, and Mestizo groups. However, in spite of these disagreements, these two pathways are, nevertheless, underscored by a shared central premise: poverty is, at its core, an experience of formlessness, an experience of *feeling* unseen and unheard. In this way, these two seemingly opposed options for responding to a sequence of crisis or transition are placed into inextricable relation with each other and, in key ways, are variants of each other. To see just how this is so, the crisis of form—the reasons why "capital fictions" and socialist realism do not (or no longer, or never did) "work" in Latin America—needs to be understood. For these purposes, it is helpful to turn to Argentina's worker- and poverty-focused experience with the political, cultural, and economic phenomenon of Justicialism (or Peronism, as it is commonly called).[14]

Juan Domingo Peron's political movement—Justicialism—is, perhaps, Latin America's most famous alternative modernity. As Luis Alberto Romero notes, Justicialism took shape as something like a strategy of survival in the context of the emerging post–World War II political and economic order. On the one hand, the political and economic power of the United States severely limited Argentina's ability to return to a nineteenth-century commodity export model. The Soviet Union, on the other hand, did not provide an attractive model for Perón. Not only would a Soviet model involve, Romero notes, "an enormous effort to finance, requiring restrictions on consumption and a 'sacrificed generation'" (106), that strategy likely would have produced high levels of unemployment and its related "social consequences" (108). These would have included social unrest, state violence, and a destabilization of his own hold on power. In seeing neither model as providing stable, plausible, or implementable norms and conventions for Argentina, Perón opts instead for the famous "third position" (104) in which, as Perón would put it in *La fuerza es el derecho de las bestias* (1956), Justicialism is understood as "neither one nor the other" (15).[15] In other words, Perón conceives of Justicialism as neither a capitalist nor a socialist modernity but instead as a modernity that lives with and alongside them (i.e., is a viable alternative for Argentina). Unlike capitalism's reliance on the market and its "universal laws" or socialism's appeal to the party with its "public values" (though both of these elements play significant roles in Justicialism), what sustains this alternative (Justicialist) modernity is the production of a *feeling*: the sense that things are moving in a just or more egalitarian direction.

As Perón states in "The Twenty Truths of Justicialism," his model is one in which no one "[feels] more than what he is nor less than what he should be"

(Perón 14). This feeling, Perón explains, is what divides Justicialism from capitalism: "When a Justicialist begins to feel more than what he is, he begins to transform into an oligarch" (14).[16] One becomes an oligarch not when one has more money; not when one controls industry, land, or labor (i.e., the means and relations of production); and not when one advocates particular political positions or maintains undue influence on the state. Instead, it is when one feels oneself to be or sees oneself as better than or superior to others. In a Justicialist modernity, everyone should see themselves or feel themselves to be equal even if actual equality has not (yet) been achieved (or, one might say, even if there actually is an oligarchy). Later in *La fuerza*, Perón likewise gives his own analysis of the failure of a socialist modernity in Argentina, explaining that it was as a product of working-class experiences of "deception" and "betrayal" (44) at the hands of socialist parties and union leaders, who, under the "gravitational pull of [the] politics" of "bourgeois managers" (44), ultimately "march[ed] through the streets [against the Justicialist poor and working class], locking arms with the crudest representatives of the conservative oligarchy" (17).

In Perón's account, socialism produces experiences of "deception" that leave workers and the poor feeling excluded and "betrayed" while capitalism produces in workers and the poor the feeling of being "less than." Those feelings and experiences of life lived on the margins of both capitalist and socialist forms of social life—the experiences of formlessness—are precisely what sustains the Justicialist "third position." The "universal laws" of the market and the "public values" of the party sustained the first two modernities, but it is the experiences of formlessness (poverty)—derived from the ever-present threat of the capitalist and socialist oligarchy's actions—that sustain the Peronist alternative. And while social relations of the first two modernities come into being via the form-giving "invisible hand" (in capitalism) or "engineers of human souls" (in socialism), Peronist social relations emerge through its "two arms[:] social justice and social assistance. With them, we embrace the People with justice and love" (14). The operation of this phenomenon is perhaps best illustrated by the familiar photographs and newsreels of Juan Domingo Perón and his iconic wife, Evita, addressing masses of workers and the poor from a stage or a balcony in the 1940s and 1950s (figures I.1, I.2).

Perón and Evita's outstretched, embracing arms convene with their words, their speeches, and their rituals all who have experienced socialist "betrayal" and capitalist humiliation. The words uttered from the balcony produce effects of identification, which is to say, the joyous experience of feeling seen or being heard. Those effects, in turn, direct the words of the leader who seeks to extend the experience. The Peróns' words elicit joyous response, which, in turn, elicits more words from the Peróns. Justicialism "works," then, because the "people"—those who have experienced formlessness, the poor—provide the material that drives the extension of the Justicialist project (the experience of Perón's "embrace") while the leader, as Perón says, "is elected to create the happiness of his People and to bring about the greatness of the Nation" (4) as he forms, shapes, and affects

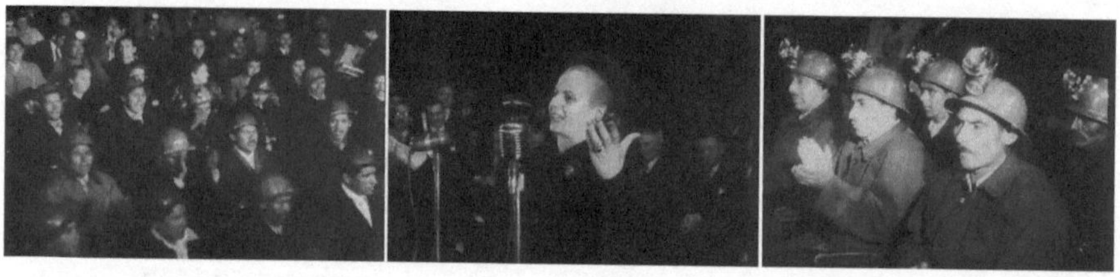

FIGURE I.1 Still sequence from *Noticiario panamericano*, no. 562 (dir. Adolfo Rossi, 1951–1952). This sequence is from a presidential event celebrating mine workers in the elegant Teatro Colón in 1952 (described as the first of its kind in the history of the country in the newsreel narration).

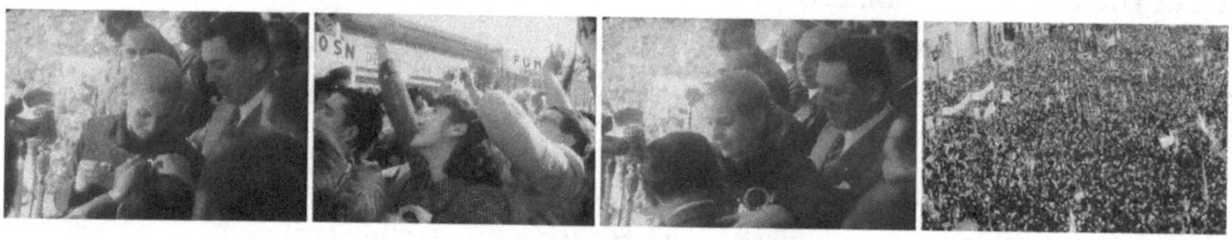

FIGURE I.2 Still sequence from *Noticiario panamericano*, no. 562 (dir. Adolfo Rossi, 1951–1952). This sequence is from the October 17, 1951 (Day of Peronist Loyalty) celebrations, where Eva Perón was honored with the Gran Medalla de Lealtad Peronista (Highest Medal of Peronist Loyalty).

those values and desires through his words and actions. These interactions congeal into the serially produced images of the Peróns addressing the masses at official ceremonies and Justicialist demonstrations.

One way of understanding Justicialist modernity, then, is as the persistent making and remaking of spaces in which no one "[feels] more than what he is nor less than what he should be" (Perón 17). That making and remaking operates primarily through the effects of language. For example, in figure I.1, we can see Evita's outstretched arms as she delivers from the stage a speech celebrating mine workers, whom we, in turn, see seated in their work clothes and protective helmets. They are not, however, listening from a far-off mine but instead seated as invited guests of Perón in the upholstered seats of the elegant Teatro Colón opera house. Similarly, we can see in figure I.2 the joyful, cheering masses at an annual demonstration of Peronist loyalty. Egalitarian feeling flows from the balcony, where the Peróns speak, to the streets and plazas of Buenos Aires, where those who have experienced feelings of being marginalized, unseen, or unheard are gathered to hear those words and have those experiences transformed.[17] Justicialist demonstrations replace "capital fictions" and the "ideological therapies" of socialist realism with the effect of the Peróns' words and actions, which is to say, the experience of the Peronist "embrace": the two outstretched arms that invite "joyous" participation as a member of the Peronist "mass" or "collective" and that positively reshape and unify the heterogeneous, negative experiences of poverty (e.g., feelings of "betrayal," abandonment, and being "less than").

That unity, however, is always temporary as the whole is persistently and repeatedly taken apart, reconstructed, and remade with each new audience, each new situation, and each new configuration of heterogeneous experiences and elements. As Ernesto Laclau explains it, the words that Perón and Evita utter and the actions they carry out (such as the outstretched arms) operate as prime examples of what he calls "empty signifiers" (*On Populist Reason* 105). These are possibly meaningful words, statements, or gestures that maintain "weak links to particular" or specific meanings or programs of action. Those "weak links"—the openness or ambiguity of those words and gestures—"[give] symbolic unity to all . . . disparate struggles" (216), thus enabling "the most contradictory contents [to] be assembled [as a whole], as long as the subordination of them all to [an] empty signifier [such as "Peronist" is maintained]" (217).

When understood as a modernity built from transforming negative experiences of life lived on the margins (formlessness) into the positive and joyous experiences of the Peronist "embrace" of "justice and love," which makes it *feel like* society is moving in the direction of an egalitarian modernity, Justicialism's contrast with capitalist and socialist modernities is clear. While the latter are premised on understanding poverty as a kind of nonnormativity or deviation from the norms and conventions thought necessary to bring about the realization of modernity, the former understands the nonnormativity or deviation from capitalist and socialist norms and conventions as productive of modernity itself. The feelings produced by the experience of formlessness are harnessed and operate as the necessary resource for the making, unmaking, and remaking of spaces for egalitarian feeling. What becomes clear in Laclau's description of Perón and Evita's words and gestures as "empty signifiers" is that Peronism approached material questions—such as the optimal structures for producing and circulating of goods, the optimal structure for managing social and political relations, the optimal model for understanding of poverty—as if they were only or merely products of "capital *fictions*" or the "*ideological* therapy" of the all-knowing party and its delegates. Indeed, what Laclau sees in Peronism is a generalizable political procedure or strategy that sustains all sociopolitical modes of organization.

The name for that generalizable procedure—the name for the process by which formlessness can move to form—is "articulation," a term Laclau develops in his work with Chantal Mouffe. This term remains an essential concept in cultural studies today.[18] For Laclau and Mouffe, generalized sociopolitical power (generally called "hegemony") is created through processes of language that engage in a "constant joining [articulation], severing [disarticulation], and rejoining [rearticulation]" (Larsen, *Modernism* xxix) of groups of people.[19] For example, in Justicialism, the antagonistic groupings created in Perón's speeches and demonstrations were Justicialists (synonymous with workers) and oligarchs, or, more simply "Pueblo" (the People) and "Anti-Pueblo" (the Anti-People). In this model, Justicialism comes to power by successfully "severing" existing groupings: workers are *dis*articulated from their association with socialist parties and "corrupted" labor unions; oligarchs are *dis*articulated from their exclusive association with the halls of governmental and cultural power. Then, those reconfigured categories enable a "rejoining" in a new articulation of power: workers, the poor, and their leader (i.e., Pueblo, Peronists) are associated with governmental and cultural power, while oligarchs along with socialists, communists, and corrupted union officials, now understood as working to "deceive" and subordinate the poor (i.e., Anti-Pueblo, anti-Peronists), are relegated to the margins. This model of "articulation" is generally understood as the creation of "hegemony": the successful joining together of social elements into a ruling order. This is the same process for creating a "counterhegemony": the effort to sever existing groups by transforming their elements through language and rejoining them into new groupings. And it is also the key procedure within the first path to an alternative modernity built from a commitment to utilizing the feelings and mindsets of the poor: the experience of formlessness as the key resource for *de*articulating a present order that no longer "works" (or never did) and *re*articulating a new, culturally appropriate order.[20] In this model, Justicialists—for whom there is "only one class of men: those who work" (Perón 14)—create new, culturally specific norms and conventions that are neither capitalist nor socialist but instead a viable alternative modernity.

In this sense, it is easy to see the connection between Laclau and Mouffe's model of "articulation" and accounts of the modernism developed in the Latin American Boom novel, which, as noted, has been understood as primarily concerned with producing "utopias of form and language" (Larsen, *Reading* 72). The Boom novel's rejection of existing ("imperialist") social forms entails the embrace of the option to utilize language, gestures, and practices from the margins of Latin American societies to construct an alternative Latin American modernity in ways that parallel the words and gestures of Perón and Evita. Thus, Larsen's assertion that the modernist Boom novel can "just as easily support a Perón or an Omar Torrijos as it does a Fidel" (Larsen, *Reading* 77) holds because the "mythical" understanding of the Boom—that is, the idea that those authors created works that disrupted colonial and imperial models of language and narrative so that buried or marginalized or subjugated regional and national identities (i.e., "cultural essence") could be expressed—shares a fundamental premise with Laclau and Mouffe's model of "articulation": material elements (e.g., structures for producing and circulating of goods, social and political structures) are treated as if they were *only* questions of language, which is understood as the mechanism by which subjugation, marginalization, and domination take place. Because power operates through language's ability to "join, sever and rejoin," both the Boom novel and a speech by Evita from the stage or the balcony have the possibility of creating more egalitarian forms of life through *re*articulation.

However, as Larsen makes clear in *Modernism and Hegemony*, the influential assertions that sustain Laclau and Mouffe's arguments are based on faulty premises. "Elements" such as "classes, means and relations of production, the state, and so forth" (xxix), he explains, are not "*constructed* through a calculated manipulation" (xxx, my emphasis) exercised through the wily opportunism of a talented *caudillo*, nor are they simply localized cultural phenomena within the intellectual field of a provincialized bourgeoisie nor, for that matter, that of the activists and apparatchiks of left-wing parties. Instead, those material elements are "objectively *given*" (xxix): for example, regardless of language or social groupings, one way of producing an item requires X number of labor hours while that production process with a new piece of technology requires *less than* X number of labor hours. This enables us to see that the transformation of material elements like the means and relations of production emerges from the effects of the interactions between those elements, which are equally objective (e.g., a transformation marked by the effects of technological innovation can lead to an "objectively given" transformation in the relations of production, such as modified managerial practices, the sidelining of workers, worker resistance, etc., all of which do not have their origin in language).

This does not mean, however, that words and gestures do not have an effect on those elements. Instead, Larsen draws attention to a fissure that opens up between the "objectively given" material elements of a society and the words and gestures thought to "articulate" or create them through the processes of language. To be clear, the fissure Larsen identifies is *not* the "permanent chasm between . . . *acts* [the words and gestures that function as 'empty signifiers'] . . . and the *contents* of those [acts]" (Laclau, *Populist* 216), which Laclau has identified as the key operational mechanism that sustains the "empty signifier" in the "articulation" model. Laclau's "permanent chasm" is internal to the word or "signifier." The fissure Larsen identifies is more in line with the phenomenon we saw Beckman describe above: Latin American elites pursued "market integration and liberalization" (x) despite evidence that suggested these narratives about how the economy operates do not "work" (e.g., "frequent [economic] disasters") (x). As Larsen explains, the fissure that requires our attention is *not* the supposed "permanent chasm" between "signifier" (word) and "signified" (multiple potential but always unsettled meanings). Instead, that fissure is the one that exists between the deeply held values, strategies, and practices of actually existing classes (e.g., "lasting prosperity can be created only through . . . free [trade]" or defeating "national or class [enemies] . . . [in the] bureaucratic administration" is the key to prosperity) and the evolving material realities of modernizing systems that are the effects of those practices and show that they do not (or no longer or never did) "work."

That fissure manifests as a crisis internal to classes as they are actually constituted. The strategies that enabled the ruling class to consolidate its power (e.g., "market integration and liberalization" or party loyalty) are no longer what is needed to continue the process of consolidating their power. Or, to put this more simply, there is a fissure that opens up between *what the ruling classes want to do*—that is, continue living with the same social structure and cultural practices that produced and have sustained their political and economic power—and *what they must do* (if they are to remain ruling classes): that is, modify their cultural practices and social structures in response to the material changes to the production and circulation of goods in a modernizing economy.

As Larsen notes, the new, necessary norms and conventions of the emergent ruling order are not at all obvious: they appear "to take on the attributes of a superordinate social agency with no fixed political or cultural subjectivity" (xxiv). In a sequence such as this, material social relations on an abstract, global scale are able to "break free from certain specific political—and in this sense, representational—relations and structures" that were the condition of their emergence and operation (xxiv). As a result, the ruling classes cannot represent to themselves what would secure their hold on power as the world changes around them in response to their own actions and activities. This marks what Larsen calls a "crisis in representation" (xxiv). The ruling classes do not claim (and perhaps even reject) the cultural practices and the social structures emerging from the materially changed and modernizing economy resulting from their own practices. Indeed, because those new social norms and conventions appear to "break free" from any connection to social structures as they actually exist (despite being the direct consequence of them), those new social norms seem belong to no one.

In a sequence structured by a "crisis in representation," it becomes possible for alternatives like Justicialism, with its proposal for new, nationally specific norms and conventions, to emerge. And it can seem plausible that such a scenario is precisely a question of language: how to make the new and necessary norms and conventions intelligible and logical for existing or emergent social groupings (i.e., how to "articulate" a new hegemony amid the crisis). However, Larsen's identification of the *material* (non-language-based) nature of the "crisis in representation" makes clear that Laclau and Mouffe's formulations are on shaky ground. If we accept that everything is simply the product of manipulated or managed language (i.e., the language of power already creates or "articulates" all social groupings and their ways of understanding the world), then how is it possible to explain changes to the system?

In formulating a version of this question as a way of critiquing Laclau and Mouffe, Larsen explains that the answer would have to be that systemic changes take place through a kind a "radical subjectivism" (xxx). What this means in practical terms is that the breakdown of something like "capital fictions" or the "ideological therapies" of socialism occurs because those systems were not total or complete. There was some social element that was "not-yet-fully-articulated": some person or social grouping was not fully graspable within the forms of language that created the society in crisis. That experience of being "not-yet-fully-articulated," which means having no language to give expression to your experience of the world, is what I am calling the experience of formlessness.[21] And it is also, I am arguing, coterminous with the conceptualization of poverty as it has operated in the development of twentieth-century modernities in Latin America.

For Laclau and Mouffe, all systems of social organization (egalitarian and inegalitarian alike) exist only as they are "articulated" by the processes of language. Because systems of language always and inevitably contain "not-yet-fully-articulated" social elements, the experience of formlessness is an unavoidable part of modern societies.[22] In this way, the inevitability of language systems containing "not-yet-fully-articulated" social elements—those who experience formlessness, the poor—finds parallels with notions that poverty is an unavoidable, seminatural phenomenon of subjective human experience. What the theory of "articulation" does, then, is transform that social element—the experience of formlessness, poverty—into a kind of safety valve against the language of power. The built-in nonnormativity of the poor is the necessary resource for the process of constructing, deconstructing, and reconstructing "society" (xxx). This is the case for both Laclau and Mouffe's model *and* the Justicialist model.

That these models structure their politics and social critique around the operation of language and its effects is what make them one of the primary targets of Jon Beasley-Murray's analysis in *Posthegemony*. Unlike Laclau and Mouffe or the cultural studies scholars he critiques in his book, Beasley-Murray does not see political promise in models built on the open-ended experience of ambiguously meaningful forms (e.g., the words and gestures of Evita and Perón on the stage or balcony; the widely circulated mass media recordings and images of those words and gestures). Indeed, this is evident in his book's memorably succinct refrain, which formulates his central argument regarding the limits to any model that asserts a central social or political role for language and its norms and conventions: "Something always escapes!" (xxi).

Beasley-Murray's point here is largely the same one Larsen derives from the logic of Laclau and Mouffe's arguments: systems of language always have elements that are "not-yet-fully-articulated"; "something always escapes" any attempt to name it or account for it in language. While the lesson Laclau and Mouffe draw from this phenomenon is that power lies in the ability of those who are marginal—those who experience formlessness, those who cannot make their needs seen or heard through available forms of language, the poor—to disrupt and *re*articulate the language of power, the lesson Beasley-Murray draws is that the power was always with the formless: no language, no norms and conventions, no forms necessary. Beasley-Murray's proposal is to move away from a focus on always insufficient forms to a concern with formlessness itself: the body-based *experience* that is poverty. In other words, where Laclau and Mouffe see language as the mechanism by which subjugation, marginalization, and domination take place and see articulation of a new, more egalitarian hegemony as the orientation of the political, Beasley-Murray sees affect as the primary social mechanism.[23]

Affect "indicates the power of a body (individual or collective) to affect or be affected by other bodies" (x–xi). It is, more simply, "our power of acting" (127). For Beasley-Murray, that power does not have its origin in language or the conscious mind but instead always comes before language and consciousness as the near-automatic psychobiological reaction to other bodies. "When our power of . . . affecting and being affected by others increases, we feel joy," Beasley-Murray explains, and "when it decreases, we feel sadness" (127–128). That power is always in a state of "constant flux. . . . If I am well-nourished, for instance, I may have greater power to affect other bodies than otherwise" (127). Above all, affect in this model is constituted by "the constant interactions *between* bodies and the resultant impacts of such interactions" (127, my emphasis). The notion of being "between" is crucial here because the key to Beasley-Murray's model is keeping things in movement, preventing them from coming to a "standstill" (127) and avoiding any and all collapse into closed forms or representations. "Capture and closure" (128) convert what is outside of language and what is uncontrollable into "habits," which can become a mechanism of control or a tool for liberation. This is why Beasley-Murray turns to Justicialism in his analysis and critique of Laclau and Mouffe's model.

If we return to figure I.2, we can see examples of what Beasley-Murray calls "the classic images of Peronism: the medium shot view (from in front and slightly below) of Evita on the balcony, her arms raised in salute, coupled with a long shot from above of the crowds in the plaza" (244). These images are constructed through "the classic cinematic device of shot and reverse shot" (243). In figure I.1, we see the miners seated in orderly rows in the elegant opera house; the camera cuts to Evita speaking with outstretched arms on the stage; we cut back to the miners seated in the audience. We see a similar dynamic in figure I.2 as the camera cuts back and forth between plaza and balcony in the shot, reverse shot structure.

While Laclau's model would identify in this the possibilities of open-ended experience (a "not-yet-fully-articulated" element that would maintain the openness), Beasley-Murray sees it as the "very picture of hegemony" (25), of capture and closure. In his assessment, these stage-managed events with their mass media distribution transform the heterogeneity of bodies in "constant flux" into a homogenized "People," or "Pueblo," created through the "inculcation of habit" (25): "the Peronist state produced its people and, reciprocally, its own sovereignty, which was then encrusted in the habit of being a Peronist" (66). The movement from formlessness to form—Justicialist "articulation"—is the movement from open-ended experience of bodies in contact to the ritual and the formulaic justification for the leader and his government's domination of the poor.

This movement from formlessness to Justicialist form—the transformation of the experience of socialist "betrayal" and capitalist humiliation into the joyous experience of feeling seen or heard—constitutes what Beasley-Murray calls Peronism's "balcony effect" (243): "Heterogeneity becomes homogeneity as its various partial aspects . . . are joined . . . through their relation with those on the balcony. . . . Shot, reverse shot[:] the [heterogeneous] multitude is represented . . . as the people whose gathering is retroactively intelligible by reference to the balcony . . . [and as] a homogenous (hegemonic) bloc" (244). As this shot, reverse shot structure is repeated over and over again in the ritualized pageantry of Peronism, these forms place a limit on the nonnormative radically heterogeneous collective of the poor, whose responses to each other in the plaza, in the streets, and in the mines are the sole source of power. The joy of those gathered in the plaza or the experiences of workers seated amid the fineries of the opera house cannot be "subordinated to the word" (244) coming from the balcony or the stage. It is rooted instead in the psychobiological experience of being with others and in being transformed through the near-automatic bodily responses to the presence of and interaction with the other bodies present in those spaces.

The challenge, as Beasley-Murray understands it, then, is not how to hear more, see more, and understand more. In other words, the challenge is not how to move "not-yet-fully-articulated" social elements (the formless, the poor) into a position in which their needs, desires, demands, and experiences disrupt the ruling order and become intelligible to it (or rearticulate it). Rather, the task is to embrace the fundamental formlessness that, Beasley-Murray argues, has always been what secures social order. As he argues in the opening words of his book, "there is no hegemony and never has been" (x). Instead, "social order is secured through habit and affect" and so too is "social change . . . achieved through habit and affect" (x). The difference between "social order" and "social change" is never "categorical" but instead "involves modulation" (169). When released from their "capture" by the figures on the balcony, the "encrusted habits" of Justicialism are simply impoverished bodies responding to other impoverished bodies. They do not need a "program" or to be seen or heard by the language of power to transform inegalitarian "social order" into egalitarian "social change," which, in the end, are "not so much distinct as approximate; one affect can always lead to another" (169).

This second pathway to an alternative modernity (posthegemony/modulation) makes important critiques of the first pathway (represented by Justicialism and articulation/hegemony). However, it nevertheless maintains the position that the experience of formlessness or the nonnormativity of poverty is an essential resource rather than a specific, historical, and material relation of economic exploitation and dispossession. In Laclau and Mouffe's model of articulation/hegemony, those who experience formlessness provide access to that which is "not-yet-fully-articulated" (or what some critics of the modernist novel of the Latin American Boom have called a cultural "essence"). Those experiences of formlessness can disrupt and *re*articulate colonial or imperial norms and conventions. In Beasley-Murray's model of modulation/posthegemony, in contrast, the experience of formlessness is a precognitive, embodied, psychobiological process (i.e., affect), which operates as the key political tool and horizon: the goal is to expand the capacity to affect and be affected by others, such as by maximizing nourishment, by reducing populist pageantry, by eliminating forms that "capture" and foreclose the spontaneity of egalitarian life in common, and by fostering encounters resistant to formulaic interactions that would stifle nonnormativity.

However, just as Laclau and Mouffe view as inevitable the presence of "not-yet-fully-articulated" social elements (the formless, the poor) in all language systems and thus transform the experience of formlessness (poverty) into a kind of safety valve against the language of power, so too does Beasley-Murray establish a model that logically requires the presence of poverty (the experience of formlessness). While Laclau and Mouffe saw "articulation" as an active and, indeed, human-made process that could be undertaken, modified, or changed once it was understood, Beasley-Murray's theoretical formulations rely on a psychobiological framework that is noncognitive, nearly automatic, and fundamentally disconnected from intelligible efforts to, say, bring processes of dispossession and exploitation to an end. "[Social] change," Beasley-Murray explains, "is not a matter of substituting one program for another" (x).

Moreover, he argues, recognizing, analyzing, understanding, and confronting the "objectively given" processes of dispossession and exploitation (i.e., the means and relations of production entering into a "crisis in representation") do not seem to lead to more egalitarian modes of social organization. "Everybody knows," he tells us, "that work is exploitation" (ix), but "nobody," he also tells us, "is very much persuaded" by the making of that assertion (ix). Thus, even though we know that poverty results from specific acts of dispossession and exploitation that are enabled by the political and economic systems that operate at the level of their actually constituted, everyday forms and at the level of their real abstraction, those systems and their conflicting sets of representation must be set aside as irrelevant. Put more simply, posthegemony's response to the "crisis in representation" is to ignore it or disengage from it by declaring it a nonproblem. Arriving at this conclusion, posthegemony leaves us with exactly the same dilemma presented by Laclau and Mouffe's model of hegemony.

As we saw, Laclau and Mouffe's model reaches its logical impasse because its structure begins to parallel notions that poverty is an unavoidable, seminatural phenomenon of subjective human experience. Posthegemony's parallel impasse is evident in Beasley-Murray's metaphorical descriptions of "modulation," that is, affect in action, or what he calls the multitude.[24] In his descriptions of "modulation" or the multitude, he naturalizes the processes of change, such as when he asserts that the multitude—or the mass of near-automatic bodily responses, the experience of formlessness that is taken as coterminous with poverty—operates like a hurricane (257). Hurricanes, of course, are natural climatological processes that emerge under specific meteorological conditions and follow from discoverable scientific principles. Hurricanes are not the creations of humans or their systems of social organization. They can, of course, have their severity, intensity, or effects "modulated" by human activity (e.g., the long-term increases in atmospheric levels of carbon created by human beings "modulate" climate patterns and the intensity of storms), but hurricanes themselves are natural phenomena that do not depend on human beings. As we have already seen, however, poverty is *not* a natural phenomenon but instead an objective relational aspect of a historically particular and specific structure of economic organization. By having posthegemony rely on "modulation" and conceiving the collective action of the poor on the model of natural phenomena like hurricanes, Beasley-Murray arrives at a position that treats structures of exploitation and structures of equality as if they also were natural phenomena, as if they, like the meteorological conditions producing hurricanes, followed some kind of universal or discoverable scientific principle.

In such a scenario, we must simply accept the naturalized presence of the phenomenon (poverty), do what we can to "modulate" its effect (e.g., reduce populist pageantry, evade all forms, embrace the near-automatic, embodied spontaneity of the poor's nonnormativity) so as to weather the "storm" for now and await the arrival of tomorrow's sunny day and its calmer sea. In this way, posthegemony returns us to a scenario that not only parallels the impasse at the heart of Laclau and Mouffe's model and the Justicialist "third position" but also is not so distant from Beckman's account of "capital fictions" and its socialist counterpart explained above.

In those scenarios of crisis, the "impoverished reality of the present" (Beckman 19) must "for now . . . [be accepted as] limitations" (13) until the market obeying its "universal laws" creates "the conditions of possibility under which social and natural landscapes might be altered" (20). In the case of posthegemony, it is the "multitude" (the embodied "power to act" that resides in the prelinguistic, near-automatic responses modulating the interactions between the gathered bodies of the poor) that "obey[s] [a] logic" (Beasley-Murray 257), or what authors of "capital fictions" might call "laws." Within this logic, which Beasley-Murray terms the "logic of resonance" (257), there can emerge "a limit, however contingent, [that can] bring death rather than life" (257). In other words, within the experience of formlessness, within the prelinguistic, near-automatic responses modulating the interactions between the gathered bodies of the poor, there are "good encounters" but also seemingly inexplicable "limits" to them, which emerge spontaneously to convert the "good encounters" into "bad encounters," a conversion that takes place according to the "logic" or laws "of resonance." The authors of "capital fictions" might call this a "crisis" that moves the market from boom (the "good encounters") to bust (the "bad encounters").

As I noted at the outset, the problem I am identifying in the models of modernity under examination here is that they understand poverty not as an *objective relational aspect* of a historically particular and specific structure of economic organization but instead as a subjective (or, in the case of posthegemony, presubjective) negative social, cultural, political, or even psychobiological *experience* of *any* economic system, an experience that is transhistorical in nature, can appear anywhere, and does appear everywhere in each and every economic system. The reliance on the experience of formlessness (poverty) as a resource to be mined (rather than a problem to be solved) becomes particularly pronounced as economic systems enter into sequences marked by a "crisis in representation," which, again, is a sequence in which members of classes as they actually exist can no longer represent to themselves the way the world "works," or what values, practices, and strategies could secure the existing modes of social organization as the world changes around them in response to their own actions and activities.

As explained above, these sequences of crisis produce an absence of *necessary* norms and conventions, often leading to the desire to produce a "third option" rooted in the experience of formlessness, which is understood as the practices, values, and experiences of the poor (those who are unseen or unheard by the reigning mode of social organization). The "third option" in these sequences, I argue, has taken at least two contrasting pathways that are linked by their shared conception of poverty: (1) hegemony's option for "articulation" and the creation of new, culturally specific (even if contingent and temporary) norms and conventions; (2) posthegemony's option for "modulation" and the rejection of all norms and conventions in favor of the embodied experience of formlessness or nonnormativity itself. As we have also seen, that commitment to formlessness returns us to the same logical dilemmas produced by the crisis in the "ideological therapies" of capitalism and socialism. Perhaps more problematically, in identifying as the essential problem the existence of *form*—either colonial/imperial forms of language and social organization or *all* forms of language and social organization—these wagers for a "third option" produce a new commitment to *maintaining formlessness*, that is, to ensuring that poverty always exists in its role as a necessary political and aesthetic resource. In other words, the "third option" cannot exist if poverty ceases to exist, and the "third option" becomes plausible only if we accept that poverty always will exist.

Because of these alternative models of modernity rest on an "antipathy to representation" (Beasley-Murray 67), the material, "objectively given" aspects of the "crisis in representation" remain inaccessible to them. Forms like the Justicialist ritual or, for that matter, the Boom novel are, in the view of these models, always tools for consolidating and managing power by "closing" or "capturing" the freedoms created by those who live in poverty (i.e., those who experience formlessness). In this way, we can recognize that what these models call for is for us to follow the path of escape from the forms that seek to capture the freedoms "modulated" by formlessness, or the path that cracks open the forms that have "articulated" them into a position of inferiority. And in understanding what these models call for, we can also recognize that they entail not only a theory of politics but also a theory of art and its role in historical sequences of crisis.

## Aesthetic Form and Antitheatricality in the "Crisis in Representation"

As we have seen with Larsen, it is possible to understand the figures on the balcony and Boom authors together. For Laclau and Mouffe, both the "balcony effect" and the Boom novel should be understood as generating cocreators who, in their dearticulation and rearticulation of the "empty signifier," could create pathways for "not-yet-fully-articulated" social elements to disrupt the closed forms of society. For Beasley-Murray, both the "balcony effect" and the Boom novel (and literature more broadly) generate oppressive habits, rituals, and formulas that must be evaded at all costs. In both cases, representation must collapse either into participatory cocreation of meaning (or what Laclau calls a "chain of equivalence") or into the natural processes of psychobiological experience (i.e., near-automatic bodily response to contact with other bodies). In these models, not only is politics fully congruent with or identical to the experience of life but so too is the work of art. Indeed, the notion of a "work" of art dissolves into experience. Mediation—the ways a story is told, the ways a work of art is put together, the mechanisms that make representation possible—is set aside in favor of subject matter and the feelings it elicits. Without mediation (or form), art, like poverty, is reduced to the experience of formlessness, located in whatever you see, whatever you feel, and however you respond.

It is the case, however, that works of art, like poverty, are not natural phenomena: they are created within specific historical sequences. Artists and authors find themselves called upon by their historical circumstances to choose or invent forms that give expression to certain subject matter *and* to choose or invent subject matter that occasions the opportunity to develop needed forms. Just as the displacement of the material and "objectively given" nature of the "crisis in representation" leads to models that produce a commitment to maintaining formlessness (poverty) as a necessary political and aesthetic resource, those models also displace an understanding of how works of art as meaningful representations can provide access to the crisis and enable us to place it under analysis.

As Larsen notes, the "crisis in representation" is accompanied by a "crisis *of* representation." That is, the apparent absence of necessary *social* norms and conventions is paralleled in the realm of art in the apparent absence of necessary *aesthetic* norms and conventions. To put this differently, just as members of classes as they actually exist can no longer represent to themselves the way the world "works," or what values, practices, and strategies could secure the existing modes of social organization as the world changes around them in response to their own actions and activities, so too can artists find themselves faced with the dilemma of seeing their aesthetic strategies and pictorial practices failing to "work" or express their vision as successfully as they had before. This situation, like the broader socioeconomic structure, is produced by the ways that pictorial practices as they actually exist transform the world around them: they make available an understanding of what no longer seems to "work" just as they make available an understanding of what is possible or coming into being.

In works of art, then, we can see a phenomenon paralleling the broader "crisis in representation": a tension or fissure between "historical subject and historical object," a fissure between the values and practices as they actually exist and the values and practices that give expression to social relations emerging from their real abstraction. By focusing on the meaning of the work of art, which is a focus on how an author or artist decides to navigate the historically specific interaction between subject matter and form, we can move toward grasping the objective nature of the tension or fissure. Artists come to the conclusion that certain ways of telling stories, telling certain kinds of stories, or organizing pictures in certain ways no longer seem to "work" under present conditions as they had before. In key ways, that basic realization is the story of modernism and modernist art. And for that reason, as this book argues, it becomes possible to recognize that the best way to approach the problem of poverty—the specific problem of recognizing how the "crisis in representation" has shaped the tendency to develop an experiential account of poverty *and* reveals poverty's status as an objective relational aspect of a historically particular economic sequence—is through indirect analysis: through an analysis of debates about the work of art and the kind of problem *it* is.

This is a point we can develop by returning to how Larsen analyzes the "crisis in representation" in his reading of a fragment of Theodor Adorno's *Minima Moralia*: "The coming extinction of art is prefigured in the increasing impossibility of representing historical events" (Adorno in Larsen, *Modernism* 6). That "impossibility of representing" is the fissure between the readily available strategies for making sense of the world and the processes of modernity that take place at an abstract level and remain inaccessible or unintelligible to those already existing practices. The modernization of social relations embedded in and driven by social relations as a real abstraction creates what appears to be a "history without events" or a social actor without subjectivity: historical changes are happening, but it seems like no one is responsible for them.

In the terms elaborated above, if not having enough to eat feels like something, understanding that feeling in its fullness—how it came to be that you do not have enough to eat and that no one sees or cares that you do not have enough to eat (i.e., what sequence of events was set into motion and made it so that you do not have enough to eat)—remains in some sense inaccessible. For example, you might continue living your life as you always have: in your daily life, you're being "responsible" in the ways that you understand responsibility and that have created stability for you in the past (e.g., working, saving, paying bills, buying a home, planting certain crops, etc.). All of a sudden (or perhaps over an extended period of years), those practices no longer secure stability. What "worked" in the past now fails to do so under shifting historical circumstances that remain outside full understanding within the context of everyday life. It could be, for example, the effects a currency devaluation (as in Mexico or Argentina in the 1980s and 1990s), or it could be technological innovations (as with the creation of artificial nitrates that severely affected Chile at the beginning of the twentieth century). That is, the "crisis in representation"—the fact that the existing classes, their social practices, their needs, desires, and so on are nonidentical with the ongoing modernization of social relations set into motion by those classes—creates a situation in which "what really happens" always remains within an "essential abstractness" (in Larsen, *Modernism* 6).

In Larsen's account, modernist aesthetics emerge as a set of practices that invert that "impossibility" by producing works of art that begin to "[occupy] the lost terrain of social representation" (Larsen, *Modernism* xxiv). In other words, modernist aesthetics compensate for the norms and conventions that no longer "work" in a sequence of crisis without, for that matter, providing full or total access to the emerging norms and conventions. Modernist artworks, like social relations in their real abstraction, are not reducible to the world as it is given. They do not give us immediate access to the world as we have understood it through the narrative or visual tradition as it actually exists. At the same time, modernist artworks are also not reducible to unintelligible abstractions: they are understandable as "works of art," which means they are rooted in a specific art-historical sequence that is in dialogue with both the present and the past as it has been handed down. In this sense, modernist works of art emerge as meaningfully autonomous: they "work" because they are not reducible to the values and practices that sustain actually existing classes but at the same time are inscribed within those values and practices. They make intelligible what "can be felt but not seen" (Larsen, *Modernism* 28). Social relations in their real abstraction might be perceived in a representation of what an individual experiences when having difficulty acquiring enough food or identifying a source of consistent and decent work.

As a key example of these phenomena, we can turn to short stories by Mexican author Juan Rulfo, an author whose fiction often focused on the lifeways and practices of Mexico's peasants and rural proletariat. For Larsen, a significant problem in understanding Rulfo's work is the critical tendency to identify his fiction with the recovery of Mexico's "cultural essence," which remains connected in the national imaginary with the rural Mestizo communities that maintain deep cultural ties with the country's past. As Larsen explains, however, "Rulfo's style owes . . . little or nothing to questions of cultural experience and everything to those of historical experience" (*Determinations* 139). Larsen argues that what appear to be depictions of cultural realities in Rulfo's portrayals of the rural poor are actually narrative frameworks structured by "negative peripeteia" (142). There is no "transparent linkage of past and present" (141): changed circumstances appear to be sudden, inexplicable and simply register at the level of the story's central narrative conflict. In this way, there is no recognition of a modernizing present and its transforming social relations: the characters interact as if their present lives and circumstances could not possibly be different from how they and their communities lived in the past.

As an example of this, we can cite Rulfo's story "Paso del Norte." Here, the narrative focuses on a father and son. The son, whose pig farming business recently failed, arrives to tell his father he is planning to migrate to the United States to look for work and asks his father to look after his affairs while he is gone.

The father initially rejects the son's request, telling the son that he (the son) should meet his own obligations rather than turning to the father for assistance. The son accuses the father of not meeting *his* (the father's) obligations to prepare the son for life by teaching him a trade. While there is more to the story than the details of the initiating circumstances of the conflict between father and son, this is enough to illustrate the basic point of what works of art can do in sequences of crisis.

The tendency in analyzing this story is to look at how it evokes the traditional "culture" of rural Mexico (e.g., family ties, the remembrance of past conflicts and their relevance in the present, etc.). His characters experience the present as if it were the past and find that what they are actually able to do (e.g., call forth expectations regarding familial obligation) or what they are actually able to acquire (e.g., unstable, inconsistent local employment) persistently remain nonidentical with what they wish to do (e.g., provide for their family). As a result, they are unable to represent to themselves the nature of this nonidentity, thinking something along the lines of the following: if I am doing everything I am "supposed" to do, that is, everything that the members of my community who came before me also did, why am I poor while they weren't (or aren't)? Neither father nor son engages in any recognition of the changed circumstances of the present. The son's pig farming business failed, which is the initiation of the story's conflict, but the broader economic climate of the period (e.g., macroeconomic changes in the circulation of pork as a commodity, the emergence of new national and transnational labor markets and their demographic effects on the countryside and its local markets) is never brought to bear on the situation. The nature of this conflict, however, is available to a reader, who can read the tension between the calling forth of preceding norms and conventions (i.e., familial obligation and small-scale farming) and those market-oriented norms emerging in the 1940s in Mexico. For Larsen, the "profound artistic truth" (*Determinations* 142) in Rulfo's narratives is not the access they provide to "cultural essence" nor their achievement of a kind of modernist "perfection" of literary art. Instead, that "artistic truth" is embedded in the structure (the literary form) of "negative peripeteia," which can be understood as a narrative representation of the socioeconomic "crisis in representation."

In practical terms, the literary form that gives expression to the "crisis in representation" operates by portraying figures who, within the narrative mise-en-scène, remain unaware of how they misunderstand the meaning of their own actions: they are not aware of the fissure between how they understand their actions and what those actions mean as a component of the work as a whole or, for that matter, "society as a whole." Indeed, they are not aware that their actions mean anything at all as they do not believe themselves to be performing for anyone (even though their actions exist solely as fictions to be read). It is literary and artistic phenomena like Larsen's account of "negative peripeteia" that compose what I am arguing is an underexamined tradition in Latin America and that serves as an alternative to the valorizations of poverty as an experience of formlessness. That tradition, as we will see in the chapters that follow, is one that maintains commonalities with the development of antitheatrical representational practices in the history of French painting.

As Michael Fried argues in his trilogy of books on this topic, the antitheatrical tradition resulted from a series of historical crises of representation that were ultimately generative of what we now call modernist artistic practice. While it is important to note that the crises of representation that Fried analyzes are not the economic "crises in representation" that sustain Larsen's arguments, the unawareness of being beheld that makes "negative peripeteia" work as a mode of access to the "crisis in representation" maintains striking parallels with Fried's examination of the strategy of absorption in painting. As Fried notes, absorption is a strategy in which figures within paintings are depicted as so completely focused or concentrated on the activity they are completing within the depicted scene that they "compel the conviction" (i.e., convince the beholder looking at the painting) that the scene as it is depicted was not put there for the beholder to contemplate. Paintings, of course, are objects created for beholders: they are objects that are made to be looked at and are objects that are received through the filter of whatever preconceptions beholders have for paintings. But these characteristics are precisely what painters must neutralize if they wish to avoid creating objects that are merely decorative and a function of the vanity and falsity of "polite society."

These crises in which the need to neutralize or "obliviate" (Fried, *Absorption* 103) the audience through strategies that "establish positively . . . [that the beholder] had not been taken into account" (103) are largely motivated by a desire to "compel conviction in the beholder" that a painting could be "a mode of access to truth" (104) about the world rather than simply the expression of "a desire to play to the crowd" (98). Rather than appealing to the exaggerations and falseness of "the manners and conventions of polite society" (99), which had become a hallmark of mid-eighteenth-century painting in France, writers like Denis Diderot argued that artists could and should reject the tendency to reproduce false and exaggerated scenes that were responses to existing social "manners and conventions." Paintings had become objects that "performed" and sought the approving applause of beholders in "polite society." Diderot argued that the "continued functioning [of painting and drama] as major expressions of the human spirit [were] held to depend upon whether or not the painter or dramatist [was] able to undo that state of affairs" (104), a state of affairs (vanity, falsity, direct appeal to the desires of the crowd) Diderot disapprovingly called a state of "theatricality."

Working against an art that was aware of its audience and was constructed precisely to elicit their praise and approval, Diderot championed works of art that could "*detheatricalize beholding* and so make it once again a mode of access to truth and conviction, albeit a truth and conviction that cannot be entirely equated with any known or experienced before" (*Absorption* 104). A classic example of this strategy, Fried argues, appears in paintings like Chardin's *The Soap Bubble* (ca. 1733) or his *The Game of Knucklebones* (ca. 1734). These paintings are successes not only because the activities they depict create a unity of action within the closed system of the painting but also because those activities require sustained attention on the part of the figure. Their absorption in a world separate from or severed from the beholder is demonstrated not only by their ignoring the possibility of a beholder but also through indicators of a disregard of social conventions (and the possibility of being seen) that govern "polite society," such as "the tear in the young man's jacket" in *The Soap Bubble* or "the upper corner of the young woman's apron that has come unpinned" in *The Game of Knucklebones* (48).

To make more explicit the connection I am drawing here, it is possible to say that the "negative peripeteia" in "Paso del Norte"—the son's engaging a global shift in commodity production as a local conflict embedded within the structures of meeting or not meeting familial obligations—can be understood as the narrative parallel to young man's "torn jacket" or the young woman's "unpinned apron," which are indicators of a "world" outside the falsity of "polite society" even as those figures are embedded within it. Of course, the "torn jacket" and the "unpinned apron" necessarily needed to be paired with the absorptive activity since they otherwise might have been received as mere violations of decorum rather than what they are: the representation of a world that exists within the falsity and exaggerated inauthenticity of "polite society," or, more simply, "a truth and conviction [about that society] that cannot be entirely equated with any known or experienced before" (*Absorption* 104). Indeed, as Fried notes, "the evolution of French painting between the early 1750s and 1781"—by which he means the development of antitheatrical strategies to establish a new relationship between artwork and beholder—cannot be understood to have taken "place in a vacuum isolated from society and uncontaminated from its stresses" (4). Instead, they make available an understanding of "the relationship between painting and beholder as laying the groundwork for a new understanding of how the 'internal' development of the art of painting and the wider social and cultural reality of France in the last decades of the *Ancien Régime* were implicated and so to speak intertwined with one another" (5). This "intertwining," Fried explains, is a creation, a human achievement: there is no automatic tie between socioeconomic process and artistic practice.

While I do not have the space to rehearse the whole of Fried's arguments about the development of the art of painting in France and their relation to the history and development of modernism, it is important to note here that I continue to refer to Fried's account of antitheatricality throughout this study as a way to name an alternative Latin American tradition that we can glimpse in "Paso del Norte" above. This tradition, I argue, does not merely reproduce "the manners and conventions of polite society" (*Absorption* 99) nor reject out of hand the need for norms and conventions to communicate a meaningful critique of them. It is a tradition that, in recognizing the "crisis in representation," also recognizes that efforts to reveal poverty as an objective relational aspect of a historically particular and specific structure of economic organization require meaningful representations that do not direct themselves to merely reproducing the everyday experiences of social relations as they exist. These works compensate for the norms and conventions that no longer "work" without, for that matter, providing a didactic or explanatory account of emerging norms and conventions. Instead, they make available "what really happens" or "what can be felt but not seen": the objectively true fissure between actually existing social relations and the emerging social relations of a modernizing economic order.

As I have demonstrated, the values, practices, "logics," and "laws" of capitalist, socialist, populist, and post-Marxist models are premised on a commitment to understanding poverty as an experience of formlessness, of not being seen and not being heard within the norms and conventions of "polite society." However, as I have also argued, the solutions proposed by those models sidestep or evade poverty as an objective relational phenomenon. Thus, the subjective and negative experience of having no place in existing social, cultural, political, and economic systems of modernity was to be solved by reserving that negative experience as a necessary resource for creating the positive experience of becoming modern. In the chapters that follow, I trace formlessness as the logic governing understandings of poverty across three political, historical, and aesthetic contexts, each with their own histories of egalitarian political movements. If we are to understand how (or if) literature and art, as I am arguing, are to contribute anything to the struggle against the poverty and inequality resulting from global capitalism, we must begin by recognizing the mistakes that stem from experiential accounts of poverty. To do so, we must turn to an analysis of theatricality and antitheatricality in Latin America, a task to which this book now turns to engage in full.

# 1

# Managing to Get By

## Lizardi, Cantinflas, and the Problem of Horizontalism

In 1939, while serving as chief of the editorial bureau of the UNAM and just beginning his appointment as a professor of Spanish American, Mexican, and Spanish literature, a position recently vacated by the Porfirian novelist Federico Gamboa (who died that same year), Francisco Monterde launched a consequential editorial series that continues to be published today: the Biblioteca del Estudiante Universitario. This series has as its primary "aim the publication of mostly historical or literary works [that are] difficult for students to approach, [and the publication of] simplified editions [of those works] with prologues written by specialists" (Pereira et al. 139).[1] As scholars have noted, this series as well as others created by the university press in this period were "fundamentally connected to a project for [teaching and creating access to works significant for] national culture . . . [that] otherwise would not be easily obtainable" (139). Perhaps emblematically marking the institutional transition from the Porfirian Gamboa to the postrevolutionary model that had been in development over the previous two decades, the first text published in the series was *El libro del Consejo*, which is obviously better known today by its title in K'iche', the *Popol Vuh*.

One of the earliest collaborators on this editorial project was Agustín Yáñez, who, of course, would go on to write influential novels about the rural and urban poor and serve as governor of Jalisco (in the 1950s) and as secretary of public education during the Gustavo Díaz Ordaz administration during the consequential year of 1968. But in the 1930s, as Yáñez tells Emmanuel Carballo, who had asked about Yáñez's "silence" in that decade, he was focused on studying philosophy and teaching rather than writing literary works (Carballo 313–315).[2] His first contribution to Monterde's editorial project—the prologue to and annotations for the second installment in the series, *Crónicas de la Conquista* (1939)—is a visible example of his essayistic production in this period. In this anthology of works from the era of the sixteenth-century Spanish invasion and military occupation of what is now Mexico, Yáñez included not only traditional selections from the *Cartas de relación de Hernán Cortés* or Bernal Díaz del Castillo's *Historia verdadera* but also selections from the *Crónica de Chac-Xulub-Chen*, which had been translated from Maya Yucateco into Spanish just three years earlier by Héctor Pérez Martínez. These first two volumes in the series, where indigenous, Spanish, Criollo, and other works were presented together in a unified way, were of a piece with approaches to national culture embedded within the postrevolutionary politico-aesthetic tradition of *mexicanidad* (Mexicanism): the term that expresses the notion of an essential Mexican identity embedded in ever-evolving processes of mestizaje and the historical continuity of a revolutionary heroism struggling against (but in the process often reproducing) the corrupt and exploitative colonial order.

Widely visible in everything from visual art and "Golden Era" film to literature and popular culture, the politico-aesthetic logic of mexicanidad was also reflected within Monterde's series. As the series developed in its first years, the unified heterogeneity of those first two installments produced by Monterde and Yáñez appeared in numerous other volumes in the series, ranging from the writings of significant figures like the Porfirian intellectual Justo Sierra, the colonial period's Carlos Sigüenza y Góngora, and the nineteenth-century conservative intellectual and politician Lucas Alamán to editions and anthologies of literary works by Sor Juana, Juan Ruiz de Alarcón, and indigenous poets.[3] It is in this Mexicanist vein that we can also read Yáñez's second contribution to the series in 1940 with his "Estudio preliminar" and annotated anthology of selected writings by José Joaquín Fernández de Lizardi, also known by the nickname he shared with the title of his newspaper, *El Pensador Mexicano* (The Mexican thinker).

Illustrated with woodcut or linocut images (perhaps made by Monterde), this volume (the fifteenth in the series) comprises Yáñez's selected narrative dialogues that Lizardi wrote in his characteristically satirical and plain style in an effort to illustrate the ideas underscoring the fight for independence. Yáñez cites as an emblematic example "[a] passage that can serve as an epigraph for the complete works of el Pensador" (*Pensador* xlvii), which he draws from an exchange between el Payo (the peasant) and el Sacristán (the sexton) in his "Constitución política de una república imaginaria" (1825):

SACRISTÁN Our way of talking about things [Nuestra conversación] certainly isn't proper [no es de lo más limpio]. . . .

EL PAYO It's true, but our way of talking about things is aimed at giving them their proper form [se dirige a la limpieza].[4] (xlvii)

What Yáñez means by noting the epigrammatic function of this passage is not only how it highlights wordplay that is characteristic of Lizardi's work but also how that wordplay expresses the political ends that Lizardi envisioned for his writing.[5] As Yáñez states, "All of the works by el Pensador [were] wholly directed at giving Mexico its proper form [la limpieza de México]: spiritual and material, ethnic and political, by overcoming the [colonial] stage" of development (xlvii–xlviii).

Yáñez identifies in Lizardi's satirical writing what he calls a "lumpen realism" (*Pensador* xxx). While some critiques of Lizardi highlighted his "vulgarity" (xxviii), "poor taste" (xviii), "impropriety," and breeches of "decorum" ("la buena educación"), Yáñez embraces precisely those characteristics of Lizardi's writing as essential for understanding and as foundational for la mexicanidad. The "improper" ("lo no limpio") was always what the colonial social order (in Lizardi's case) or the Porfirian social order (in Yáñez's case) saw as shiftless, useless, or dangerous, and therefore it was also what could "sweep away" those oppressive social structures: "Our way of talking about things certainly isn't proper . . . [but it] is aimed at giving things their proper form," which is to say, the "spiritual and material, ethnic and political" forms that can "[overcome] the [colonial] stage" of development.

What Yáñez seizes on in Lizardi's writing is the notion that colonial (or Porfirian) "ways of talking about things" or ways of doing things or ways of seeing things (as "vulgar" or in "poor taste" or "improper" or "lacking decorum") are responsible for creating existing, unequal "social divisions" (*Pensador* xix). Like Lizardi, Yáñez believes that making visible what is "improper" is the primary and best tool for tearing down the hierarchies that produce poverty. If, as Yáñez argues, "poverty is a cancer plaguing societies [that] is created by . . . three causes," which are "opulent overconsumption, profligacy and exploitative financial schemes" (xxxix), then the solution is to make visible how existing social hierarchies (existing "social divisions") talk about things, do things and see things. While this logic is embedded in the particular works Yáñez chose for the anthology, such as "Los paseos de la Verdad" (1815), he actually spends the bulk of his introductory study developing an argument about Lizardi's multivolume serialized picaresque novel *El periquillo sarniento*, in which Lizardi's politico-aesthetic model is most extensively developed.[6]

In this chapter I analyze the links between Lizardi's writings—especially *El periquillo,* which is treated extensively in the "Estudio preliminar"—and Yáñez's thinking. The goal in that analysis is to elaborate the "lumpen realist" aesthetic that structures the relation Yáñez builds between postindependence Mexico (Lizardi's era) and postrevolutionary Mexico (his present). As we will see, that aesthetic is premised on Yáñez's account of the figure of the *pelado* in Lizardi's writing (particularly *El periquillo*), a figure that is structured by a conceptualization of poverty defined as the experience of formlessness, or, the experience of being seen (if seen) by society as "vulgar" or in "poor taste" or "improper" or "lacking decorum."

This conceptualization is directly tied to the cultural politics of mexicanidad in the nascent era of the PRI. Notably, as we will see, it is shared by a related and significant film released the same year as Yáñez's "Estudio preliminar" and his anthology of Lizardi's writings: *Ahí está el detalle* (1940), one of the most iconic of the more than fifty films in which Mario Moreno appeared as the *peladito* Cantinflas. By reading the relationship between Yáñez's account of "lumpen realism" (i.e., our improper way of talking about things is aimed at giving them their proper form) and Cantinflas's own verbal strategies for evading oppressive structures to meet his needs and reveal the "impropriety" of the supposedly "proper" and egalitarian forms of postrevolutionary social life, it is possible to see a confluence between the structuring logic of Mexico's state-financed mass culture and the intellectual and artistic works created by Yáñez, one of the PRI's devoted bureaucrats.[7]

Cantinflas's films, of course, have been critiqued by scholars such as Gareth Williams for the ways they reinforce the norms and structures of the Mexican state. Williams roots his critique of Cantinflas and his cinematic "peladito" in his championing of a horizontalist, dehierarchizing project rooted in the poor's (or, the pelado's) actions, which are seen as a threat to social stability and produce in the poor negative social, cultural, political, and even psychological experiences that should be recovered and reoriented toward a new egalitarian project. In other words, the critique of Cantinflas and his films' reinforcement of the Mexican state's increasingly oppressive structures is rooted in a politics that always and only emerges from the raw, subjective, negative experiences of the poor that cannot be given forms sanctioned by the state. However, as we will see by reading a film like *Ahí está el detalle* in its relation with Yáñez's affinity for the pelado in a Lizardi-inspired "lumpen realism," it is possible to recognize that a political model built from experiential accounts of poverty (i.e., built from what is seen as "improper," what is formless) not only fails to critique the historically particular and specific structure of state capitalism that creates poverty as an objective relational aspect of that system but also is essential to the construction of that system.

Put more simply, reading *Ahí está el detalle* with Yáñez's account of Lizardi's "lumpen realism" makes it possible to understand how the conceptualization of poverty in a horizontalist, dehierarchizing model (i.e., as an experience of formlessness) emerged as essential to the single-party state (the PRI) as it began to develop a state capitalist model in the 1940s. Moreover, that conceptualization of poverty underscored the political project of the single-party state as it consolidated its structural power through the party's association with and use of notions of mexicanidad. As an author, a politician, and a bureaucrat, Yáñez, of course, actively participated in the building of these structures. This context and analysis will enable me to conclude the chapter by positing an alternative to the PRI's Mexicanist politics of poverty as the experience of formlessness. I will do so through a reassessment of Alfonso Reyes's reading of Lizardi's work. Reyes's contrast with Yáñez enables us to see not only how an analysis of Lizardi opens up new understandings of both the PRI's Mexicanism and the cinematic works of Cantinflas but also how Reyes's analysis of literature and poverty posits a productive alternative path for turning away from the mistakes embedded in Mexicanism's structuring logic, which, at its core, valorizes the experience of formlessness.

## Lizardi and Formlessness as Form

In his excellent reading of the prologue to *El periquillo sarniento*, Samuel Steinberg argues that Lizardi's novel thematizes not only the problem of poverty as experienced by its central character but also Lizardi's own problem of poverty: how to finance the creation of the novel we are reading is a central part of the novel's structure (appearing in serialized installments) as well as its opening conceit (its prologue). As Steinberg explains, in place of the wealthy patron, who customarily financed the production of artworks and was consequently praised in an opening literary dedication, Lizardi instead dedicates his novel to a heterogeneous reading public who will buy the novel's installments over time: "peasants and workers; Indian, Mulatto and Black [populations]; drunks and layabouts; simpletons and fools."[8] As Steinberg argues, Lizardi's prologue to *El periquillo*, which was "the first Latin American novel" ("Originary" 55), is one that equally establishes a foundational logic for Mexican literature and Latin American literature more broadly. While Steinberg sees in the prologue to *El periquillo* the foundation of "the symbolic rule of the State" (54) by subordinating the freedom of artistic creation to literature's "duty" to construct "a people," Yáñez pushes back against an account of Lizardi as establishing or securing any kind of literary formula, obligation, or duty. Rather than reading the prologue as the imposition of a duty on literature, Yáñez, in what can be read as a kind of reply in advance, understands Lizardi (el Pensador) as producing his literary work within a sort of populist unity with the "marginal subjects" who will be his readers. Duty, Yáñez says, resides not in literature but instead in wealth: "wealth has a social function and brings with it duties" (*Pensador* xxxix). And the product of the collective wealth of "marginal subjects" who finance the labor of the writer (i.e., literature) becomes a mechanism by which wealth can be made to carry out its duties and social functions.

This notion of wealth and its social duties, and literature's role as a tool to make wealth (rather than "the people") carry out those social duties, is one that is embedded within *El periquillo*. Indeed, the novel's structure is one in which Lizardi builds a five-volume response to the conventional understandings that organized colonial and early national social life. As an example of those social conventions, we can cite what Pedro's father tells him in the novel's first volume regarding the expected behaviors of a young Criollo like Pedro:

> [I will] not . . . tell you that poetry and the other areas of study I have described to you are not useful; indeed, many of them are not only useful but instead absolutely necessary to certain professions. . . . A poor boy like you who decides to study [the humanities] (las letras) in order to make a living will find himself needing to become a priest or a practitioner of canon law; or in the secular realm, a doctor or a lawyer. . . . What is important is that children are not lazy and unreliable but instead dedicate themselves to becoming useful to themselves and the state [and] never become a burden to society as a member of the idle classes. (212–214)

What is most important, Pedro's father says, is to have the products of labor and collective wealth (i.e., "poetry and [the products of] other areas of study") be directed toward giving form to the formlessness of life: to make "useful" what would otherwise be "unreliable," "lazy," or "idle." Of course, the point of the novel's five volumes is that Pedro, who is narrating his autobiography to his children from his deathbed, demonstrates all the ways in which he did not follow his father's advice: he became a petty thief, swindler, and *pícaro* who is in no way "useful to himself or to the state." Indeed, in episode after episode, we are shown the extent to which Pedro is a drain on his family and his society as well as a continuing threat to their stability (e.g., in the third volume, his swindling ends up producing an indigenous rebellion in Tula).

There is a developmentalist logic embedded within Lizardi's work, one that is, however, not identical to Pedro's father's model of development, despite the resemblance it might bear. In Yáñez's account, what Lizardi envisions is not carrying forward a kind of noblesse oblige in an uninterrupted chain of "decorum," social conventions, and duty to the state but instead showing how what is "vulgar" or in "poor taste" or "improper" or "lacking decorum" can found a *new* order by making wealth, rather than "the people," fulfill its social obligations. Pedro occupies again and again the margins of society as what one character, in the third volume, calls his demonstrated ability to be a "jack of all trades but master of none" (570). Pedro's "ill use" or "improper" use of the bits and pieces of religious, medical, social, or other kinds of knowledge acquired in the process of surviving his experience of the margins of colonial and early national social life (i.e., his experience of formlessness as a Criollo who cannot or will not take a "proper" place within the divisions of social life) are essential, in Yáñez's view, to understanding Lizardi's importance to Mexico's artistic and literary tradition.

What Yáñez highlights is that the novel shows that regardless of his many years of impropriety, vulgarity, and petty crime, Pedro's "lack of decorum" is "redeemed by the labor he performs" (xxxix). By rejecting "decorum" and "duty," which require him to operate outside the "obligations" and privileges of the ecclesiastical or professional or aristocratic spheres that organize his father's developmentalist imagination (linked to structures of decorum, propriety, duty and obligation), Pedro, like every poor person in the colonial and early national period, only has the options to work or to steal. In other words, they only have the option to create a more proper order through an existence that demonstrates the current order's "impropriety" and its hierarchical ways of seeing, being, doing, and knowing. The unacceptability (in Lizardi's view) of Pedro's path of petty crime and the inevitability of Pedro's "redemption" via labor ultimately drive the creation of a new order in which there is a place not only for him as a delinquent, impoverished Criollo but also for the "peasants and workers; Indian, Mulatto and Black [populations]; drunks and layabouts; simpletons and fools" who had, along with Pedro, experienced formlessness, which is to say, had the experience of not being seen, not being heard, or being heard as only threat or noise.

For Yáñez, literature (the product of the labor performed by Lizardi) is a mechanism to "redeem" the collective wealth of those who experience formlessness. Lizardi, in this reading, is interested not in transforming a "non-people" into a "national people" but instead in *making use of*—making useable—the beings, doings, sayings, and knowings of that "non-people." What is essential about Lizardi, in Yáñez's view, is his focus on Pedro's being outside and also within the existing social order. What is also essential is the experience of being unseen or formless because that experience can function as a mechanism to reveal the corroded structures of supposedly "proper" systems of colonial and early national governance. The problem is not the particular actions taken by a pícaro like Pedro but instead the ways of seeing, being, doing, and knowing that occasion the need for those actions. In other words, both Lizardi and Yáñez see Pedro's "improper" use or "ill use" of the social order as essential to recognizing the fundamental deficiencies within that social order. This is what Yáñez means when he says that the passage from Lizardi's "Constitución" could serve as an epigraph for his complete works: our improper way of talking about things is aimed at giving them their proper form.

The supposedly "improper" figures within the colonial and early national system—"peasants and workers; Indian, Mulatto and Black [populations]; drunks and layabouts; simpletons and fools" and also, yes, impoverished Criollo delinquents like Pedro and his fellow pícaros—are only "improper" insofar as their ways of being, doing, saying and knowing fall outside the formulas and conventions of "decorum" that organize the supposedly "proper" system of colonial and early national governance. In that sense, the point of Lizardi's writing, in Yáñez's estimation, is not to change the behavior of someone like Pedro but rather to change the ways of seeing, being, doing, and knowing that ascribe to that behavior the categories of "improper" or "vulgar." As Yáñez points out, "Fernández de Lizardi's passion was giving national life its proper shape as it charts a new path" (*Pensador* xv), and the mechanism for giving "national life its proper shape" was Lizardi's "progressivist idealism" and his "lumpen realism" (xv). Yáñez compares the function of Lizardi's "lumpen realism" to the function of *corridos* and other popular art forms in postrevolutionary Mexico, art forms in which there is a new "norm established as a guide for conduct" and one that would "make clear how to travel from what is to what should be" (xv).

Lizardi's project, in this reading, is one in which a new set of national norms are being established, and these norms necessarily differ from merely following the colonial norms exemplified by someone like Pedro's father. But those norms also are not merely replications of delinquent actions that meet short-term needs for survival. The "improper" and the "vulgar" can achieve a kind of "redemption" through "labor." New norms and new structures created by *making use of* the beings, doings, sayings, and knowings of those who are seen as "vulgar" or "improper" enable the production of a kind of equilibrium between resistance to an existing unequal order and the establishment of a new order that meets the needs made visible through that resistance. This is what Yáñez means when he highlights the epigrammatic nature of the passage from Lizardi's "Constitución," which can be reexpressed, in Yáñez's view, as the observation that "what is"—*both* the "vulgar"/"improper" *and* that which is "in good taste"/"proper"—is not "what should be." That opposition, in Yáñez's reading of Lizardi, is one that must be persistently interrogated and "redeemed" through "labor." While this does include the labor of other workers occupying the margins of any and every iteration of Mexican society, particularly important is the labor of an artist like Lizardi or others mentioned in the study (like the muralists, corrido singers, and even Yáñez himself).

Art and literature can operate as a mechanism—a set of practices, structures, and strategies—to make the experience of formlessness—the experiences of the poor—visible so that the deficiencies of the existing ways of seeing, being, doing, and knowing (i.e., "what is") can be reworked and reorganized (i.e., be transformed into "what should be"). That "what should be" cannot be set up in advance but instead is revealed in the spontaneous happenings of everyday life experienced as formlessness.

For Yáñez, *El periquillo* is the story of how poverty (what is "vulgar" or "improper") reveals the way existing colonial and early national social structures (or "what is") reproduces poverty (new experiences of formlessness). In Yáñez's study, then, he argues that the genius of Lizardi is the way that his "lumpen realism"—that is, the "impropriety" of the poor shown not as in itself "improper" but rather as the created result of problematic structures of "decorum"—can be attached to a permanent "revolutionary" project. Yáñez identifies a structure of persistent or eternal revelation: in each and every organization of life, there will be an experience of formlessness: someone will always be deemed "vulgar" or "improper"; someone will always be formless, someone always poor. This leads to a reorganization of existing forms, but that reorganization, nevertheless, maintains an element of formlessness that will require the new "what is" to be reorganized again. Yáñez understands this dynamic as synonymous with la mexicanidad: the term that expresses the notion of an essential Mexican identity embedded in ever-evolving processes of mestizaje and the historical continuity of a revolutionary heroism struggling against (but in the process often reproducing) the corrupt and exploitative colonial order. As we will see, Yáñez's interpretation of Lizardi is guided by his commitment to the Mexicanist project. But as we will also see, his Mexicanism—expressed both in his literary production and in his work as a politician and high-level government functionary who was an important contributor to the consolidation of the PRI's power in Mexico—was shaped by his understanding of poverty as an experience of formlessness, an understanding developed in dialogue with his reading of Lizardi.

## Yáñez and Lizardi's "Lumpen Realism"

To understand what, precisely, Yáñez envisions as the characteristics of Lizardi's "lumpen realism" and therefore also how the internal logic of postrevolutionary (PRI-dominated) Mexicanism is shaped by an understanding of poverty as an experience of formlessness, it is important to examine a couple of key examples from Lizardi's writing. Some do appear in works Yáñez chose for inclusion in the anthology he contributed to Monterde's series. These include, for example, "Diálogo fingido de cosas ciertas, entre una muchacha y Tata Pablo" (1813) and "La ciega y su muchachita" (1813). However, the clearest articulation of Lizardi's "lumpen realism" as what Yáñez envisions as a permanent revolutionary process is most fully developed in *El periquillo*, and for this reason it is relevant to examine two episodes from the novel that can serve to elaborate what Yáñez calls Lizardi's ability to "[portray in his novel] . . . the realities of life lived in poverty" (*Pensador* xv).

The first takes place at the outset of the second volume, where Pedro outlines his profligate use of his family's resources, which, when accompanied by the death of his parents, ultimately leaves him without housing, with mounting debts, with no skills or trade that would lead him to a regularized stream of income and with no support from his extended family: "The pícaro deserves to suffer the consequences of his criminal actions" (475), his uncle tells him in a letter. The result is that he reconnects with Januario, better known by his alias Juan Largo, a petty criminal he had met by chance during one of his parents' earlier attempts to lead him down a productive path.

Pedro and Juan Largo begin a period in which they travel around to low-stakes gambling games in order to cheat and steal their way into a more comfortable economic situation. Aided by the new clothing they purchased with their ill-gotten gains, they were able to generate trust—being seen and heard as legitimate or trustworthy gamblers—and thus find their swindling and their schemes to have short-term success. But when Juan Largo, with another accomplice, proposes to Pedro (who had only recently left the hospital after a brawl) that they commit more serious crimes, such as armed robbery and murder, Pedro parts ways with them. But before doing so, they exchange tokens of friendship (rosaries), a fateful decision that leads the police to conclude that Pedro was involved with a robbery and murder committed by Juan Largo and his accomplice. Pedro ends up in prison with a cross-section of the population of the poor in New Spain, where the logic of poverty structuring Lizardi's world begins to become clear after having been obscured by the colonial logic embedded in combinations of parental advice and parental indulgence (which Lizardi rejects).

While in prison, Pedro observes that, in being the only Criollo in the basement cell, there is an expectation from his fellow Indigenous, Mulatto, Black, and Mestizo cell mates that he have some money he could wager in the low-stakes card game they are playing with a partial, beaten-up deck. When he admits that "[he] didn't have a penny to his name" (425), they refused to believe him, asserting instead that his decision not to play was motivated either by his desire to treat them cruelly or his desire to maintain himself in a position of superiority over them (425). What begins to come into view from this impoverished group's reaction to Pedro is that, despite what his father said about the importance of being "useful to himself or to the state," the axis of colonial social relations hinges on structures of seeing (something already suggested by the decision Pedro and Juan Largo made to purchase new clothing as one of their first tasks after successfully cheating and stealing money from the gambling games). The alternative to the social norms and conventions of colonial and early national governance, that is, the new set of national norms that could be established through an engagement with the experience of formlessness, emerges in Pedro's interactions with a Mulatto prisoner named Aguilucho.

What Aguilucho makes clear to Pedro is that the norms of colonial life (built on hierarchical ways of seeing) are not, as Pedro's parents presume, a singularly rigid structure with immoveable and unavoidable obligations, responsibilities, liabilities, and (lack of) privileges. Instead, Aguilucho shows how the multiracial and multiethnic group of impoverished inmates (including Pedro) demonstrates how easily and often those supposedly rigid hierarchies built on prescribed ways of seeing, being, doing, and knowing are reorganized. Importantly, Aguilucho also shows how this fluidity—the episodic elimination of hierarchical ways of seeing—functions as a mechanism to impose or reestablish those hierarchies (though with individuals like Aguilucho occupying a higher rung of the existing set of "social divisions").

The most immediate example of this phenomenon is the way that Pedro is immediately confronted with its factual nature in his dialogue with Aguilucho. Pedro describes and confronts his own surprise at hearing the Mulatto prisoner so eloquently explain an understanding of the operation of the system of social hierarchies: "I never thought that a man like you would be able to speak with such reason; because, truth be told, and without desire to anger you, members of your class never speak on any topic in the way you just have" (450). Aguilucho doesn't take offense and, in fact, responds that this supposed "rule"—that the colony's "lower *castas*" lack the ability to produce persuasive and reasoned argument—isn't "as generally true as you suppose" (450) and that, to the extent that these groups do have difficulty articulating their beliefs, arguments, and points of view, this supposed difficulty "is not due to an inability to understand but instead due to their lack of culture and education" (450). A statement like this one succinctly summarizes what Yáñez, the future secretary of education, sees in Lizardi's writing. The so-called inability to produce reasoned argument is not congenital but rather the product of the social structures and divisions that tend to place some above (e.g., Criollos) and others below (e.g., Indigenous, Mulatto, Black, and Mestizo populations), a notion that was as relevant for Lizardi's independence era narrative as it was for Yáñez's postrevolutionary Mexicanist narratives.

Aguilucho's point in explaining this idea to Pedro is to show precisely how the dehierarchizing prison cell makes the pliability of that broader social fabric intelligible. As he introduces prison life to Pedro, he emphasizes the ease with which the supposedly rigid colonial hierarchy—the supposedly generalized rule—is reordered and eliminated within the context of the prison:

> In prison it is only by drinking and gambling that you can manage to get by, because there is nothing to do and no way to keep yourself busy. Here, the blacksmith, the tailor, the weaver, the painter, the military horseman, the tinsmith, the carriage builder and practitioners of many other trades, once they find themselves deprived of their freedom, also find themselves deprived of their trade, and as a result see themselves and their families reduced to an immiserated state from this forced idleness; and those who have no trade suffer in the exact same way. (449)

The prisoners Aguilucho describes (who occupy the same social status as the readers of the novel identified in Lizardi's prologue) are deprived of any ability to practice their trade, and as such they are, through their poverty, made indistinguishable from "those who have no trade." This dedifferentiation and dehierarchization of tradespeople and workers, on the one hand, and vagabonds and the poor, on the other, is a product of the colonial system's highly structured and hierarchical ways of being, seeing, doing, saying, and knowing.

The dehierarchization within the prison walls has the same effect as the hierarchical social divisions outside the prison: impoverishment and family members who are victims of the idling of the primary earners of income in the family. This is a notion echoed in a text like "Diálogo fingido de cosas ciertas" (included in Yáñez's anthology), where Lizardi critiques the effects that the monopoly system has for small-producing tradespeople in a way that parallels what Aguilucho describes as the effect that the prison cell has on tradespeople: you're poor whether you can be of use or you can't. Under the colonial system made visible inside the prison cell, there is no difference between the painter and the blacksmith (who have worked hard every day of their lives for what little they have) and the profligate Criollo, who ate, drank, and gambled his way to the same status. The colonial system makes "beggars of us all," Lizardi seems to be saying.

Aguilucho's point here is not a moral one, despite the many moralistic readings of Lizardi's writing that would suggest otherwise. His point instead is that the negative horizontalism within the prison is no different from the verticalized hierarchy outside the prison (hence the replication of its logic in Lizardi's critique of the monopoly system in "Diálogo fingido"). People are poor "due [not] to an inability to understand but instead due to their lack of culture and education" (450). In other words, the producer of poverty, whether inside the prison or outside the prison, is the failure to adhere to the normative set of cultural and social expectations. It is the experience of formlessness—having one's ways of being, doing, saying, or knowing not seen or heard or having them be seen or heard as out of place—that leads the vagabond, painter, blacksmith, and idle Criollo to be placed in prison together (i.e., their behavior is out of place, a violation of governing norms). What Aguilucho's analysis makes clear is that it is this dedifferentiating "out-of-placeness" that is the source of poverty. Regardless of one's "casta," regardless of one's trade (or lack thereof), they are all in prison together seeing themselves and their family suffer the same poverty: "[They] find themselves deprived of their trade, and as a result see themselves and their families reduced to an immiserated state from this forced idleness; and those who have no trade suffer in the exact same way" (449).

Importantly, Aguilucho also shares what he argues is the solution to the experience of formlessness, which is produced through the confluence of the vertical social hierarchy outside the prison and the impoverishing negative horizontalism within the prison. Aguilucho offers this solution twice in this initial conversation with Pedro: "Here [in prison], what matters is not whether you're refined or you're crass when you speak. What matters is not whether your skin is light or dark. It doesn't matter if your clothes are ragged or if you're well-dressed. *What matters here is seeing how you manage to get by*, and [also] winning some coin off our cell mates. So, let's go play [cards], Periquillo" (451, my emphasis). The solution Aguilucho identifies for the impoverishing effects of the experience of formlessness is "seeing how you manage to get by." Whether in its form as a differentiating hierarchy (normative "social divisions" with some above and some below) or as a negative horizontalism of carceral dedifferentiation (the inability to "make use" of anyone rendered "useless" because of the fundamental sameness of nonnormativity), that colonial system that "makes beggars of us all" can be counteracted by "managing to get by" ("pasar el rato").

The solution that the prison cell makes available—the notion of "pasar el rato" or "managing to get by" or "managing to get from here to there"—is articulated as an alternative to both the "decorum" of existing "social divisions" (a vertical hierarchy with obligations, responsibilities, and [lack of] privileges that locate some above and others below) and to the supposed "violations" of "decorum" that create the dedifferentiated community of the poor in the prison cell (a negative horizontalism with its impoverishing effects). This alternative seeks to circumvent, on the one hand, notions of "good use" (which would reproduce the colonial hierarchy by seeking to have one's ways of being, doing, saying, or knowing recognized and accepted within its governing norms and structures) and, on the other hand, notions of "bad use" (which would be to simply accept the colonial order and its decisions to ascribe a status of delinquency to certain ways of being, saying, doing, and knowing). The goal is to posit a new kind of category that neither seeks inclusion within the colonial hierarchy nor accepts poverty as an unchangeable status of dedifferentiated formlessness.

As already suggested above, Lizardi's goal is to utilize literature as a mechanism by which wealth can be made to meet its social obligations (i.e., making use of "our [improper] way of talking about things . . . [so as to give things] their proper form"). Lizardi's project, expressed through the observations made by a Mulatto prisoner, is to *make use* of what is seen as "improper." In other words, Aguilucho, like Lizardi, identifies the solution to the colonial system as a kind of "ill use." "Pasar el rato"—"managing to get by" or "managing to get from here to there" or, more simply, "ill use"—is not a program set up in advance in which a person is either refined or crass, well-dressed or in rags. Instead, it is finding a way, within the colonial system that makes "beggars of us all," to rework and reorganize social systems so that, even if only episodically, wealth can be directed toward meeting its "duties" and obligations to the social: "What matters is not whether your skin is light or dark. . . . What matters here is seeing how you manage to get by, and [also] winning some coin off our cell mates."

As I have argued elsewhere, Yáñez's embrace of Lizardi's aesthetic of "lumpen realism" rests on his enthusiasm for the idea of "ill use." As I said there, what Yáñez values most is the moment in which "others *see* and *say* that one is 'making ill use,' that one is out of place, that one behaves outside the formulas of 'decorum' that are used to exploit the poor and maintain privileges for the 'respectable'" (Buttes, "Partition" 42). As noted there, Yáñez organizes his understanding of "ill use" in Lizardi under the figure of the impoverished urban migrant: the pelado. The pelado, for Yáñez, is "a haphazard disruption of . . . 'prevailing habits and conventions' [and] is a direct challenge to 'the conservative, the man of status, the man of privilege, the man who exploits'" (42). For this reason, Yáñez asserts in his reading of Lizardi that "synonymy exists between '*pelado*' and '*igualado*' [one who asserts his or her equality], [because] '*pelado*' is often used to address, insult, reproach or threaten anyone presumptuous enough to declare him or herself another's equal" (42).

What Yáñez sees in a novel like *El periquillo* is that so-called pelados like Pedro or Aguilucho come into visibility precisely because they "declare [themselves] another's equal" (an "igualado") in the moment of their choosing. As Yáñez says (and as I have highlighted previously), "the *pelado* experiences a discomfort with any and all predetermined practices habits or formulas... he breaks with every type of tyranny; *he desires to live as he pleases*" (Yáñez in Buttes, "Partition" 42, my emphasis). This, of course, approaches very closely the lesson Aguilucho gives to Pedro in prison: "What matters is not whether your skin is light or dark.... What matters here is seeing how you manage to get by, and [also] winning some coin off our cell mates." And it is here in Aguilucho's observations that we can clearly see how a poverty novel like *El periquillo* (Latin America's first novel) gets so clearly linked to the conceptualization of national culture embedded both within Monterde's editorial series but also within what, in 1940, were the emergent structures of what would become the PRI and its consolidated single-party system.

To clarify what I mean and demonstrate how the experience of formlessness (which is made available in Yáñez's equation of poverty with the pelado via his reading of Lizardi) is essential for understanding Mexicanism as the reigning postrevolutionary cultural logic, it is worth quoting one last time my previous arguments:

> In Yáñez's reading [of Lizardi] ... the term "*pelado*" names the accumulation of unplanned, spontaneous assertions of more egalitarian partitions in each and every era of Mexican history. Beginning with indigenous rebellions and spiraling out into an expansive historical reading of post-Independence Mexico, there is no coherent program emerging from the heterogeneous faces attached to the term "*pelado*." Instead of naming a particular programmatic tradition, the actions are seen as "one-off" performances of an ever-evolving logic of equality. This meaning only materializes in specific moments of spontaneous assertions of equality and dissipates as a new order is established. As [Yáñez] notes, Hidalgo, Morelos, Guerrero, Santa Anna, Juárez, Porfirio Díaz, Madero, Carranza, Villa and Zapata were all called *pelados*, along with rebellious indigenous communities. (Buttes, "Partition" 42)

Now, while Yáñez identifies an egalitarian logic within the pelado's solutions to the experience of formlessness, it is also immediately possible to see the problem with this dedifferentiating horizontalism. It makes the peasant revolutionary Emiliano Zapata indistinguishable from the dictator Porfirio Díaz and collapses the actions of the bourgeois-liberal Francisco I. Madero into the actions taken by indigenous communities rebelling against land seizures and the destruction of the *ejido* system.

What is important to note here is not the ideological or political incoherence of such a claim but instead that what unifies them, in Yáñez's account, is not an ideological program set up in advance. The dedifferentiating horizontalism posited by Yáñez through his recovery of the figure of the pelado is not an attempt to develop some kind of expansive narrative linking that demonstrates how the country has taken various steps or passed through various stages in the "inevitable development" of capitalist or socialist modernities. Instead, his point is to demonstrate how this single figure makes intelligible a whole range of historical actors who, in one way or another, made use of their negative experiences of existing hierarchical "social divisions." Those figures make visible their deviation from the supposedly proper forms of social relations that would bring about varying desired forms of modernity. In his embrace of those who were "presumptuous enough to declare [themselves] another's equal" and who momentarily dedifferentiated existing social hierarchies in order to posit more egalitarian organizations, Yáñez establishes the utility of formlessness (poverty) to securing the impossibility of any inegalitarian form. While inequalities (new norms and social hierarchies) will, inevitably, be reestablished following horizontalist moments of egalitarianism created by those seen or heard as pelados, the newly formless (or those who continually experience formlessness from one set of hierarchies to the next) will emerge as new expressions of the pelado's lack of "decorum" in a new historical sequence and thus assert an egalitarian logic once again. What Yáñez envisions is a formlessness without form, that is, the experience of the egalitarian without the need to appeal to specific inegalitarian forms set up in advance: "he desires to live as he pleases" with no need to appeal to capitalism, socialism, or another socioeconomic system.

Yáñez's appeal to the pelado is an effort to conceptualize a formlessness without form, that is, an experience of not being seen or heard that is not conditioned on nor determined by a relation to any specific set of norms and conventions producing modernity. It would appear in the world as an accumulating series of "'one-off' performances [that produce] an ever-evolving logic of equality." In this context, it is possible to understand Aguilucho's observations more fully. In the narrative retrospect that is the novel we read, Pedro is able to see and say that his past behavior was nonnormative and not of benefit to himself or society. At the same time, however, in his seeing and saying that his behavior was nonnormative and even harmful to society, he also demonstrates the harm created by nondeviant, normative behavior filled with decorum that benefits and sustains the existing, unequal colonial "social divisions" and their hierarchies. In making visible his breaches in the vertical hierarchies of colonial decorum through the narrative account of his swindling and scheming with Juan Largo, his time in prison shows hierarchy's horizontalist counterpart through carceral dedifferentiation (the painter and blacksmith rendered as "useless" as the swindling, profligate Criollo).

If we accept Yáñez's account of Lizardi (which would be to accept the Mexicanist cultural logic that governed intellectual exchange in Mexico after the Revolution), the idea of "managing to get by" or "managing to make it from here to there" ("pasar el rato") would be the strategy that alters the negativity of this momentary horizontalism. "Pasar el rato" would be the term that expresses the logic of the pelado's behavior when it remains outside structures of visibility. Within the prison cell where verticalized "social divisions" dissipate amid the dedifferentiating logic of "getting by," Aguilucho works with other cell mates to swindle Pedro out of the food, clothing, and other resources he receives from don Antonio, a recently released Criollo inmate he had met in the prison yard. While some critics have described Aguilucho's behavior as an expression of "a revanchist attitude" (Ramírez 79), from Yáñez's point of view in 1940, the actions resonate differently: they are the logic by which wealth can be made to perform its social functions. In making material fact his observational assertion that "what matters is not whether your skin is light or dark . . . [but instead how you] manage to get by, and [also] winning some coin off our cell mates," Aguilucho executes a momentary tearing down of the particular (hierarchical) ways of seeing and hearing expressed in Pedro's surprise at Aguilucho's eloquence and the cell mates' conclusion that Pedro wishes to maintain himself in a position of superiority over them.

As noted, these hierarchical ways of seeing, being, doing, and knowing are understood to be the source of poverty. What this prison sequence suggests in the way it foregrounds Aguilucho's behavior and experience is that, for a Mexicanist critic like Yáñez, Lizardi creates a model in which there are no predetermined forms of "decorum" (and no programmatic form of modernity) that would guarantee success or survival. Instead, what Yáñez takes from Lizardi by generalizing the literary logic of *El periquillo* as the cultural logic of the pelado is that what is most essential for Mexican modernity is the concept of "getting by": creating a situation in which a hierarchy can be leveled, temporary equality established, and then advantage gained before the inequalities of a hierarchy are reestablished. Formlessness (poverty) does not exist in relation to specific forms of social life: it has a nonrelation to those hierarchies and merely needs to level the hierarchy and its norms when those norms seek to assert themselves. Formlessness, in this model, does not depend on form: it is a poverty that is detached from any specific set of social relations and an egalitarian procedure that can appear spontaneously with no need to appeal in advance to existing social norms or historical sequence that conditions that experience. In Yáñez's view, poverty is transhistorical and transcends the specificities of material social relations. What Lizardi makes available is, in essence, a formlessness conceived without form.

While it might seem obvious that formlessness is always *without* form, the scenario that Lizardi envisions and that Yáñez adopts as his politico-aesthetic model is one in which it is formlessness ("ill use" not set up in advance) itself that enters as the productive motor of modernity with no need to appeal to preexisting norms or conventions: "our [experience of formlessness] is a way of giving things their proper form." In the transformation of the experience of formlessness from a problem defined by its specific, material and historical relation to the "proper" forms of sociality (i.e., a problem of social and economic relations) into the open-ended, essential resource that keeps all forms open, the experience of formlessness paradoxically takes on a kind of form-giving role. In the context of *El periquillo*, it is possible to see this dynamic in (1) the existing "decorum" and "necessary" norms and conventions that sustain colonial "social divisions" (which Yáñez takes as a proxy for Porfirian "social divisions"); and (2) the negative effect of deviating from those supposedly necessary norms and conventions (the carceral dedifferentiation that Aguilucho describes).

As noted in the introduction to this study, when formlessness takes on the political roles ascribed to social norms and conventions in capitalist or socialist models of modernities, we enter into the logic of the "third" or populist position. The experience of being seen as "improper" or heard as "vulgar" is transformed into the valorization of nonnormativity and the experience of *deviating* from existing norms and conventions becomes a key mechanism for producing modernity. In this way, the third position is articulated as the conversion of the negative horizontalism of the prison cell into a generalizable strategy: the experience of formlessness (persistent and permanent "ill use") takes on an episodic structure, which enables that experiential account of poverty to take on a kind of form-giving role without, for that matter, setting up new hierarchical, inegalitarian forms. There will always be a "next episode" to level whatever inequalities were created in the sequence of "ill use." In championing Lizardi as a model for Mexican literature and Mexican culture, Yáñez seeks to generalize and make permanent the egalitarian logic of "ill use" we see in *El periquillo*. It is the lesson Pedro learned from Aguilucho in prison, one that guided his actions over the course of the novel's remaining five volumes and, in key ways, is what he imparts to his readers: the persistent "ill use" of existing "social divisions" that require a temporary (often more egalitarian) reorganization can be utilized to his benefit before the hierarchy and its inequalities are reestablished and Pedro is punished.

Swindled out of his remaining belongings and tricked by Aguilucho into believing there are special punishments for Criollo prisoners, Pedro ends up being exonerated by the corrupt prison *escribano*, Chanfaina, who brings Pedro into his service. Pedro witnesses all sorts of malfeasance on the part of this official: from having an indigenous prisoner serve the sentence for his mistress's brother to falsifying documents to wage theft (i.e., refusing to pay Pedro for more than a year). Pedro is able to learn "everything that a notary (*escribano*) can do" (483) and eventually seduces the sister of Chanfaina's mistress, whom Chanfaina had brought to his home as a domestic worker and concubine. Asserting himself as Chanfaina's equal in both professional and personal contexts, Pedro is eventually discovered and chased out of Chanfaina's home. This eventually leads him to a series of additional apprenticeships, such as one with the barber-dentist don

Agustín Rapamentas, a friend of Pedro's father, and another with the infamous *boticario* Doctor Purgante.

In each of these cases, Pedro engages with the profession just enough "to get by," establishing the repeated structure that Yáñez values: the persistent "ill use" of existing "social divisions" that require a temporary reorganization (a dedifferentiation between the impoverished Criollo and the corrupt professional), which Pedro utilizes to his benefit before the hierarchy and its inequalities are reestablished and Pedro is punished. For Yáñez, this structure is a rejection of "a 'good taste' [that] requires euphemism, circumlocution, fabrication, detachment and a disregard for reality" and inserts in its place the cultural logic of the pelado that rejects "every kind of artifice" (*Pensador* xix). Yáñez values what is an "inevitable" nonnormativity as a source for persistently generating a horizontalist leveling of false hierarchies. Yáñez sees Lizardi as generating a model in which dedifferentiation can be shifted from the purely negative experience of formlessness and the material impoverishment that follows from it (the blacksmith collapsed into the vagabond) into a positive one: a structural or institutional process for leveling false hierarchies through political systems, education, and literary form. As Yáñez clearly states at the outset of his essay, "Political independence reinvigorated literary independence" (vi). That political system and that literary independence rest on the pelado's ability to level hierarchies and on the ability to prevent the experience of formlessness from ever emerging as a negative experience because it was measured against predetermined and preexisting norms. Establishing the experience of formlessness (poverty) as a mechanism to negate the form-giving role of modernizing norms and conventions is essential to the forms Yáñez himself seeks to develop in his political, educational, and literary work. Those forms, as noted, are constituted by the accumulation of serial experiences of nonnormativity.

Because Yáñez's essay appears as the prologue to an anthology meant to serve educational purposes in Mexican universities, it is necessary to consider how he understood the task of education as paralleling the task of politics: knowledge must be made to perform its social obligations in the same way as wealth. Hierarchies are inevitable. As such, the primary strategy for undoing their inequalities is an awareness of them and a recognition that persistent "ill use" and the temporary (hopefully more egalitarian) reorganization of those hierarchies occurs before they are reestablished. As Yáñez notes in the closing of his essay, "José Joaquín Fernández de Lizardi . . . is Mexico's teacher and the teacher of our youth. Accept your responsibilities! Live with an awareness of social hierarchies and your position within them so that, whether high or low, they remain honorable because we identify with them!" (*Pensador* l).

What Yáñez seems to be saying here is what can be generalized from Pedro's experience in the prison cell: by being aware of how the hierarchy functions, it can be temporarily reorganized, positions within it flexibilized, and the negative experiences of formlessness transformed into positive experiences of creating an "honorable" hierarchy with which we can, temporarily, identify before it needs to be reorganized again amid novel experiences of formlessness. This serial structure is present in Lizardi's novel and, as we will see, equally part of a certain variant of populist logic that structured the PRI. And yet while it nominally seeks to conceptualize a formlessness without form, that is, a nonnormativity that is transhistorical and transcends the specificities of material social relations, this appeal is, nevertheless, structured by repeated formulas like those of the "balcony effect" that structured the Peronist ritual, which was analyzed in the introduction.

## Cinematic Formlessness and la Mexicanidad as Commodity

One of the clearest examples of this comes into view when examining another work that was released in 1940, the year Yáñez published his anthology of Lizardi's works. That work is the film *Ahí está el detalle* (1940), starring Mario Moreno as the peladito Cantinflas. As Jeffrey Pilcher has pointed out, what would eventually be filmed and released as Cantinflas's first commercial success, *Ahí está el detalle* was actually initially conceived as a filmic adaptation of Lizardi's *El periquillo sarniento* (71). The cost-prohibitive sets eventually led the scriptwriter to create a screenplay based on his own early experiences working as a pro bono lawyer for impoverished defendants from Peralvillo and Tepito (72). But, the "successful formula" (xxiv) that Cantinflas developed with *Ahí está el detalle* became a model for films that were some of the biggest commercial successes in 1940s Mexico when the market for film was rapidly expanding, growing to a hundred million annual ticket sales by 1947 (84).

The series of films that began in 1940 with *Ahí está el detalle* "usually featured two female leads, one plebian, the other wealthy" (Pilcher 67), and the films "explored the ambiguity of identity within Mexico's social hierarchy by having the pelado mistaken for popular heroes and authority figures" (68). Pilcher explains this structure away as simply "unrealistic depictions of revolutionary social mobility" (68), but as we have seen above, the dedifferentiation of social hierarchies is essential to the Lizardian tradition that Yáñez recovers for a 1940s Mexicanist cultural logic through its association with the figure of the pelado, a figure with which Cantinflas has become synonymous. Perhaps even more importantly, given that both Cantinflas and Lizardi produce works of humor, it is important to highlight the fact that, as Dianna C. Niebylski has noted, the effects of porosity are often essential to the success of comedic or satirical approaches to the social (*Humoring* 10). Indeed, she points out in her analysis of Lizardi's novel *La Quijotita* (produced at the same time as he was writing installments of *El periquillo* as well as other works Yáñez included in his anthology), Lizardi "[avails] himself of the comic figure of a would-be *pícara* (Quixotita) to boost his book's popularity even while condemning comic women as misguided at best and immoral at worst" (23). What Niebylski points out, of course, is the logic Yáñez finds embedded in the epigraph he selects for Lizardi: our improper way of talking about things is a way of giving things their proper form. And that logic is one that is extremely popular with audiences, whether it be in the context of Lizardi's newspaper or Cantinflas's films.

I will return to Lizardi's popularity at the end of this chapter, but it is important to note here that the popularity of Cantinflas's Lizardi-style impropriety was developed into a set of formulas that were organized not only for comic effect but also for commercial success as a cinematic commodity that circulated widely and successfully in Latin America and Spain. The current study does not have space for a full consideration of the commodity nature of the formulaic films Cantinflas made in this period, since that would require analysis of his later films, which have often been described as lower in quality and criticized as too overtly supportive of the PRI and its increasingly authoritarian approach to politics. I will, however, return to the question of the commodity in the next chapter. What I highlight in my analysis of *Ahí está el detalle*, instead, is the ways that the most common elements in Cantinflas's cinematic commodities find pairing with both Lizardi's literary model (valued by Yáñez) and something like Perón's cultural-political rituals. Indeed, those connections connect quite clearly to what Steinberg, citing Roger Bartra, calls a process of self-inscription through the ritual repetition of the "Mexican Office," the tropes of mexicanidad that would manage and police actions, behaviors, and thoughts (i.e., ways of being, doing, saying, and knowing). The challenge, however, is recognizing that this logic is horizontalist in nature and rests on conceiving poverty as a problem of formlessness and its solution as the rejection of all norms and conventions in favor of the experience of formlessness or nonnormativity itself.

*Ahí está el detalle* is a film that features Mario Moreno in his classic role as the street tramp Cantinflas who, in the film's opening, arrives at the wealthy household where his girlfriend, Paz (Dolores Camarillo), is employed as a domestic worker. This scenario sets into motion a series of events that produce multiple instances of mistaken identity and its correlated processes of dedifferentiation that sees the jovial but penniless Cantinflas treated, at differing points in the film, as a loafing nuisance, a feared home intruder, a beloved brother and brother-in-law, the heir to a fortune and rightful "señor de la casa," the estranged father of some eight or nine illegitimate sons, a murderer, an (almost) newlywed, and a prisoner. Cantinflas's wealth and, indeed, his very identity come and go in the blink of an eye. One minute he is Paz's loafing boyfriend Cantinflas, who pockets a dropped wallet just before he's asked to euthanize a rabid dog (a task given to Paz) in exchange for a free meal from the kitchen where she works. The next minute he is hiding in a storage closet when don Cayetano (Joaquín Pardavé), the owner of the house, unexpectedly returns home and, in what Pilcher would call an "unrealistic" turn, becomes convinced that the man he discovers drinking his liquor and smoking his cigars is not the penniless boyfriend of his domestic worker but instead don Leonardo del Paso, his long-lost brother-in-law and the true heir to the family fortune.

It is worth pausing for a moment to recognize what happens in this moment. This ruse that repositions Cantinflas in the social hierarchy is one that is generated so as to avoid disclosure of Paz's improper behavior (she brought her boyfriend into the home for a free meal) as well as the improper behavior of doña Dolores (Sofía Álvarez). Unhappily married to don Cayetano, Dolores had an affair with a mobster named Bobby Lechuga (his first name is the same as the rabid dog Cantinflas killed), who goes by the street name "the Fox-Terrier" (which is also the breed of the rabid dog). Bobby, who is the owner of the wallet Cantinflas snatched from the ground in the film's opening sequence, threatened to disclose their affair before he is killed in a business dispute. Confusion over the identity of Cantinflas, which converges with the confusion over the identity of the two fox-terriers, leads to a significant number of the comic sequences that find Cantinflas accepting and refusing the various identities assigned to him from one moment to the next, each time with an eye on making it from one point to the next with a full stomach and as little discomfort and responsibility as possible. That everyone (including del Paso's common law wife) insists that Cantinflas is Leonardo del Paso and the fact that Cantinflas possesses the mobster's wallet ultimately lead to the police, acting on a tip regarding del Paso's involvement in the murder, arresting Cantinflas and placing him in jail. This, of course, leads to the hilarious courtroom sequence that is often cited as the most emblematic example of the brand of humor Cantinflas practiced.

The parallels between *Ahí está el detalle* and *El periquillo sarniento* are undeniable. Aside from the narrative device of circumstantial evidence that lands both Pedro (with Juan Largo's rosary) and Cantinflas (with Bobby Lechuga's wallet) in prison, the behavior of each of them is structured by a logic Yáñez associates with the pelado: "A synonymy exists between '*pelado*' and '*igualado*' [one who asserts his or her equality], [because] '*pelado*' is often used to address, insult, reproach or threaten anyone presumptuous enough to declare him or herself another's equal" (Yáñez in Buttes, "Partition" 42). If, in Yáñez's reading, this is what structures *El periquillo*, it is also what structures the comic sequences between Cantinflas (as pelado) and Paz (as domestic worker) in *Ahí está el detalle*.

This working-class couple are social and economic equals. But once the existing "social divisions" undergo "improper" use, Cantinflas, newly empowered by being misidentified as the long-lost heir to the family home, accepts the privileges associated with being seen and heard as the wealthy don Leonardo. He relaxes on a sofa in the sitting room, openly drinking don Cayetano's liquor and smoking his cigars just as don Cayetano himself would (figure 1.1). This, of course, is precisely what Cantinflas was already doing when he was first discovered by don Cayetano, though in that case he remained unseen and (mostly) unheard while hidden in the storage closet. Having not been witness to the sequence of events that led to the mistaken identity (or, from Yáñez's point of view, how the pelado-igualado revealed the instability of supposedly rigid and immovable social hierarchies), Paz panics when she sees Cantinflas openly behaving as he would

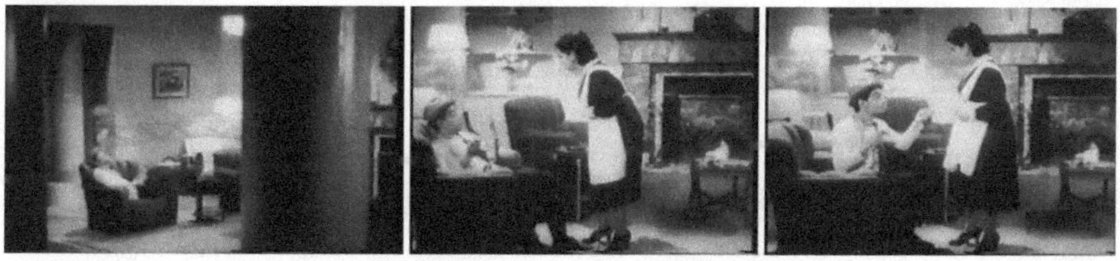

FIGURE 1.1 Still sequence from *Ahí está el detalle*. Cantinflas openly lounging, as seen from the servant's point of view.

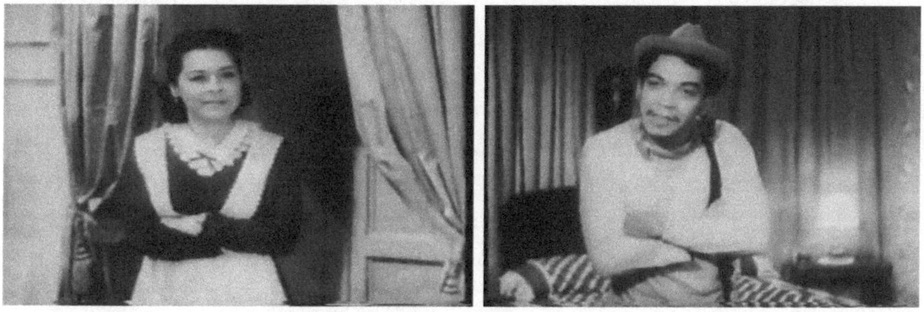

FIGURE 1.2 Still sequence from *Ahí está el detalle*. Shot, reverse shot structure of conflict between the "servant" (Paz) and the "boss" (Cantinflas).

when hidden out of sight. She fears reprisal from her employer, not recognizing that the sitting room, like the prison cell in Lizardi's novel, had become a space in which nonnormative behavior (by Paz, Dolores, and Cantinflas) had temporarily leveled hierarchies, enabling positions and identities to shift within it before the hierarchy was restored. It is in this context that Cantinflas protests, plainly explaining that he had already been discovered by don Cayetano and that he, Cantinflas, is now the owner of the house. Obviously assuming that this claim was simply another of Cantinflas's jokes, she tells him to come with her to the kitchen. Cantinflas responds to this by saying, "No, why would I go to the kitchen? I don't need to. That's only for the servants!" And when Paz insists he accompany her by grabbing him by the arm, he refuses, pulling his arm away and telling her, "Do not touch me because *we are not equal*. If you could be so kind, please refrain from addressing me as you have been looking down at me for quite some time now" (my emphasis). A similar sequence (figure 1.2) occurs upstairs when Paz is asked to prepare a bedroom for "don Leonardo" (Cantinflas). Frustrated at the turn of events that has her boyfriend now improperly assigned a position of authority over her, Paz asks in exasperation if "el señor" might need anything else before she leaves. Cantinflas, wanting to have no obstacles to continuing his improper use of the house and other resources (now made temporarily "proper" by don Cayetano), he tells her that he won't be needing anything else other than for her to take herself and her "igualada" attitude out of the room.

Aside from the hilarious verbal sparring between Moreno and Camarillo (who was coming off an award-winning performance as a supporting actress in a film released a few months earlier), the visual structuring of these two sequences is important. In the first sequence, the camera initially takes the working-class viewpoint (that is, Paz's viewpoint) in order to organize our understanding of both the pelado's impropriety and its effect on the existing order: our first view of Cantinflas as beneficiary of the "*jerarquía* igualada" is a glimpse from the kitchen (or an adjacent location). Seeing Cantinflas lounging on the sofa and carrying on as if he were still hidden away in the storage closet, that is, seeing that Cantinflas's "improper" behavior can be easily seen, Paz enters the scene because she cannot make sense of what she is seeing. This, in some sense, parallels Pedro's inability to make sense of Aguilucho's eloquence in the prison cell. And Paz's response to this counterpart to the very familiar "social divisions" of the existing hierarchy (i.e., the negative horizontalism that leaves the verticalized hierarchy intact) parallels Pedro's as well. She insists on applying the "rule" that she understands as governing the scene by seeking to relocate both of them to the working-class space of the kitchen that remains hidden from view. Visually, then, she is placed above the lounging Cantinflas, urging him from her place on a sort of pedestal or "balcony" to bring order to the scene.

While the viewer can see that the structure of the balcony effect here is to position Paz (the working-class figure) above the figure of the "out-of-place," impoverished pelado in an effort to restore the existing order after it has been interrupted by the impropriety of the behavior of both herself and her employer (Dolores), what Cantinflas's response reveals is that the balcony is actually inverted. The "out-of-place" Cantinflas, who did not need to change his ways of being, doing, saying, and knowing to occupy the space on the sofa, is the one who actually restores the hierarchy. His position on the sofa is not one of "inferiority," or what Yáñez would call a pelado "buried in a chasm" (*Pensador* xx), but instead the position of authority: the "señor de la casa" who can and does discount the ways of being, doing, saying and knowing expressed by the working class, which are also his own. Like the shot, reverse shot structure of Peronism discussed in the analysis of posthegemony in the introduction, the command "Do not touch me because *we are not equal*" "both joins and separates: the multitude's heterogeneity becomes homogeneity as its various partial aspects . . . [become] dependent upon their relation with those on the balcony" (Beasley-Murray 244).

In this case, however, it is not the leader-artist but instead the pelado, or, more specifically, the peladito Cantinflas, who "joins and separates": he is dedifferentiated from the Criollo ruling class (as he is seen as "don Leonardo") as well as from the working class (as he is just as easily returned to his impoverished [and imprisoned] status later in the film). In this sense, the peladito refusing to be relegated to the working-class spaces of servants and at the same time insisting that everyone has a place (as long as his isn't with the servants), the logic of the sequence in the sitting room of don Cayetano's house parallels the visual structure of Diego

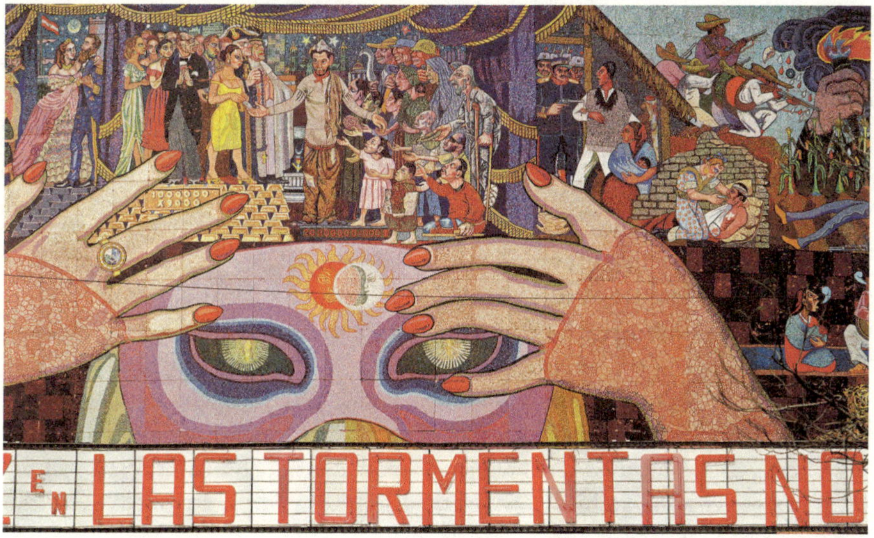


FIGURE 1.3 Detail of Diego Rivera, *Historia del teatro*, mural, Teatro de los Insurgentes, 1953. Copyright Historia del Teatro: Banco de México Diego Rivera Frida Kahlo Museums Trust (Printed with permission of Artist Rights Society). Photo credit: Schalkwijk / Art Resource, NY (Printed with permission of Art Resource, NY).

Rivera's 1953 mural at the Teatro de los Insurgentes (figure 1.3). Here, we see Cantinflas squarely in the center, on a pedestal slightly elevated above the poor on the right-hand side and slightly below the ruling class on the left-hand side. Cantinflas serves here as the Mexicanist expression of formlessness without appeal to form: a permanent experience of dedifferentiation (formlessness) that temporarily levels hierarchies before they rematerialize. If we accept the absent couple of don Cayetano and doña Dolores (who remain upstairs) as an added component of the sequence featured in figure 1.1, we can read Rivera's work as a muralist repetition of the "balcony effect" we see developed in this first iteration of Cantinflas's commercially successful formula.

As Carlos Monsiváis notes, Cantinflas brings into being a series of films in which he produces "300 identical jokes" while playing, year after year, an unending series of professions: "fireman, musician, film extra, a student in remedial classes, bell boy, a mailman" (*Escenas* 96). Like Aguilucho's complaint about the dedifferentiating effects of the prison cell, this dedifferentiating unity does not bring "social divisions" to an end but instead operates as a negative horizontalism. Indeed, like Peronism, with its ritualized public spectacles organized by what Beasley-Murray calls the shot, reverse shot structure of the "balcony effect," the "300 identical jokes" that structure Cantinflas films as profitable domestic and exportable commodities are similarly premised on the shot, reverse shot structure that achieves a dedifferentiating separateness. Indeed, the second sequence in *Ahí está el detalle* (figure 1.2) not only finds Cantinflas repeating a hackneyed joke about the poor's (and his own!) lack of hygiene while also reestablishing the social distance between him and Paz (calling her an "igualada") but also is quite literally a shot, reverse shot sequence.

Now, given the parallels I am drawing between Peronism, on the one hand, and, on the other, the Mexicanism developed out of Yáñez's reading of *El periquillo sarniento* and in my reading of Cantinflas's *Ahí está el detalle*, it should come as no surprise that many scholars who have considered the problems embedded in works like those of Lizardi and Cantinflas (i.e., dedifferentiation that simply accepts or actually reestablishes hierarchies) often seek to locate a solution to those problems in the figure of the pelado himself (or in the concept I have been calling the appeal to formlessness without appeal to form). Key examples of this appear in the work of Carlos Monsiváis and in the scholarship of Gareth Williams. While I have written in more detail about Williams's arguments elsewhere, it is worth pausing here to consider the solution Monsiváis proposes for the hierarchies reestablished by the work of a comedian whose "smiling picaro from the slums" transformed "the fierce and dangerous pelado" into the "tame and harmless peladito" (*Escenas* 88).

For Monsiváis, one way of understanding the persistence of Cantinflas as a figure is to recognize "his incoherence as the coherence of the multitudes, his aggressiveness as the unawareness of hierarchies, his jokes' memorizability as its guarantee to be repeated with success" (*Escenas* 94). But Monsiváis emphasizes that understanding Cantinflas would be to contextualize more fully the myth that emerged in "the forties [when] Cantinflas becomes synonymous with Mexico's poor and the representative defender of those who come from humble origins" (94–95). Instead, Cantinflas must be recognized as what Roger Bartra calls "a conformist critic" (*Cage* 126) and as the creator of films that Ilan Stavans describes as "[lacking] an ideologically charged message inviting the unhappy to rebel" (83). In other words, Monsiváis emphasizes that the image Cantinflas developed as the impoverished man fighting social injustice by making nonsense of power was "at the same time . . . itself a branch of the cinema industry and popular culture: there are figurines of Cantinflas available in markets and shops in various sizes and made from various materials" (95). Indeed, for Monsiváis, the key event that helps us understand Cantinflas took place the year before *Ahí está el detalle* was released: the 1939 founding of Posa Films (Publicidad Organizada, S.A., or Organized Advertising Incorporated), as the production, distribution, and branding company for Cantinflas. As Monsiváis notes, "Some journalists and—in private—many producers see in Cantinflas the entry point for North American capital into cinema" (*Escenas* 93–94). What Monsiváis suggests is that in Cantinflas, as in Yáñez's account of *El periquillo sarniento*, we see a temporary leveling of "social divisions" before hierarchies are reestablished in a slightly reorganized set of traditional "social divisions": "at first, Cantinflas is a success because his comedy is innovative; afterward, his successes are premised on expressing a new traditional cultural consciousness" (94).

And what enables the construction of that new set of traditional "social divisions" is the work of Posa Films: "Cantinflas owes his success to the wide distribution Posa Films gave him . . . and to the skills of his agents and partners Santiago Reachi and Jacques Gelman" (92) as well as his earliest routine directors (Fernando A. Rivero and Carlos Toussaint) and scriptwriter (Estanislao Shilinsky).

As Pilcher notes, Posa Films made Cantinflas "a brand name in its own right" (68), something that was initially achieved through the early work in 1939 of creating advertising shorts in the lead-up to the writing and production of what would be *Ahí está el detalle* (which, as noted, was previously slated as an adaptation of Lizardi's *El periquillo*). In that year before *Ahí está el detalle*, Cantinflas filmed five short films, where he starred in plots that hinged on his use of particular commercial products. For example, *Siempre listo en las tinieblas* was a promotion for Eveready batteries and had those batteries function as a key plot device. A similar structure was used in other film shorts from that year, such as *Jengibre contra dinamita* (for Canada Dry ginger ale) or *Cantinflas ruletero* (for General Motors's Chevrolet brand). As Pilcher points out, the 1940s saw Cantinflas serve as pitch man for a department store, Coca-Cola, razor blades, cigarettes, and tailor shops, among other commodities (71).

What Aguilucho identified in Lizardi's novel as a kind of negative horizontalism in carceral dedifferentiation is redeployed in the work carried out by Cantinflas as a positive logic of formlessness in the ways it was connected to "selling the consumer dream" (Pilcher 71), which was a key component of sustaining the political program and cultural logic of the PRI's Mexicanism. In other words, if in Peronism the key to "populist modernity" is the nonnormative, participatory, and egalitarian experience cocreated by leader and people, Monsiváis sees the production of what he calls "Mexico's essence" ("el ser mexicano") (*Escenas* 94) in the interactions between Cantinflas as the "comedian-businessman" (94) and his viewers: "Cantinflas is the authentic Man of the People, an idiosyncratic expression that will be the essence of [a] new tradition" (94). That "new tradition," of course, is the postrevolutionary Mexicanist politico-cultural logic that underscores the structures and activities of the PRI, which, with the emergence of the presidency of Miguel Alemán (1946–1952), took a more concerted turn toward championing a consumerist commodity logic that would be connected to the ritual repetition of the "Mexican Office," the tropes of mexicanidad that would manage and police actions, behaviors, and thoughts (i.e., ways of being, doing, saying, and knowing). While the confluence between poverty as a renewable resource for producing formlessness without appeal to form and the commodity as a similarly positioned concept will be explored in the next chapter in more detail, it is important to explain the solution Monsiváis imagines for the ritualized Mexicanism that is embedded in the "300 identical jokes," which enable the logic of antihierarchical dedifferentiation and the logic of the commodity to coincide in Cantinflas.

The central problem with the Cantinflas approach to "social divisions" in Monsiváis's account is as follows: "The poor cheer in [Cantinflas] what it is they recognize and identify with . . . [which is a] festive and vindicative portrayal of poverty. The rich appreciate the opportunity to laugh at the [satirized] demagogues and the poor . . . [all the while claiming] to 'normalize' the revolutionary period" (*Escenas* 91). While Monsiváis is specifically talking about *Así es mi tierra* (1936), Cantinflas's debut where he played a supporting role in a postrevolutionary narrative that takes place in a rural setting, the point that Monsiváis makes with this and other Cantinflas films is that, in spite of living "in a country without comedic traditions" (94), Cantinflas was able to create a categorical notion of "the Funny at a national scale" (94).

It was that organization that was the central problem for Monsiváis. It was able to be ritualized: "[Cantinflas] appears on screen, moves, begins to weave his verbal tangles, confuses his interlocutor, and makes fun of him for never grasping the knowledge embedded in those linguistic deviations . . . and the viewing public is pleased, enjoying the opportunity to feel happy, delighting in the humorous situation" (*Escenas* 94). And then it was commodified ("300 identical jokes" in a serial production of increasingly formulaic films exported around the Spanish-speaking world). As ritual and commodity, the cinematic practice of Cantinflas formed a part of steps to "'normalize' the revolutionary tradition," organizing conventions where none existed before and removing formlessness and nonnormativity from lived experience in favor of formlessness as a kind of form: *cantinflismo*, the disconcerted figure of authority dedifferentiated from the pelado who (temporarily) steps into his shoes before order is reestablished, requiring a new act of dedifferentiation (i.e., a new film to be released next year).

The solution for Monsiváis, then, is a rejection of that organization and a pushing off of any and every form and formula. This strategy would be as relevant for contesting the ritual as it is for contesting the commodity. In this sense, his argument parallels the view of the pelado Yáñez develops in his analysis of Lizardi: "the pelado experiences a discomfort within any and all predetermined practices, habits or formulas . . . he breaks with every type of tyranny; he desires to live as he pleases" (*Pensador* xxii). In Yáñez's account, the pelado is the figure "[who] dares to think and act with spontaneity, outside the confines of reigning habits, prejudices and conventions" and, in many cases "[they are] unknown men from the lower classes" (xx). For Monsiváis, the pelado is "the shadow of poverty lurking in the city . . . the nameless threat" (*Escenas* 88). For Yáñez, the pelado is able to "[take] reality as a whole . . . make do in order to get by" (xxiii), while for Monsiváis he "is the figure [who threatens] violence, robbery or assault" (88). In other words, the alternative to both Cantinflas and Pedro from *El periquillo* is a figure like Aguilucho.

## Aguilucho and the Direction of Poverty

In the novel's final volume, Aguilucho reappears as a *cazador* or bandit. It is in the interpretation of a character like Aguilucho that the horizontalist models advocated by Monsiváis and Yáñez arrive at mistaken conclusions regarding poverty. Upon initially seeing Pedro (recently impoverished anew), Aguilucho mistakes him for an indigenous peasant. He eventually recognizes Pedro, and when Pedro also sees that it is Aguilucho, he once again listens to Aguilucho's advice, this time a practical iteration of his earlier lesson that taught Pedro that "what is important here is how you get by": "for now, get back on the horse, which is what is important" (834). The importance of getting on the horse is so that they can easily and quickly move off the main road, where they will be easily seen and heard (and therefore also easily apprehended by the authorities or challenged by rivals). Aguilucho takes Pedro with his crew of bandits to a hillside hideout "[where] we seat ourselves in a thicket from which we could see the road very clearly but could not ourselves be seen" (834). In this thicket hidden away from view, which can be said to parallel to the prison cell, Pedro narrates the misfortunes that have guided his life since prison (i.e., how he has put into practice what Aguilucho taught him, or, *cómo pasó el rato*). Aguilucho similarly explains what he has been doing, and more particularly, he gives details about the dangerous activities associated with his work as a cazador. When Pedro expresses trepidation at the possibility of working alongside the group of bandits, Aguilucho reproaches Pedro: "It seems to me that you're not so much a coward as you are someone who clings too closely to conventions, wanting a fine life without risking anything; but let me tell you something: that idea misses the mark, because he who doesn't risk anything can't cross the sea. These tasks were made for men" (837).

Including in this reproach the *machista* bravado that would be so common in postrevolutionary descriptions of the pelado, Aguilucho pursues here an argument like the one Pedro first heard in the prison cell. His is a call to "ser muy hombre" and level hierarchies: Pedro's cowardly love of comfort and wealth should be torn asunder and give way to courageous acts of redistribution, like those carried out, in Yáñez's account, by figures like Villa, Zapata, and rebellious indigenous communities but also by figures like Francisco I. Madero and Porfirio Díaz. In Yáñez's account, what Lizardi provides in a figure like Aguilucho—in both his eloquence and his refusal to accept unequal structures—is a model for transforming the negative horizontalism of carceral dedifferentiation and the verticalized hierarchies of colonial "social divisions" into a positive horizontalism that, like *El periquillo* itself, makes the egalitarian logic of "ill use" a generalized, structural element of the whole. In other words, for Yáñez, what Lizardi teaches to Mexico's youth is that there is not only what is "proper" (which, in this interpretation, Lizardi associates with the colonial order he rejects) and "improper" (which is simply the other side of the colonial order). For Yáñez, there is a third option made intelligible by Lizardi's epigrammatic rule: our improper way of talking about things is a way of giving things their proper form.

The permanent process of making "proper" what is seen and heard as "improper" does not cease with a single episode: it is not reducible to the eloquence of one Mulatto prisoner who ran afoul of existing "proper structures," nor would it be reducible to the "300 identical jokes" that structure the cinematic commodities that created a new comic tradition and made Cantinflas a "brand." Indeed, in Yáñez's view, the permanent process of making "proper" what is seen and heard as "improper"—a process that, in his account, is synonymous with both the figure of the pelado and egalitarianism more generally ("[the pelado is] the person who, have been assigned to an inferior social level, asserts himself as equal"; *Pensador* xxi)—has infinite ways of manifesting itself within existing "social divisions":

> "Pelado" is the term for a politician who gets rid of special deals (*privilegios*), who imposes new taxes, who recognizes the truth in the abuses that the poor and the indigenous report. . . . [Pelado is the term for] the worker who goes out on strike, the peasant farmer who stakes a claim to land, the servant who appeals to the courts for his rights and talks back to his employer. . . . [Pelado is the term for] the writer who tells the unvarnished truth and calls out corruption. . . . [Pelado is the term for anyone who] does not mince words or rely on affected or pretentious behaviors and conduct. (xxi)

If this long list of examples of behavior connected with the figure of the pelado seems to echo the long list of professions in Aguilucho's account of carceral dedifferentiation, the point Yáñez makes here is that dedifferentiation—a horizontalist logic that levels hierarchies that see certain ways of being, saying, doing, and knowing as inferior—can be made positive by being connected to an entire tradition, a corpus of serial acts. Linking rebellious indigenous communities to Hidalgo, Morelos, and Guerrero; to Santa Anna; to Benito Juárez and Porfirio Díaz; to Carranza, Villa, and Zapata; to striking workers, assertive domestic workers, and radicalized peasant farmers; and also to well-heeled but resistant politicians, writers, and artists, Yáñez creates a positive version of the horizontalist leveling of hierarchies that poverty as formlessness makes available. There is no single set of ways of being, doing, saying, or knowing—there is no single formula or set of habits—that would make this egalitarian logic available. Instead, the experience of nonnormativity and the experience of deviating from capitalist (or socialist) norms and conventions are *the* form Yáñez champions: the experience of formlessness (poverty as the experience of not being seeing and not being heard) as form with infinite, unending potential or possible conventions that can be permanently constructed and deconstructed.

This is why something like Aguilucho's lessons—"get back on the horse, which is what is important" and "what matters here is seeing how you manage to get by"—make Yáñez's arguments so clear. Managing to get by, getting from here to there, seeing without being seen, and thus making an "improper moment" an imminently "proper moment" in which to act: these are all instances in which an egalitarian order is declared. Thus, when Aguilucho is killed in an armed robbery gone wrong, his death does not mean the tragic end of the possibilities of positing an egalitarian order.

The same is true when Pedro learns in Teotihuacán that a whole group of bandits had been brought to justice, and he subsequently encounters, on the outskirts of Mexico City, the corpse of their leader (none other than Juan Largo) who was left to rot, fastened to "a pole and supported with a stake . . . [with] his hands fasted to it" (856). Juan Largo, here, functions as a symbol of the ruling order's brutal imposition of the rule of law against the poor who, as Aguilucho helped both Pedro and the novel's readers understand, are the product of a negative horizontalist order that stands alongside the verticalized hierarchy of "social divisions": the "pole" and "stake" that dedifferentiates the blacksmith or painter from the beggar or profligate Criollo even as the social hierarchy and its divisions are maintained. But this is also a central moment for understanding how Lizardi's novel serves to support Yáñez's conceptualization of postrevolutionary Mexicanist culture.

For Yáñez, the deaths of Aguilucho and Juan Largo (however traumatic for Pedro) would not be occasions that should be mourned by any single individual but instead opportunities that could be *made useful* by being converted or transformed into what he understands as an episode within a broader egalitarian logic of formlessness. While Aguilucho and Juan Largo, like Zapata and Villa (mentioned in Yáñez's "Estudio preliminar"), are figures who "do not mince words or rely on affected or pretentious behaviors and conduct" (Yáñez, *Pensador* xxi), they are also not individually necessary figures because their leveling of hierarchies can be achieved by other means: "the writer who tells the unvarnished truth and calls out corruption" (xxi). In the context of Lizardi's novel, those other means are initially articulated by Pedro himself, who carves into the bark of a tree by Juan Largo's corpse a sonnet in which he imagines Juan Largo to be providing him with a life lesson that would enable him to "learn from the wickedness and misdeeds of men" (857), a notion that parallels Yáñez's epigrammatic account of Lizardi's work.

As noted above, Yáñez's reading of Lizardi is one in which "el Pensador" is producing his literary work within a kind of populist unity with the "marginal subjects" who will be his readers. His goal is not to transform his readers but instead to transform the surrounding social structures that view them as inferior, thus creating the unequal social order in which they act on what Pedro calls their "mala disposición." The result of this transformed social order would be that instances of "a disposition to commit misdeeds" would not condemn someone to a life of dispossession but instead could be *made useful* to a project dedicated to reorienting wealth toward its social function. In the context of the prologue, the wealth of "marginal subjects" who finance the labor of the writer (i.e., literature) becomes a mechanism by which wealth can be made to carry out its duties and social functions. In the context of the deaths of Aguilucho and, especially, Juan Largo, Pedro transforms Juan Largo's death from a symbol of negative horizontalism into an episode within the history of the positive horizontalism of an egalitarian logic. The point of the encounter between Pedro and Juan Largo's corpse is that, from Lizardi's view, neither the supposedly "superior" colonial authority nor the supposedly "inferior" outlaw is an order to be followed. Instead, it is Aguilucho's lesson that governs Lizardi's novel: "What matters is not whether your skin is light or dark . . . [but instead how you] manage to get by." What is important is "cómo se pasa el rato," how one can make "ill use" of existing "social divisions" so as to persistently disestablish or "unmake" those "social divisions," which is also to accept that "social divisions" will once again be made in the process of unmaking.

Thus, when Yáñez embraces Lizardi as "Mexico's teacher and [the teacher] of our young people" (*Pensador* l) in the closing paragraphs of his essay, that praise is not to form a normative set of prescriptive formulas for behavior (e.g., a new "*manual de urbanidad*") that Mexican youth should internalize as their own. Instead, it stands as a guide for conceptualizing the task of politics and daily life as one of persistent "unmaking" or dedifferentiation. It is only by continuing the never-finished practice of leveling "social divisions"—which are always the establishment of some ways of being, doing, saying, and knowing as "superior" (or what Yáñez characterizes as being "in the clouds") and others as "inferior" (or what Yáñez characterizes as being "in the chasm")—that wealth can be made to fulfill its social duties and egalitarianism be made "permanent" (though never actually achieved).

As we will see in more detail in chapter 3, this logic of unmaking is what guided some forms of resistance to the PRI and its authoritarian approach to a supposed "revolutionary egalitarianism." Monsiváis's critique of Cantinflas developed above is mirrored in his critique of the PRI in other contexts. Similarly, his solution resides in an emphasis on this logic of unmaking, of resistance to form as a formal structure of action. Ironically, that supposedly antiauthoritarian mode of thinking is precisely what structured the making of the PRI's authoritarianism, something that was possible through the work of a devoted PRI apparatchik like Yáñez. As I have been arguing, both of these logics have shared roots in what I have been describing as the misconceptualization of poverty as a subjective experience of formlessness rather than as an objective relational aspect of a historically particular and specific structure of economic organization. The point that I am making, then, is that to associate Aguilucho's lesson (or Lizardi's literary project) with an idea of formlessness (that is, with the notion of unmaking or horizontalist dedifferentiation in its positive transformation) would be to miss the forms of social organization that he proposes based on his understanding of his material situation. This mistaken conceptualization, I am arguing, is often why solutions to the problems that generate and are generated by Mexicanist authoritarianism themselves seem to reproduce the very inequalities they ostensibly wished to resolve, a phenomenon already examined in the context of Peronism.

As we saw earlier, Bartra is a critic who argues against Mexicanism for the ways it serves as the "odious, legitimating source of a dominant, exploitative system, which seeks to justify deep inequality and injustice through the imposition of uniformity on political culture" (*Cage* 175). At the same time, it "is also the source of a succession of transfigurations and transpositions that have resulted in a political culture which no longer corresponds to the needs for expansion within the system of exploitation itself" (176). While Bartra calls this the "crisis" of "Mexican nationalism" (175), it is clear that his description (made in 1987) has certain parallels with the "crisis in representation" Larsen tracked throughout the 1980s. But, despite correctly associating "revolutionary nationalism" with both the violent actors of "imperialist capitalism" and the resistance against those actions that had been "domesticated by the *caciques*, workers' movements ringing with Cantinflas's puns, and inefficiency and corruption in the name of a cohort of pelados" (176), the solution Bartra identified fails to address the underlying issue of how poverty is conceptualized within these traditions.

As he notes, the generation of Mexicans coming to question the PRI in the 1980s (in the wake of the student-popular movements of the 1960s and 1970s) were a group that came to reject what had become formulas for revolutionary nationalism's valorization of formlessness: "Without ever having been modern, they are de-modern . . . they are other people, they are different" (*Cage* 176). Their difference, however, resides in the practice of decanonizing what he calls the "canon of the axolotl," the Mexicanist melancholic narrative of metamorphosis in which there is a notion of an essential Mexican identity embedded in ever-evolving processes of mestizaje and the historical continuity of a revolutionary heroism struggling against (but in the process often reproducing) the corrupt and exploitative colonial order. Bartra's option for the "postmodern or *demodern* idea" (9) of "a heterogeneous and divided world" (10) is one in which the only solution is difference and resistance to the Mexicanist formulas and habits that are understood to be the "odious, legitimating source of a dominant, exploitative system, which seeks to justify deep inequality and injustice through the imposition of uniformity on political culture" (175). What I have shown in this chapter is this logic that is supposedly critical of the PRI is one that is embedded, as we have seen in Yáñez's embrace of his interpretation of Lizardi, in the logic that the PRI and their devoted apparatchiks put into practice through their commitment to the experience of formlessness as *the* form for an institutionalized revolutionary politics.

## Confronting the Theatricality of Mexicanism

While an important part of this study is to point out the underexamined confluence of these logics, another equally important component is to highlight the fact that there were Latin American artists and intellectuals who were critical of this mistaken conceptualization of poverty and the ways it underscored both politics and aesthetic practice. Many of these figures were deeply interested in and concerned with the nature of artworks and often sought to produce normative accounts of meaning. This also involved critiquing what could correctly be termed "improper" accounts of literary projects or literary interpretation. Indeed, the origin of Yáñez's essay on Lizardi for his anthology, aside from his need to produce a text for Monterde's editorial series, was his critique of the arguments advanced by just such a critic: Alfonso Reyes. Reyes's approach to Lizardi (and literature more broadly) gives us a different account of Aguilucho's lesson and Cantinflas's commodities, one that will serve as important context for the next chapter.

I have detailed the specific aspects of the debate Yáñez establishes between himself and Reyes elsewhere, but what is important for the present study is the way that Yáñez misunderstands what he calls Reyes's disrespectful and disparaging attitude toward the poor. Specifically, Yáñez denounces Reyes's looking down on uneducated readers who were unaware that Lizardi's nickname, "el pensador mexicano," was not a reference to his ideas or his genius but instead to his newspaper, which itself was an adaptation of the title of a periodical publication from Spain. As I argued, however, Reyes's critique of this particular instance of popular "use"—or "ill use"—of the literary tradition is but one example of a broader phenomenon he seeks to criticize.

The key example I cite in the earlier study is Reyes's discussion of an episode in which *El periquillo sarniento* "was censored 'because it contained an attack on slavery' (171) and its price 'on the market' skyrocketed: 'from that moment on, [the novel contained] something like a martyrdom for freedom; it suffered for the ideals of the people' (171)" (in Buttes, "Partition" 54). For Reyes, the problem with this understanding of Lizardi is that it has almost nothing to do with the "artistic value" (54) of Lizardi's work, which requires that someone has read Lizardi's work. Instead, this approach to Lizardi has everything to do with "the mandates of the market and the whims of political structures" (54). A more productive approach for interpreting the work of Lizardi would be to "[understand] the tradition in which [his] particular work[s] [were] developed in order to move beyond [them]: to identify and understand, to confront and overcome political and aesthetic problems in a given historical moment" (55). This alternative approach to understanding Lizardi's literary works emphasizes that "critics intervene politically with judgments that, as normative, universal claims, may be right or wrong" (55). And I argue that the approach Reyes articulates is one that "points to an alternative path for a literary politics of poverty" (54), an alternative that will be explored in the remaining chapters of this book.

Within this alternative, what is important is not that individual readers buy a book because it was censored or because of its antislavery point of view. Similarly, understanding a book like *El periquillo* does not hinge on understanding how readers (such Pedro's children, who are the intended recipients of the narrative) use the book's words or how many copies of the book readers (such as those

Lizardi mentions in his prologue) ultimately purchase. Those kinds of considerations may be relevant for understanding how Lizardi's works remained (or failed to remain) in circulation or, to apply the observation to another example examined in this chapter, why the "300 identical jokes" that composed Cantinflas's serially produced films functioned as a successful "branding mechanism" that could launch numerous other products onto the Mexican market.

Reyes's point, however, is that these kinds of considerations—how someone uses a book or whether they buy a book—does not tell us whether or not the book is any good. Similarly, a reliance on those considerations alone—how someone makes a book useful—would be to disregard any truth about the world that the book might communicate. In other words, the categories that are relevant for assessing the success of Posa Films (did people buy a ticket or not) are not relevant to assessing the success of the work of art. And it is to that kind of evaluation that Reyes was responding in his essay, noting that Lizardi's approach to art and narrative did not merit the significant place it was given in a two-volume anthology that was published three decades before Monterde's series: the *Antología del Centenario* (1910), which was overseen by Justo Sierra, Luis G. Urbina, Pedro Henríquez Ureña, and Nicolás Rangel. Asserting that a work of art—a Cantinflas film or a Lizardi novel—is good is a normative claim that rests on arguments that place those works into relational sets of value.

A simple version of this kind of claim would be the following comparative analysis of two Cantinflas films: *Ahí está el detalle* is a better film than *El señor fotógrafo* (1953). In this scenario, the claim emphasizes aspects internal to the works that produce a qualitatively better film: the composition of scenes, the quality of photography, the precision of actors' performances, the coherence of narrative sequencing, the ingenuity of wordplay, and so on. In other words, we could make arguments regarding the difference between the meaningfully arranged visual sequence in figure 1.1, where Cantinflas is glimpsed from the kitchen doing in the open precisely the same thing he would be doing if hidden from view, and the hard jump cut that ends *El señor fotógrafo*. That more people might have bought tickets to see the latter film (released toward the end of the period of prolific production in serial and in the same year as Rivera's completion of the controversial mural featuring Cantinflas) or vice versa isn't relevant for understanding the above claim. Similarly, it's not relevant if more members of the poor and working class saw the latter than the former in a movie theater. However, for Santiago Reachi and Jacques Gelman, Mario Moreno's business partners in Posa Films, the only thing that matters is whether or not people buy tickets and whether or not Moreno "lives the brand" and continues to give "the people" what they want: more of the "300 identical jokes" so that the poor and the working class continue to buy tickets. The distinction elaborated here regarding a potential line of analysis of Cantinflas films—one concerned with the cinematic and artistic quality of two films and the other with ticket sales and advertising—is one that very much parallels the debate between

Reyes and Yáñez. Of course, in the case of Yáñez's critique of Reyes and his championing of Lizardi, the choice isn't posited as between "artistic quality" and sales/advertising but instead between disparaging elitist hierarchies (Reyes) and affirmational/positive horizontalist dedifferentiation.

There is not a disconnect, conceptually speaking, between Yáñez's positive horizontalist dedifferentiation, with its emphasis on respect for the poor's "ill use" of Lizardi, and the brand-oriented production of cinematic commodities by Cantinflas and Posa Films. For this reason, Reyes's emphasis on "artistic quality" makes possible an alternative pathway to develop a critique of the inequalities that capitalist commodity production created. As Nicholas Brown points out in his analysis of art and commodities, there is a "distinction between an object whose use (or purpose or meaning) is normatively inscribed in the object itself [with] a meaning that is universal . . . [and] available for everyone and not therefore a private matter" (loc. 181), on the one hand, "and an object whose use is a matter of indifference from one standpoint and a matter of possibly intense but necessarily private concern" (loc. 188), on the other. That difference is one that is, as Brown explains, embedded within the distinction Marx draws between objects within "a society of commodity producers" (the latter) and objects within a society with another (noncapitalist) sort of organization (the former).

In noncapitalist systems "the problem" that objects solve is "the satisfaction of 'universal' or social needs through individual labor, through irreducibly particular talents and drives" (loc. 154), which means that the qualities an object has are tied to its use value, purpose, or meaning. For example, a shovel might have the shape and be made of the material that best serves the removal of the kind of soil present in the community where it has been traditionally made and used; a tomato will have the texture and flavor it has because it can be used to create certain dishes linked to community practice; bread will be made with certain grains because they provide certain durability in the product or because those grains grow well in the soil or climate of a particular location; and so on. The particular qualities the shovel, the tomato, or the bread have are made to be used in particular ways or for particular purposes that have a normative use within a community. Those qualities are intimately tied to the "universal or social needs" of the community that makes and uses them.

In capitalist societies, however, there is a process of dedifferentiating those qualities because the owner of a commodity has an object that "has no qualities" (loc. 116). What Brown means is that all the qualities a commodity object might have—the shape of the shovel, the texture of the tomato, the grain chosen to make the bread—are dedifferentiated from each other and reduced to the "one quality that matters," which is "its qualitative equality with other commodities: its exchangeability" (locs. 116–122). Under the capitalist system, the use value becomes dedifferentiated from the object's exchangeability or exchange value: the only use it has is its ability to be linked to and exchanged with other objects. Thus, what is important is not whether someone is going to use the shovel to plant a garden or whether they're going to use it to stage a still life they will photograph: what is important is that it sells because it "is a use value for others" (loc. 131). The buyer *makes use* of the object, and that use does not require approval by the commodity owner, who does not "legislate what its actual use value should be" (loc. 139).

The difference Brown articulates here is the "distinction between an entity that embodies, and must seek to compel, conviction and an entity that seeks to provoke interest in its beholder—or, perhaps, all kinds of different interest from different beholders" (loc. 188). That distinction, I am suggesting, maps onto the difference between Reyes's approach to Lizardi—which emphasizes "artistic quality" and Reyes's estimation that Lizardi's appeal to his readers undermines his ability to compel conviction—and Yáñez's approach to Lizardi—which emphasizes that nonnormative, ill use should not be disparaged or disrespected. Indeed, the key point for Yáñez is that to do so would be to miss the vast collection of pelados that such disrespect would erase from view. As Brown notes, the above distinction between an "entity that embodies conviction"—the "distinction between an object whose use (or purpose or meaning) is normatively inscribed in the object itself [with] a meaning that is universal" and available to everyone—and an "entity that seeks to provoke . . . all kinds of interest from different beholders" is the distinction between art and objecthood that Michael Fried elaborated in his analysis of art amid the crisis of painting in the 1960s. I am arguing that the debate between Reyes ("artistic quality") and Yáñez (respect for the experience of formlessness [the poor]) can be understood in parallel terms. The logic of the commodity and the social logic of the PRI converge in their respect for the poor and their indifference to addressing the objective relational aspects of the economic system that produce material inequality.

For this reason, I would argue that reading *El periquillo sarniento* today would be important precisely because it is a work that is concerned with the variables I have been analyzing here. What is poverty? What is a work of art? What strategies can be utilized to eliminate the former and execute the latter? These questions come to a head in the final chapter of the fifth and final volume of the novel where, three years after Pedro's death, Lizardi the narrator acquires Pedro's manuscript, corrects it, and proposes to Pedro's wife the idea of publishing it. Appalled at the possibility of defaming Pedro's memory by making known his scandalous past, or what she calls his "gracias" (938), Lizardi, the skillful narrator, explains that Pedro's children already benefited from hearing these stories from their father and that "in Mexico . . . and in the whole of the world there are a number of Periquillos for whom this story could be of the utmost use in its imparting of morality and good conduct" (938). What Lizardi wishes to make clear to Pedro's widow is that Pedro's work is not reducible to Pedro's autobiographical indiscretions, to accumulating layers of meaning, or to myriad readerly uses and experiences of his text. As the narrating Lizardi points out,

> A book like this one will be gobbled up by misbehaving children, profligate young men, frivolous young women and even shameless pícaros and unrepentant rogues. When these individuals read it, they are not the least bit interested in learning any lessons as they do so. They open the book out of curiosity and they read with pleasure, believing that they are only going to enjoy reading a few entertaining stories and that [entertainment] was the author's sole purpose for writing it. . . . [But] when we read [this book], it seems that we are almost watching the events take place, [and] we retain them in our memory. . . . We remember this or that character from the story when we see others behave in a similar manner, and we benefit from the instruction that the story had given us. And with that, ma'am, it should be said that it would not be just to leave your husband's work to be forgotten, locked away in a trunk. (939)

In this passage, there always seems to be the possibility that this meaning-bearing work (Pedro's manuscript) can be transformed into a meaningless object or into a multiply meaningful textual encounter, much like characterizations of Cantinflas's speech and his serially produced films. Indeed, Lizardi would seem to provide evidence for the populist logic Yáñez imagines. For example, there is the suggestion of a role for an active reader hinted at in the possible effects of leaving the manuscript "buried and forgotten," and Lizardi goes out of his way to cite the varied reading experiences that would take place if Pedro's widow would consent to publication: "misbehaving children," "frivolous young women," "profligate young men," "shameless pícaros," and "unrepentant rogues" would all love this book and would have a variety of uses for it.

Yet regardless of those individual experiences and regardless of whatever analogies any reader might make "when we see others [in the world] behave in a similar manner . . . [as] this or that character from the story" (939), Lizardi's point is that when Pedro makes the choice to write his manuscript with "familiar and everyday language that we all use in regular conversation" (which, of course, is Lizardi's description of his own style and his own goals for this novel we are reading), he is also insisting that his work is not reducible to the reactions of scandalized censors, to the demand for the novel and its high prices, to the pure entertainment of the "shameless pícaro and unrepentant rogue," nor to "[children who] already have a well-formed sense of being" (938). As Lizardi says in one of the last paragraphs of the novel, "this little work may have many flaws, but these will not undermine the merit contained within the morals it expresses, because what is true is true regardless of who says it and regardless of the way they say it" (940). Or, to make the same point via Brown's formulation, this novel has a "use (or purpose or meaning) [that] is normatively inscribed in the object itself [with] a meaning that is universal . . . [and] available for everyone and not therefore a private matter" (loc. 181). What the work means has nothing to do with reader experiences of it (scandal, enjoyment, praise, and so on).

Indeed, as Lizardi says in the last line of this lengthy novel, "Let us hope the novel's success mirrors the praiseworthy intentions of the author!" (940). Rather than understanding the novel's "success" as a proxy for reader experience (they buy it, they read it, they cite it, etc.), Lizardi makes the point that the novel's meaning is not reducible to its success or failure on the market. Even if it were to remain "buried and forgotten" it would still communicate whatever truths and whatever falsehoods it contains even if no one ever read it. So, for example, once Juan Largo's corpse is removed and Pedro's sonnet, carved in the bark of a tree, is all that is left of this encounter, the use or meaning of that sonnet—the ways that Pedro utilizes the fate of Juan Largo and Aguilucho as a lens through which he can reveal the truth of his own situation and relationship with the world—would continue to be available. Even though any individual reader may misunderstand the meaning of Pedro's sonnet and even though Pedro himself might misdiagnose his own situation and relationship with the world, his sonnet would nevertheless reveal the truth about a moment in history in which that mistake (if a mistake) was both plausible and necessary.

This is exactly the lesson we should learn from Aguilucho. Unlike Yáñez, whose reading of Lizardi would spin the deaths of Aguilucho and Juan Largo out into the dedifferentiated history of nonnormative pelado-igualado acts that are different from but interchangeable with each other, the approach Reyes advocates would be one in which the qualities of the work are what is important. We need not agree with Reyes's judgments regarding Lizardi to acknowledge that Reyes's mode of conceptualizing aesthetic judgment as a normative claim is correct. And in this way, we can read Aguilucho's lesson differently.

We could discard a reading that highlights a logic of horizontalist dedifferentiation that in its negative articulation makes blacksmiths and beggars the same kind of social problem and in its positive articulation provides them temporary reprieve from the effects of social divisions. Instead, we could read his lesson as a normative, perhaps even programmatic, claim set up in advance that posits an alternative social order organized not by exchangeability but instead by collective effort to meet "the satisfaction of 'universal' or social needs through individual labor, through irreducibly particular talents and drives" (Brown loc. 154). That order, nevertheless, is derived from the lived material circumstances of the poor and projects the material obstacles that would threaten its realization.

As Brown points out, a key to generating the creation of this kind of social organization is to recognize moments within the historical development of capitalism in which creators are able to establish relations between objects and those who behold (or use) them that are not reduced to their exchangeability. Instead, those entities "embody and seek to compel, conviction" within the beholder (or "user") by confronting them with a "use (or purpose or meaning) [that] is normatively inscribed in the object itself [with] a meaning that is universal" and available to everyone. The challenge, as Brown points out, is that the social relations that would make meaning, use, or purpose irreducible to exchangeability are not always available as they actually are but instead must be presented as truth that, though derivable from history and material conditions, becomes available in that entity ("art") "as never before" (Fried, *Absorption* 79): "an ideal that . . . [newly imagined and social relations] must presuppose but can only realize in an unsatisfactory, contradictory, and unstable way" (Brown loc. 147). Such is the multiracial egalitarian order Aguilucho describes within the prison, one that is placed under pressure by actual material inequality between the impoverished Criollo Pedro (who receives food and resources from his Criollo acquaintance) and his impoverished Mulatto, Indigenous, and Mestizo cell mates, who swindle him out of what he does not share.

The key point to take away from this discussion for the subsequent chapters in this study is that the kind of political-social sets of distinctions that Yáñez sets up are not only conceptually relying on a certain account of what poverty is, but they also rely on a certain account of what a work of art is. And those two conceptual ideas—what poverty is and what a work of art is—are not always (perhaps not usually) treated together. The argument of this book is not only that we should treat them together to understand each of the concepts more fully but also that artists and intellectuals in Latin America, such as Reyes, have already done so. The challenge is whether and how we choose to read and understand the arguments and connections they've made, a challenge that the next chapter begins to take up in earnest.

# 2

# Icons of the Everyday

## Calculating Poverty in Pablo Neruda's *Odas elementales*

In February 1954, the anticommunist and antifacist Chilean political satire magazine *Topaze* published, as it often did throughout the 1940s and 1950s, a caricature of Pablo Neruda in which his politics and poetry are mocked.[1] On this occasion, the magazine was lampooning the recent publication of *Odas elementales* (*Odes to Everyday Things*), which represented a significant shift in his poetic method. The image (figure 2.1), carrying the header "he no longer praises the oppressed," shows two impoverished Chileans engaged in conversation while observing an oblivious Neruda who is either reciting poetry or lost in thought. One of the men, Juan Verdejo, asserts that he no longer likes Neruda because he has become a poet concerned only with luxury ("poeta de lujo, poeta suntuario"). Confused, the other asks why he might think that, to which Verdejo replies with the punch line: "Don't you see that he now praises celery, onions, and potatoes?"

The joke, of course, works at the level of politics and aesthetics. Neruda is mocked for what his new poetry collection represents: a series of long, simple poems about mundane, seemingly nonpoetic objects like bread, yarn, artichokes, and tomatoes, which exist in stark contrast with the historical and continental arc of his political poetry collection *Canto general* (1950). The choice for praising the sumptuous pleasures and "benign majesty" of the tomato instead of the violent exploitation of the colonial and capitalist system would seem to confirm what Neruda's critics always suspected: he is a hypocrite who enjoys as

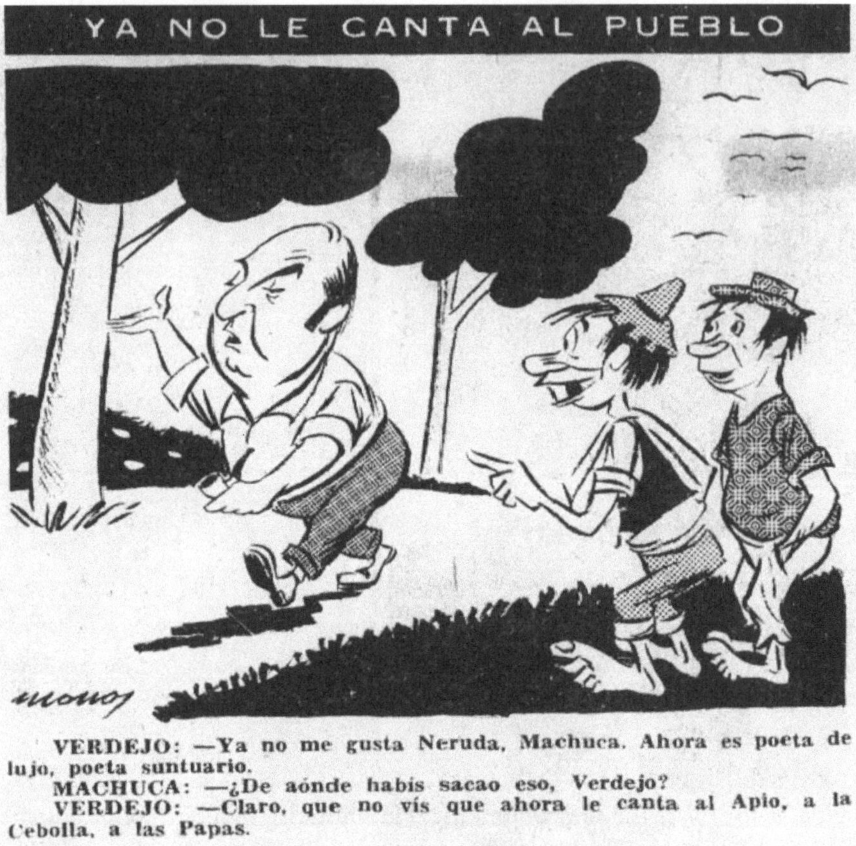


FIGURE 2.1 "He no longer sings the praises of the poor." *Topaze*, February 12, 1954.

"everyday things" what the working class and the poor could consider only as luxuries. The punch line here cuts more deeply because the impoverished men identify the most humble of food items as luxuries.

Regardless of whether the joke makes a reader laugh, it is important to note that it is based on a fundamental misunderstanding of the collection. As Greg Dawes notes in his book *Verses Against the Darkness*, the seeming simplicity of the *Odas* is "deceptive": "[The poems] give the impression that Neruda is merely praising these natural objects [as] . . . objects whose commodification is accepted. However, that interpretation is only possible if the reader . . . perceives no exit from the drive for profit in capitalist society. Any attentive reader will readily note that the interpretation only holds on the level of appearance" (284). *Topaze*'s editorial staff in this period without a doubt "perceives no exit from . . . capitalist society," and given that their parodies often operate at the level of appearance, there is little surprise that they do not recognize its deceptions. Nevertheless, reading this anticommunist parody with Marxist criticism on Neruda's navigation of the deceptions of "appearance" does productively draw out some disagreements between those critics, which the following chapter will analyze.

As we will see, Neruda's new poetic practice ultimately produces a situation in which the poetic-political activity that guarantees the end of exploitation can be sustained only by the continued existence of exploitation as it is transformed into the valorization of the experience of formlessness as necessary political resource. This transformation becomes possible through the operation of his new aesthetic practice: aesthetic transparency. Transparency emerges through the dual-level mechanism of the aesthetics laid out in "The Invisible Man," the prologue-poem that opens the *Odas*. The poet's work is what he calls a "terrible obligation": "I must tell about/account for (*contar*) [the pain and the joy of the workers]" (*Obras completas* [*OC*] 45). The poet thus describes an obligation to self-multiply or self-divide so as to unify his verse with the voices of workers.

On the one hand, Neruda sees his task as fully enumerating, calculating, and accounting for the capitalist system that exploits workers and converts everyday objects into commodities. His aesthetic transparency reveals these objects as locations in the world where social forces are "congealed" (Dawes, *Verses* 94) and the structures of capitalist exploitation can be fully brought to light. On the other hand, however, if Neruda's aesthetic transparency means that the poet is only ever looking out at the world and taking in the experiences of exploitation workers share with him, it would seem to make the misunderstanding in figure 2.1 impossible. How could a transparent denunciation of exploitation—what Dawes calls Neruda's "ode to the dialectic" (283)—*appear* to be an ode to the commodity? How could a poet fully embedded in the experiences of working-class suffering *appear* to be self-absorbed in his own enjoyment of "luxury" as "everyday things"?

To answer this question about the paradox at the heart of Neruda's poetic-political aesthetic transparency, which hinges on how these "everyday objects" *appear* to readers, I first analyze some disagreements between materialist interpretations of the *Odas*. While these scholars are mostly in agreement with each other, a closer examination of their competing analyses reveals contrasting readings of the *Odas*. Building on these debates, I then turn to analyze the dual-level mechanism of his "terrible obligation" to "*contar*": (1) to enumerate or account for the totality of capitalist exploitation and (2) to tell about or narrate individual experiences of exploitation. That "terrible obligation"—the mandate to "contar"—involves both economics and aesthetics just as it involves production and circulation. These poems, as "everyday things," are fully embedded in the world of capitalist exploitation but also are envisioned as essential tools for creating an alternative. As Dawes notes, Neruda's aesthetic transparency is marked by a desire to "see beyond poetic form and its own fetishism" (*Verses* 95), represented by avant-garde or modernist poetry, while also rejecting "naïve realism" (95).

The dual-level mechanism of aesthetic transparency (the economic and aesthetic; to account for and to tell about) is premised on critiquing "the self-absorbed poet [who] loses himself and fails to notice fellow human beings who suffer . . . [and who has] lost sight of reality completely" (95). In doing so, Neruda's poems proceed by addressing readers directly and presenting them with usable objects, an approach that carries out that "obligation." In other words, Neruda's conceit is to give the worker words of sustenance just as the worker gives the poet the "everyday things" (bread and tomatoes, wood and stone) that sustain the poet's material life. However, it is precisely the politics of this aesthetics—the ways that the direct address of reader reimagines the position of the poet—that underscores the disagreements regarding aesthetic transparency. In developing the *Odas*, is Neruda "dissolving" the "self-absorbed" poet's forms that deny the presence of workers in favor of producing objects that are *useful* to workers? Or does the direct address of the reader and the effort to "dissolve" the object's *aesthetics* ultimately undermine the relation between the poem and the worker that the poet seeks to create?

Understanding the debate about aesthetic transparency in these terms makes it clear that Neruda's concerns in the *Odas* are in dialogue with the issues of theatricality and antitheatricality, in Michael Fried's sense of those terms as they were discussed at the end of the previous chapter.[2] Neruda's pursuit of aesthetic transparency in his 1950s verses places him on a path to the dedifferentiation of art and life and of realism and the avant-garde. In this way, we can read Neruda's *Odas*, published amid economic stagnation and the first applications of what would eventually be termed neoliberal reforms, as a prefiguration of contemporary debates about the literary and its political possibilities under neoliberalism.[3]

Neruda attempts to solve the problem of the "self-absorbed poet" and his subjectivity as an obstacle for encountering the "light" of the workers. Neruda understands aesthetic transparency as a vector of encounter with workers' experiences of formlessness in the capitalist economy and as a tool for transforming that world into a place of egalitarian plenty. This poetic structure, however, which Neruda views as existing in full unity with utopian political structures, requires someone or some group to continue to carry out the role ascribed to poverty, one Neruda's aesthetic transparency ultimately associates with the poet as "invisible man." The "many things [workers] do/make" (the products emerging from their *hacer*) are contrasted with the transparency of the artist's poetic activity, which is taken as an invisible mechanism for worker expression. That aesthetic transparency (the poet's "invisibility") is what can be called the *no hacer*, or nondoing or nonmaking, of his poetry. Neruda eventually links that nondoing and nonmaking with the idea of poverty he develops in the *Odas*. As we will see at the end of the chapter, there are political consequences that emerge from this linking of aesthetic transparency with poverty.

## The Poet's Objects

As noted at the outset, the image of a poet who is oblivious to the suffering of the impoverished world that surrounds him could not be farther from the project Neruda sets out to complete in the *Odas*. This is most certainly evident on the first page of the collection when he critiques poets (himself included) who write poetry in which "with each step / something is happening to them / it is always 'I'" (*OC* 39). In this prologue-poem, "El hombre invisible" (The invisible man), Neruda famously critiques poetic worlds where "through the streets / only [poets] walk / or the woman of their heart's affection, / no one else, / no fishermen go by, / nor any booksellers, / no construction workers pass through, / no one falls / from the scaffolding, / no one is suffering, / no one experiences love, / only my poor brother, / the poet" (*OC* 39). He uses this critique to begin clearly marking out a project in which the poet is no longer alone. A new, simplified verse structure whittles away the self-absorbed poet oblivious to the suffering of others as he loses himself in the mundane details of working-class life. Neruda seeks to erase the distance between his poetic world and the world of capitalist exploitation and to collapse the difference between poetic practice (aesthetics) and active worker solidarity (politics).

We can see this clearly expressed in an emblematic poem like "Ode to Bread," which, according to Robert Pring-Mill, is among the first ten of the *Odas* Neruda composed. Beginning, as he often does in this collection, with a direct, apostrophic address of this simple everyday object, Neruda quickly converts the material base that opens the poem—"Bread, / with flour, / water / and fire / you rise" (*OC* 182)—into an object of poetic description paralleling the women at the heart of so many of his verses. What is notable in the first long stanza of this poem is that the second person address—"*you* rise"—is carried out by an observing poetic voice that absents itself from the page. There is no "I" visible to the reader in this poem. This technique is carried forward from the first stanza into the following two stanzas where poetic description is converted into political action. That action is led not by an intellectual or an artist but rather by a collective, laboring "we": "Oh bread of every mouth, / no / we will not beg you, / men as we are / we are not / beggars . . . the bread of every mouth, / . . . will arrive because we came / and planted it, / and made it, / not just for one person but rather / for everyone" (*OC* 183–184).

This unification of poetics and politics—the "you" (bread) that exists because of the "we" (workers)—operates through "[a] making or doing" that is able to continuously multiply: it is "not just for one person [*un hombre*] but rather / for everyone [*todos*]." The labor that produces the world will not be just for the poet or the landowning oligarch ("un hombre") but instead for workers and a transformed humanity living in radical equality ("todos"). In that transformed world, "All beings / will have a right / to land and to life" (*OC* 185). In this way, the poet brings to light the multiplicity of life embedded in the singularity of each "everyday thing," which is presently produced and consumed in a stratified economic and political system. In representing inequality and solidarity through a single object, Neruda envisions not a poetic transformation of bread via the special vision of the poet but instead the everyday object's transformation of the poetic object. He envisions poetry becoming equated with the worker's "daily bread": both of them serving as the sustenance workers need so as to engage in "the longest and most difficult / struggle of humankind" (*OC* 185).

This is the poetic vision of aesthetic transparency, and it appears to approach the idea of immediacy at the heart of the avant-garde. But in Dawes's reading of the *Odas*, the poetic objects created by the "invisible man" are not "a prisoner of [the] immediacy [of] avant-gardist form" in which "the poet's inner life [is revealed] in a heavily constrained and distorted content" (*Verses* 102). Opposed to the imperatives of "distorted" avant-gardist or modernist practices that would "make the rose bloom in verse," as Vicente Huidobro famously put it in his "Creationist" poetry, Neruda instead pursues a strategy in which the form of the poem would not become "a fetish [that] loses its concreteness and becomes abstract . . . [and yielding] to the spontaneity of individual motivations" (102). Rather than seeking the "avant-garde fetish," Neruda opts to make the poem as much like an everyday object as he can: visible, understandable, usable.

In this way, Dawes builds on the past four decades of reading Neruda's aesthetic transparency, which has been understood in a fairly consistent way from the early readings developed by Jaime Alazraki (1973) and Robert Pring-Mill (1979) to more recent interventions by Hernán Loyola (1999) or Dawes himself. As Loyola points out in the introduction to his edition of one of the volumes of Neruda's complete works, echoing the earlier critics, Neruda's work in the *Odas* hinges, on the one hand, on "consistently making more visible the dreams and desires, conflicts and struggles, defeats and victories of Man, of the human community, and on the other hand, pursuing the poetic *inventory* of the world, a lyric register or repertoire of the 'elements' [that are] the most immediate and simple" (28).

This critical consensus on the visibility and political utility of the verses in the *Odas* is connected to what Neruda, in the "Ode to Clarity," would call his "obligation to the light" ("obligación de luz"). That obligation was to make it impossible not to see the exploitation, suffering, and inequality that are ignored by the "self-absorbed poets." As Saúl Yurkievich notes in his prologue to the *Odas*, "Poetry descends from its rarified territory to the table of the poor. It is no longer a solipsistic object limited to private consumption" (14). Arriving at emphasis on simplicity and collective use in the everyday through an imagery of light, Yurkievich sees the essence of the *Odas* in a poem like "Ode to Clarity": "Neruda imagines himself a realist poet, a photographer who documents, who gives a true version of the world" (Yurkievich 15). Though Marxist critics would likely critique Yurkievich's approach as of a piece with liberal efforts to evacuate Neruda's politics or reduce them to Soviet formulas, Yurkievich's identification of a realist aesthetic in the *Odas* is actually largely in line with the insights of materialist critics. Dawes, for example, asserts that "Neruda's poetry strove increasingly toward the approximate comprehension of the totality of reality via the mediation of language" (*Verses* 264). In both cases—"[the] true version of the world" (Yurkievich) and "the totality of reality" (Dawes)—we are to understand the poems as a product of a poet who engages in the act of "distributing myself" ("repartirme"). The absent "I" that is dissolved into the "we" of workers would seemingly bring all readers to a clarified understanding of the mechanisms that stratify capitalist society and the multiplicity of lived realities. It is the collective action of "fishermen" and "bakers," "miners" and "boilermakers," "night washer women" and "busied bureaucrats working with statistics" that would bring that stratification to an end.

But if "clarity," "transparency," and "invisibility" are the aspects of the *Odas* that make them usable at the "table of the poor," this "simplicity" also produces a paradox that is difficult to explain. On the one hand, aesthetic transparency is the mechanism by which "any attentive reader" (Dawes, *Verses* 284) can see that Neruda, through the activity of workers he brings to light, is destroying "darkness" and bringing about "joy on the earth" (*OC* 77). On the other hand, however, at "the level of appearance" aesthetic transparency can also *produce* all the deceptions of the commodity for a reader "inattentive" to their meaning: "[The poems] give the impression that Neruda is merely praising these natural objects [as] . . . objects whose commodification is accepted" (284).[4] This leads to an obvious question: if transparency is what enables "poetry to [descend] from its rarified territory to the table of the poor . . . [and] no longer a solipsistic object limited to private consumption" (Yurkievich 14), if transparency is what dissolves the individual into the collective "we" that can take action to bring exploitation to an end, then how is it possible for the *Odas* to be received by readers at "the level of appearance" (284) as if they were praising the commodity and its inegalitarian social system?

The answer resides in Neruda's political conviction that his poems should be understood as concrete objects that should be *used* rather than *interpreted* for what they communicate about "the totality of reality." As Robert Pring-Mill notes in his widely cited study of the *Odas*, Neruda's efforts in this collection are summarized "precisely" (Pring-Mill) in a section of Neruda's Nobel speech, "Discurso de Estolcomo": "Every one of my verses was meant to be installed as a palpable object: every one of my poems sought to be a useful tool for work: every one of my hymns aspired to serve in space as a site (*signo*) of gathering where all paths cross, or as fragments of stone or wood in which someone, others, those who will come after me, could deposit new signs" (Neruda in Pring-Mill 297). In reducing these poems to simply one more object in the world—to "fragments of stone or wood" or, as in "Ode to Bread," to the "form of bread" that could be reworked or completed or consumed in "innumerable" (*OC* 185) ways by others—we see a tendency to emphasize experience of the object over interpretation of meaning. The movement of aesthetic transparency between "clarity" and "deception" should not be understood as a mechanism dependent on the identity of the reader. Instead, the movement that takes place is the shifting relation Neruda imagines between poem and reader, or, more broadly, the way he conceives the role of the artwork in the world.

As Dawes notes, if we operate as an "attentive reader" (*Verses* 284), if we are working to understand what these poems mean, it would clearly be absurd to think that Neruda is uncritically praising the commodity in the *Odas*. But if we operate at "the level of appearance" (284), if we take seriously Neruda's call to "deposit new signs"—to *use* these poetic objects rather than interpret or understand them—the sense that this might be Neruda's acceptance of commodification enters as a possibility. Indeed, if these poems really were to operate like "fragments of stone or wood," their users could direct them toward decidedly nonrevolutionary ends without contradicting Neruda's project for aesthetic transparency. In other words, the paradox Dawes brings out in his reading of the *Odas*—the poem's denunciation of capitalism can be mistaken for praise of the commodity—is possible only if we privilege the poem's appearance over its interpretation and only if the reader's experience of the poem is exchanged for their understanding of its meaning.

It is just such a dynamic that Neruda's aesthetic transparency calls forth. With the *Odas*, Neruda seeks to eliminate the difference between the artwork made by the poet (intellectual labor) and the everyday objects made by workers (manual labor). The making of artworks that are no different from (or are indistinguishable from or are interchangeable with) "everyday objects" in the world is understandable within processes of "dedifferentiation," which, as Scott Lash has noted, is a key dynamic of "postmodernization," which is often associated with "late capitalism" or neoliberalism. Dedifferentiation involves the effort to negate any special or "autonomous" status for the work of art through a "refusal to separate the author from his or her oeuvre or the audience from the performance" as well as through "[the] transgression of the boundary . . . between high and popular culture, between what is properly cultural and what is properly social" (Lash 174). To this (following Michaels and Brown), we can add the effort to "transgress" what is properly economic and what is properly aesthetic, or, following Fried, the effort to collapse art into objecthood.

This politically driven impulse to eliminate form in the favor of experience enables us to see how the problem of theatricality and antitheatricality is at play in Chile in a way that dialogues with the dynamics we tracked in Mexico (chapter 1) and Argentina (introduction). For the purposes of understanding how the *Odas* emerged as a response to the concrete situation of 1950s Chile, it is important to note that Neruda's embrace of the political promise of aesthetic transparency as dedifferentiation (form dissolving into the experience of formlessness and the "totality of reality" in working-class life) is given important critical scrutiny in Alain Sicard's *El pensamiento poético de Pablo Neruda* (1981). Though Dawes points out that he "agree[s] with most all of Sicard's analyses of Neruda's work" (*Verses* 63), it is important to draw attention to their disagreements as it concerns their reading of aesthetic transparency.

As noted above, Dawes identifies a resolution to the paradox of "clarity" and "deception" in the dialectical movement between positioning oneself as an "attentive reader" and positioning oneself as a user of objects at "the level of appearance" (*Verses* 284). Sicard, however, identifies problems with Neruda's insistence on the pole of "appearance" and the utility of his verses, which is what Neruda understands as enabling him to "dissolve" the forms that separate him from workers. In Sicard's analysis, the "appearance" of the poem as an everyday object, which is premised on making the poet's activities invisible so as to provide a direct encounter with the world, ultimately leads Neruda right back to fetishistic avant-garde or modernist forms he critiques in "El hombre invisible" and works to dissolve in the *Odas*. I quote Sicard at length:

> Poetry will be useful or it won't exist at all. Writing not only attempts to define itself as a job, but also suggests that there is nothing that distinguishes this job from that of the worker or the artisan. In fact, that dream of the dissolution of the poem into the ocean of human labor only expresses that of a total communication between the poet and other human beings. . . . By reducing itself to the dimension of communication exclusively, poetry deprives itself, paradoxically, of its specific power to communicate. By confusing itself with other forms of human labor, by renouncing its constitutive difference, poetic labor denies itself as labor. In this way, there is a risk that a poetry without a [writing] subject might substitute itself for the utopia of a poetry that creates its object. Taken to its logical end, the realism of [aesthetic] transparency converges, though through a different path, with the idealism of the "poeta pequeño dios" [Vicente Huidobro's Creationist maxim of the poet as a little god] so often criticized by Neruda. (611)

By reading the *Odas* as dissolving form into content, we confuse "the specificity of poetic labor" (618) with mere "communication" (618) carried out by everyone. This risks giving Neruda's works "an ideological treatment as pure 'creation' . . . [that] separates the poet and the worker as a consequence of the division of labor in a capitalist society" (618–619).

More than substituting the poet's own voice for the worker's, accepting aesthetic transparency (or poetry more broadly) as mere "communication" makes inaccessible the actually existing divisions between worker and poet. Imagining that the social leveling that takes place through the labor of the poet actually is transparent or dedifferentiated from the labor needed to create any other "everyday object" is to fail to acknowledge the specific place that "poetic labor" occupies in the relations of production. That failure would require us to imagine that the work that the poet has undertaken to "mine," "fish for," "form," "work out," or "calculate" the details that we read as simple or transparent poems cannot itself be registered as labor. In other words, we have to imagine that mediation—the poet's labor—is not taking place, that the poet makes nothing, and that the poet does nothing. To do so, however, is to be "deceived" by the commodity form. Indeed, as Sicard points out, Neruda himself is just as deluded as "the old poets" if we take his claim for "clarity," "transparency," "invisibility," and "simplicity" at face value: "he leaves behind one [avant-garde] illusion only to enter into another that will be called 'the invisible man' or 'transparency'" (624).

Where Dawes sees dialectical movement between the positions of "attentive reader" and user of "appearance," Sicard's skepticism of transparency leads him to an alternative approach. In his reading of "The Absent Ones" ("Ausentes"), a poem included in the volume *Las manos del día* (1968), Sicard highlights the fact that Neruda contrasts the multiplicity of the world of workers—"they all did something"—with the poet's own lack of labor: "since I did nothing / gazing in the darkness at so many absences / . . . they have turned me into a shadow" (in Sicard 617). Here, Sicard identifies an emphatic contrast between the "hombre invisible" of the *Odas* and what Sicard calls "el hijo de la luna" ("the lunar child"), which is the poetic voice organizing *Las manos del día*. While the "terrible obligation" facing the "hombre invisible" is to bring the multiplicity of the workers' "making or doing" to the light of day, the observations expressed by "el hijo de la luna" focus on how poetry is precisely not like the labor of other workers: "they all did something" while "I did nothing." The difference, then, is between the "making and doing" of workers (*hacer*) and the poet's nonmaking or nondoing (*no hacer nada*).

Unlike the proliferating multiplicity of the *Odas* with the presence of workers at every turn, in "The Absent Ones," "There is no one" (344), as the opening line tells us. There is a clear difference between the "making or doing [something] / not just for one person but rather / for everyone," as in the *Odas*, and the not making or doing anything for anyone (*no hacer nada para nadie*) in *Las manos del día*. But what Sicard identifies is a consistency in the illusion of invisibility, transparency, and clarity in the *Odas* and the (at least partial) recognition of poetic specificity in *Las manos del día*. With his emphasis on having light eliminate the shadows that occlude exploitation and on operating as an invisible or transparent presence that serves as a vector for encountering the voices that express those experiences, the "hombre invisible" imagines his poems as workers' own objects. They are made not by the poet and what he does but instead by the experiences and effects of the light of workers' labor.

In *Las manos del día*, however, "el hijo de la luna" is perhaps less deluded or less engaged in self-deception than the "hombre invisible." He recognizes his nonmaking or nondoing (his poetry) as limited and problematically separated from the world of workers: "[the workers] all did [or made] something" but "[the poet] did [or made] nothing." In Sicard's account, then, the paradox of "clarity" and "deception"—the possibility of reading the *Odas* as "odes to the dialectic" or odes to the commodity—is present but unresolved within the poems themselves. The poems are structured by an engagement with the tensions between light—the egalitarian world the workers create—and shadow—what the capitalist system occludes. It is in this sense that we can understand the paradox of "clarity" and "deception": like the commodity defined by the labor relations it obscures, the aesthetically transparent poem must also occlude the labor relations underscoring it (the labor of the poet).

In confronting this paradox, Dawes sees the resolution in the activity of the reader (the worker) who can successfully navigate between "attentiveness" and application, between meaning and experience, between interpretation and use. Sicard's reading, however, suggests that a focus on the application, experience, or use of aesthetically transparent "objects," which Neruda advocates, has significant limits. Aesthetically transparent "objects" as Neruda envisions them exist only if someone or some group resides in the shadows or outside the light of day: the *Odas* are needed because capitalism occludes the exploitation of labor; the *Odas* exist because the poem occludes the labor of the poet.

Thus, while Sicard and Dawes agree that the poet acts in the same divided capitalist system as other workers, they disagree regarding the political utility of aesthetic transparency. On the one hand, we can see the poet's form that must be dissolved and the commodity form that must come to an end (shadow) as being resolved through the light emergent from the uses workers make of those objects. On the other hand, we can see shadow as the irresolvable and inevitable presence of the exploited, solitary individual. In both scenarios, aesthetic transparency operates through a logic of dedifferentiation that valorizes the experience of formlessness and demonstrates that the project of invisibility and transparency requires both light and shadow.[5]

What Dawes and Sicard enable us to see, I am arguing, is that aesthetic transparency and its politics operate through how Neruda envisions the relation between the poem and the reader. These materialist critics show us that Neruda's emphasis on what I am calling dedifferentiation as a poetic method is one that leads him to an irresolvable paradox that will continue to play out in his poetry for the remainder of his life. As I demonstrate in the next section, that paradox is irresolvable not because poverty and exploitation (understood as formlessness) are inevitable but instead because of a mismatch between the aesthetic problem Neruda identifies and the political problem.

As we saw in the introduction, sequences marked by a "crisis in representation"—which is to say, sequences in which the ability to represent to oneself how the world "works" comes into question—are also sequences in which there is a tendency to appeal to an experiential account of poverty as a necessary resource. This is what we see in Neruda's contrasting imagery of light and shadow. While the light and movement associated with the multiplicity of workers' "making and doing for everyone" (their *hacerlo para todos*) create the forms of a more egalitarian world, the motor for those forms is what remains in the shadows: the formlessness associated with the exploitation hidden by the commodity form *and* the formlessness of the poet's objects (the poet's nonmaking or nondoing, his *no hacer nada para nadie*). Aesthetic transparency operates on a logic that dissolves shadow into light, but light, on this logic, can exist only if the workers have the objects (the "fragments of stone or wood," the raw materials) they need, which are always emergent from the formlessness of the shadows.

Neruda attempts to solve the political problem with aesthetic tools, attempting to merge shadow and light, experience and meaning, interpretation and use through his poetic method. As we see in the next section, that effort and its limits are most clearly visible in the dual-level mechanism of aesthetic transparency embedded in his "terrible obligation" to *contar*. This involves the poetic act of creating meaningful forms that can be interpreted (i.e., narrating, relating, telling a meaningful story that is not reducible to mere "appearance" but instead can be understood by an "attentive reader") and the economic act of *contar* (i.e., enumerating, summing up, calculating the ever-evolving processes of social relations and their effects that persistently change over time). In working to resolve the tensions he identifies between his embeddedness in an actually existing historical sequence and his desire to contribute to the creation of a more egalitarian world that could (and should) come into being (but is not yet discernible), Neruda opts for dissolving what is for what could (or should) be. And that involves his appeal to theatricality: appealing to the shadows (the experience of formlessness) as the necessary resource for producing the aesthetically transparent objects workers could use in any and every situation they might face.

## Nerudas's Theatricality

To see how this dynamic of theatricality operates, it is helpful to turn first to the poem "Ode to the Simple Man" ("Oda al hombre sencillo"). Often considered a second thesis poem for the *Odas*, the "hombre sencillo" serves as the figure of the worker paralleling the figure of the poet ("el hombre invisible") in the prologue. Indeed, the "hombre invisible" begins the poem by speaking directly to the worker (the "hombre sencillo"), explaining how these poems should function: "I am going to tell you in secret / who I am / so that, in a voice that can be heard [*en voz alta*] / you will tell me who you are" (*OC* 121). As the speaking "hombre invisible" notes midway through the first sixty verses that compose the first sentence of "Simple Man,"

> I search until finding / the deep tissue, / so that I also find / the unity of all human beings, / and in bread / I search *beyond the form*: / I like bread, I bite it, / and then / I see wheat, / I see budding wheat fields, / the green shapes of spring, / the roots, the water, / and for this reason, / *beyond bread* / I see the earth, / the unity of the earth, / the water, / human beings, / in this way I try everything / *searching for you* / *in everything*, / I stroll, I swim, I travel / until *I find you* (*OC* 122, my emphasis)

What we see in this section of the text is that the poetry that Neruda seeks is "beyond the form," something that clearly parallels what we see in the prologue poem: "no one lives [in the poetry of the old poets] / . . . / no one suffers in the poetry [of the old poets] / . . . [we do not see when] there is a strike / [when] the soldiers come / and fire / fire on the *workers* / which is to say / [fire] on *poetry*" (*OC* 40, my emphasis). There are no workers and no one suffering poverty in the poems written by the "old poets," but because workers *are* poetry, there is no poetry in those poems either. The poetry the "hombre invisible" seeks is outside the forms of the "old poets": it is formless. And as we hear him say in "Simple Man," poetry is a discovery that is "beyond form" and is not accessible in actually existing literary forms.

With this in mind, it is important to see how Neruda begins and ends that sixty-verse sequence that opens the poem, one in which it appears as if the poetry he seeks lays outside all poetic *forms*. In the verses that immediately follow the cited passage above, which is to say, immediately following the poet's "encounter" with the worker ("I stroll, I swim, I travel / until I find you"), the "hombre invisible" initiates a conversation with the worker: "and so I ask you / for your name, / for your street address, / so that you can receive / my letters, / so that I can tell you / who I am and how much I earn, / where I live, / and about the life of my father" (*OC* 122). While this conversation serves to reference the "terrible obligation" described in the prologue, it also mirrors the very first lines of "Simple Man":

> I am going to tell you in secret / who I am / so that, in a voice that can be heard [*en voz alta*] / you will tell me who you are, / I want to know who you are, / how much you earn, / in what shop you work, / in what mine, / in what store, / I have a terrible obligation / and it is to know everything, / to know everything, / day and night to know / what your name is / that is my duty (121)

The information the "Invisible Man" possesses and plans to share in "[his] letters" with the "Simple Man" is the mirror image of the information the "Invisible Man" seeks to collect from his conversations with the "Simple Man." What we see in the examination of the beginning and ending of that first sixty-verse sequence is that the poet, who in "old" poetry was the only figure present in poetic *form*, passes into the invisibility of the shadow and into *formlessness*: "you can receive my letters [*private correspondence* from me], / so that I can tell you / who I am." Equally, we see that the worker, who in the "old" poetry was always outside poetic forms and resided in the experience of *formlessness*, crosses into the light of *form* once the poet resides in the shadows: "in *a voice that can be heard* / you will tell me who you are; I am going to tell you *in secret* / who I am" (my emphasis).

If, as Dawes has suggested, we can understand Neruda's "objective" with his aesthetic transparency as an effort "to [create] communication between equals regarding the struggles [for] equality in the Americas" (*Multiforme* loc. 1965), it is clear why Neruda would view this transpositional poetic method as an effective strategy. By passing into "secret" or into shadow, the "Invisible Man" shares the experience of formlessness with the "Simple Man," and by placing the "Simple Man" and his struggles in a "transparent" or "invisible" poetic form (the worker speaks "in a voice that can be heard" [*en voz alta*]), the self-absorbed poet does not blot out the light: the self-absorption associated with capitalism's poetic forms is displaced to the shadows. "Ode to the Simple Man" begins, then, with an insistence on the invisibility of form and the visible or audible presence of formlessness: the poet's life remains a "secret" shared in the shadows of capitalism while the workers' struggles and collective resistance in the common spaces of the factory, the mine, and the shop floor are what we are meant to see and hear. And yet the tension embedded in this model is the one that turns on the role of poetic labor.

There is a demand that the poem come into being through the "nonmaking or nondoing" (the *no hacer*) of the poet: a poetic silence that would not obscure or block or overinterpret—that is, not transform into a controlled or manipulated representation—what it is that the workers are saying, doing, and making. This "nonmaking or nondoing," however, can come into being only if he fulfills his "duty" as a poet and meets the requirements of his "terrible obligation," which is "to know everything": "who you are, / how much you earn, / in what shop you work, / in what mine, / in what store." The internal aesthetic requirements of the task—the *no hacer nada para nadie*, the poet's nonmaking, nondoing, and self-dissolution into the shadows amid the activities of the active, light-producing working-class collective—are at odds with the political or economic requirements of the task: "I stroll, I swim, I travel / until I find you," activities that require the poet's material resources and labor time. In this way, the "terrible obligation" to "know everything" and *contarlo*, or "account for everything they make and do," requires the poet's own "making and doing": a searching, a gathering, an encountering, an accounting that serves "not just . . . one person"—the poet's own individual, private universe—"but rather / . . . everyone" (the world lived in common).

The paradox emerges, then, in the dual-level mechanism of aesthetic transparency. To *contar*, as an effective political fulfillment of his "terrible obligation," requires concrete labor on the part of the poet: a making and doing for everyone (an *hacerlo para todos*). To *contar*, as an effective aesthetic fulfillment of that obligation, requires the poet to be invisible or transparent: a nonmaking or nondoing (a *no hacer nada para nadie*). Neruda's resolution of the paradox is located in his effort to negate what Sicard calls "the specificity of poetic labor" (618) in order to insist on the "Ode" as an object in the world like any other: an "everyday thing" that, like bread or tomatoes, like "fragments of stone or wood," is raw material in which relations between workers are "congealed." Those materials aren't meaningful but instead are vectors for encountering the relations between workers, which are always beyond or exceed any concrete form in which they are "congealed": "beyond bread / I see the earth, / the unity of the earth, / the water,

/ human beings" ("Ode to the Simple Man" 122). In this way, the only thing that matters is an awareness of those relations (understood as graspable in a transparent way through the experience of formlessness [the shadows]) and their transformation through the uses workers develop for those materials.

Dawes sees Neruda's resolution of the paradox in the envisioned movement from interpretation (an "attentive" accounting for "congealed" social relations) to workers' transformative use. This model (which Dawes reads as entering into significant complications after 1956) locates the fullness of that dialectical movement within the use value of the poems. Sicard's critique brings forward "the specificity of poetic labor" (618), which shows that the leap to aesthetic transparency's utopia of use value does not neutralize the other side of *contar*—the apparent nonmaking or nondoing of aesthetics—as labor.

In other words, Neruda's appeal to what we can call, following Michael Fried, the "objecthood" of the "Ode" enables Neruda to construct a political-poetic self-conception as a kind of baker, farmworker, logger, or miner: he presents the raw materials of life in a way that can be infinitely used by workers in their daily lives. The central idea structuring this specific aesthetic of "light"—these objects are merely gathered or found materials that are presented to workers for them to use—is one that requires him to deny that these objects are, in fact, aesthetic. The materials he gathers, collects, and accounts for—the "unity of the earth, / the water, / human beings" *he* sees or discovers and makes visible or audible through his meaningful representation of "everyday things"—are presented as if they really were accessible transparently. Imagining that these poetic objects exist for workers only to the extent that they "deposit new signs" or use them as tools to create lived equality in everyday situations, Neruda's aesthetic transparency is premised on a full embrace of objecthood and theatricality.

The consequence here is that the poet's labor—his interpretation and expression of the meaningful relations between people and things, his effort to bring to light the "true version of the world" (Yurkievich) and "the totality of reality" (Dawes)—is disavowed for the experience of what exists "beyond the form" ("Ode to the Simple Man" 122): in whatever "new signs" are "deposited" when workers use these poetic objects. For aesthetic transparency to "work," then, Neruda must find a way to mask and confine the processes of aesthetic labor to the shadows so as to foreground workers' infinite uses of these objects, their response to these objects, and their creation of "light."

The possibilities embedded in aesthetics—what is available *within* the form—are set aside and are relegated to the shadows. Understood as a boundary or separating mechanism that severs the relation between the poet from workers, the appeal to theatricality and objecthood in aesthetic transparency operates a transposition. The unity of form and light—the inegalitarian forms of the commodity as all we see and hear—are reconfigured as the unity of formlessness and light: the innumerable uses and infinite responses of workers to objects and materials create the egalitarian world we will be able to encounter. Form is understood to establish difference and division where there should be unity, so it must be relegated to the shadows, which is where the "Invisible Man," whose labor interprets and expresses the unity of and meaningful relations between the people and experiences he gathers and observes, must also ultimately reside. The problem, however, as we saw above with Sicard, is that by "renouncing its constitutive difference," by placing the political object in the light and locating aesthetic labor in the shadows, "poetic labor denies itself as labor. In this way, there is a risk that a poetry without a [writing] subject might substitute itself for the utopia of a poetry that creates its object" (Sicard 611). In other words, aesthetic transparency's embrace of the poem's objecthood and its foregrounding of theatricality create the very separation Neruda seeks to avoid.

We can see the perils of aesthetic transparency's embrace of theatricality in Neruda's reflection on and critique of quantitative data in "Ode to Numbers." In a structure paralleling the opening conversation between the "Invisible Man" and the "Simple Man" in the previously analyzed poem, the final stanza of "Ode to Numbers" describes the world he envisions emerging from the workers' use of aesthetically transparent poetic objects:

> for you / I want all things. / All numbers / that are placed in prison cells, / that they move / in closed columns / procreating / until giving us the sum / of the totality of the infinite. / For you I only want / that all of those / numbers you meet on the trail / defend you / and that you defend them. / *That the weekly number on your paycheck / grows until it covers your chest.* / And from the number 2 that ties / your body to that of the woman you love / that there might emerge pairs of eyes belonging to your children / who will count once again / the ancient stars / and the innumerable / corncobs / that will fill a transformed earth. (174, my emphasis)

Here we see form appear as the "numbers / that are placed in prison cells," which is to say, are constrained by the balance sheet of a mine or factory that must reduce or contract labor costs and maximize profit. Form here operates as a problematic boundary or separating mechanism: "the weekly number on your paycheck" directly correlates to the insufficient quality of life for the worker who cannot "[cover his] chest." Because those needs exist "beyond the form" and beyond the numerical calculations on the balance sheet, Neruda's "Ode" imagines "movement," "procreation," "growth," and multiplication of those forms (those numbers) until they are sufficiently expansive: "I want . . . / That . . . weekly number on your paycheck / [to grow] until it covers your chest." But as the poem approaches its end, the process of expansion continues, with numbers continuing to grow beyond any form that could contain it: "the totality of the infinite" and "the innumerable / corncobs / that will fill a transformed earth." While "Ode to Numbers" treads a path similar to "Ode to the Simple Man," where the poet must appeal to the unifying experience of formlessness "beyond bread," the contrast between its opening and its ending demonstrates the perils of theatricality more clearly.

As we just saw, the "transformed earth" of "Ode to Numbers" imagines a solution to concrete situations of poverty—insufficient clothing, insufficient food—in the dissolution of all forms: everyone has all that they want. With endless food, the worker and his or her child will eat until they are content, counting the finished corn cobs in pleasure as they gaze, bellies full, at the uncountable stars. In the "transformed earth" that ends the poem, the act of *contar*—accounting for, calculating, measuring, budgeting, and so on—is no longer necessary or even possible. The balance sheets of capitalism—the forms supporting the sustenance of the commodity—dissolve into the activities of the worker, organized for their own purposes and at their whims. But if the poem ends with the elimination of the act of *contar* as one necessary for sustaining life—the "totality of the infinite" is located in life experienced "beyond form"—the poem's opening suggests that the act of *contar* (the creation of forms, the full accounting for and relating of the rhythms of life) is the only thing that could produce that encounter with the experience of formlessness: "What *thirst* / to know how much! / What *hunger* / to know / how many / stars are in the sky!" (*OC* 172, my emphasis).

The basic experiences of poverty—hunger and thirst—are associated with the production of form, which, in turn, is related to the natural impulse transform the world around us into the numbers that represent some idea of a desired form or stage of life: "We spend / our childhood / counting rocks, plants, / fingers, grains of sand, teeth / our adolescence counting petals and strands of hair" (*OC* 173). The natural processes of thirst and hunger for knowledge, which lead children and adolescents to transform "rocks," "fingers," and "petals" into representations of their current or desired life experiences, parallel the task that faces the poet as "Invisible Man": the "terrible obligation" to create "fragments of stone or wood," to present "palpable objects" that could be "useful tools for work." That "obligation" in the prologue-poem and in "Ode to the Simple Man" operates like the "thirst" and "hunger" in "Ode to Numbers." In an important sense, then, the creation of aesthetically transparent objects meant to dissolve existing forms in favor of the experience that lays "beyond" them comes to be associated not only with the poet who gathers, accounts for, and relates those experiences but also with the experience of poverty itself.

If this seems implausible, we need only examine the fate of poverty at the end of "Ode to Poverty." In a poem that closely parallels both "Ode to Numbers" and "Ode to the Simple Man," the speaker ends in apostrophic address of poverty: "I with others, / with others, many others, / will expel you / from the earth to the moon / so that there you will stay / cold and *imprisoned* / watching with your one eye / the bread and bounty / that will fill the earth / of tomorrow" (*OC* 197, my emphasis). Like the numbers on the balance sheet above, poverty is also "imprisoned" in this poem. However, while the numbers will be liberated as they dissolve into the light of the uses workers make of them, the expulsion of poverty from the earth and its imprisonment on the moon appear to be permanent. The poet finds no place for poverty amid the "bread and bounty / that will fill the earth" once worker experience dissolves the darkness and stasis that characterize imprisoning forms. In this way, Neruda rightly defines poverty as a form of exploitation that should be eliminated. But the mechanism he imagines as key to accomplishing that elimination is the active and infinite uses workers make of "everyday things." Within that mechanism, poverty is under lock and key ("cold and imprisoned . . . [on] the moon"), but it is not eliminated: it still exercises a kind of invisible gravitational force in ways that parallel the moon's effects on the earth and perhaps also in the ways that natural impulses of "thirst" and "hunger" drive the creation of forms. In other words, poverty, imagined as exercising, from the moon, an invisible influence on the activities of the earth, can be understood as unifying the dynamics of the two sides of aesthetic transparency: the "Invisible Man" ("hombre invisible," bringing to light the *hacerlo para todos* of the workers) and the "Lunar Child" ("hijo de la luna," residing in the darkness of a *no hacer nada para nadie*).

That unity is clear if we reimagine the opening lines of "Ode to Poverty" not as a conversation between the "Invisible Man" and a personified poverty but instead as one in which the worker responds to the activities composing the "Invisible Man's" "terrible obligation" to *contar*. In the passage that follows, the second person address in which the "Invisible Man" speaks directly to poverty is maintained exactly as it appears in the poem with the only change being the insertion of "Invisible Poet" in the place where "poverty" appears, to transform this passage into a worker's response to the activities of the "Invisible Man": "When I was born, / ['Invisible Man'], / you followed me, / you watched me / through rotting walls / during the deepness of winter. / Soon enough / those were your eyes / that were watching me through those holes. / The leaks, / at night, / repeated / *your first and last name . . . / . . . /* there you were / *searching for me, / following me* / from my birth / through the streets" (*OC* 194, my emphasis). The activities of personified "poverty"—"following" the worker, "searching for" the worker, sharing in secret the "first and last name" of the poet—are all hallmarks of what characterizes the "terrible obligation" of the poet creating aesthetically transparent objects. These fundamental aspects of poverty, which can be experienced only negatively, are transformed by the "Invisible Man" through the effort to unify the dual-level mechanism of his "obligation" to *contar*: the specificity of the poet's labor (an *hacerlo para todos*) that must be disavowed in order to secure the execution of his poetic method (a *no hacer nada para nadie*).

As we have seen, that unity is developed through the exercise of a logic of dedifferentiation: the dissolution of darkness into light, the artwork into life, meaning into experience, form into formlessness. That dedifferentiation operates through the ways aesthetic transparency reimagines the relation between the poem and the reader. Forms—numbers and poems as much as bread and tomatoes—are always points where there is a "congealing" of the social relations and a stasis. Neruda wishes to return all those seemingly stable forms to the active and mobile life "beyond form" through the appeal to theatricality: providing workers with access to aesthetically transparent objects. The political and poetic method depends on the persistent valorization and transformation of the experience of formlessness. Aesthetic transparency relies on the need to convert the negative experience of formlessness under capitalism (poverty) into its positive variant (the infinite things workers will "make and do" with the aesthetically transparent objects made available by the poet).

Neruda, without a doubt, viewed aesthetic transparency as a promising pathway for resolving both the problem of poverty (e.g., insufficient food, housing, clothing, land, work, etc.) and the problem of literature (e.g., self-indulgent forms of self-absorbed poets). However, his valorization of the experience of formlessness and his commitment to an aesthetics of theatricality (creating "palpable objects" in space that transform and are transformed by the encounter with workers) made the possibilities of securing egalitarian modes of social organization a persistent challenge. Thus, while this mode of political aesthetics seemed at odds with the way the world seemed to "work" in that period, Neruda, nevertheless, remained convinced that aesthetic transparency is what the historical moment called on him to create.

At the same time, however, as both Dawes and Sicard demonstrate, we know aesthetic transparency was, on some level, felt to be an unsatisfactory response. Neruda continued to develop and modify his aesthetic method through the 1960s and into the 1970s. As Dawes notes, Neruda experienced another poetically, politically, and personally influential crisis in the wake of the Soviet invasion of Czechoslovakia in 1968. Seeing a problematic "Neo-Stalinism" emergent under Brezhnev, Neruda experienced a "lacerated engagement" (Hernán Loyola's term) on the model of what transpired after 1956. But, as Dawes notes, "unlike his reaction to the crisis of 1956, the events of 1968 produced in Neruda's poetry an open defense of the Prague Spring, opposition to U.S. imperialism in Vietnam, and opposition to the nuclear arms race and the Cold War" (*Multiforme* loc. 4258). Thus, while he sees a pathway for his poetry to engage directly with the politics of the moment, Neruda continues to find himself in the same paradox we saw at the outset of this chapter with the satirical cartoon: a poet fully embedded in the struggles of the working class *appears* to be a self-absorbed, individualist poet focused on his own enjoyment of "luxury."

This dilemma is clear in Dawes's analysis of Neruda's poem "Possessions" from *Geografía infructuosa* (1972). As he explains, it is possible to read the poem as Neruda's defense of "individualism" and the "commodity fetish" (*Multiforme* loc. 6028), though he finds that reading improbable. Noting Neruda's advancing age in 1972 (he was sixty-eight), Dawes turns instead to Erich Fromm's explanation of why humans fear death. In Fromm's account, it is the fear of "losing what I have: the fear of losing the body, the ego, possessions, and identity; the fear of finding oneself in the chasm of non-identity, of 'losing oneself'" (Fromm in Dawes loc. 6037). Rather than an ode to the commodity fetish, Dawes argues that the appeal to possessions is a proxy for the expression of the fear of death, or, in Fromm's description, the fear of the loss of self. In the context of Neruda's poetic method, it would also be the loss of the "Invisible Man," which is understood as the mechanism by which politics and art can take place (i.e., making objects useful to workers seeking to express their needs, desires, and demands). And, as we have seen, the persistent threat of the loss of possessions—the "rotting walls" of one's home "during the deepness of winter" ("Ode to Poverty"), the military's strike breaking ("Invisible Man"), or the factory's contracting balance sheet that leaves workers unable to buy the food and clothing they need ("Ode to Numbers")—is also what characterizes a poverty that, paradoxically, must be maintained in Neruda's poetic method.

While it may be that Neruda never fully worked out the paradox he is interrogating in his work from the 1950s forward (and, in fact, may not have been fully conscious of or have fully understood the paradox in the terms being described here), his poetry does make that paradox available to readers for analysis. Aesthetic transparency is Neruda's effort to create art that meets the political moment, but it is also what a full embrace of theatricality looks like. Neruda could not perceive or intuit antitheatrical alternatives as viable options. Though antitheatrical strategies were not among the resources Neruda sought to employ nor likely the terms he would have used to describe the paradox he was interrogating, the reconfigured relationship between poem and reader (or artwork and beholder) he sought was one that was deeply engaged with the issues surrounding theatricality and antitheatricality, objecthood and art. Recognizing those issues in Neruda's aesthetic transparency and the limits to a politics that martials an aesthetics embracing theatricality enables us to see and grasp the impact and promise of artists who did recognize the force of antitheatrical commitment in the wake of the events of 1968, which are examined in the next chapter.

# 3

# The Afterlife of Mexico, 1968

## Posthegemony and Its Antitheatrical Alternatives

On October 2, 1968, the Mexican state massacred students, workers, and bystanders in the Plaza de las Tres Culturas (Plaza of Three Cultures) where a group associated with the student-popular movement had gathered to protest the Mexican state. The movement was heterogeneous. However, protestors' written demands were largely organized around the concept of "autogestión"—self-management or autonomy in social life—as a strategy that could dismantle Mexico's hierarchical, programmatic, and institutionalized revolutionary party (the PRI). They, for example, sought immediate action against state repression, moved to undermine state-directed labor and student organizations, and proposed resistance to both the U.S. and Soviet models of industrial development that found support in various factions within the PRI. In the years since the massacre, the student-popular movement, which until that moment had been referred to by numerous names (e.g., Movimiento Estudiantil julio-agosto, the revolution, Comité de Lucha, Consejo Nacional de Huelga, etc.), became forever associated with the massacre and known by the name Tlatelolco, the neighborhood where the plaza is located. As Samuel Steinberg notes, the student-popular movement's "own event" became eclipsed by "the state's 'event,' its criminal actions" (*Photopoetics* 51).

This dynamic is what drives and structures Steinberg's *Photopoetics of Tlatelolco: Afterimages of Mexico, 1968* (2016), an important reassessment of what 1968 was and meant. Steinberg argues against an archival logic and its aspirations to provide a "legible image" or "classifiable body" (35) that could name, give voice to, or fully capture, order, and organize the student-popular alliance that was murdered that October day. In very clear ways, this reading of Tlatelolco, which Steinberg calls the "an-archival" reading of Tlatelolco, is one that merges with Jacques Rancière's concept of politics (the practices of "the part who have no part") in the context of police (the reigning "partition of the perceptible"). The "legible image" or "classifiable body" that is the massacre belongs to what Rancière would term "police." This term is one iteration of the "partition of the perceptible," which is the term he used to describe how a society organizes "ways of doing, ways of being, and ways of saying" and determines who and what can appear in a given community as well as what they are allowed to do and say. As Rancière says, it gives to each "the part that is his due according to the evidence of what he is" (*Disagreement* 27). In the context of "police" logic, in which Rancière locates most modes of critical thought today, he posits as an alternative the notion of "politics" or "dissensus." This would be the "action of uncounted capacities that crack open the unity of the visible, in order to sketch out a new topography of the possible" (49).

As I have argued elsewhere, Rancière's notion of "politics" or "dissensus" largely parallels the Mexicanist notion of "ill use" as elaborated by authors like Agustín Yáñez (see chapter 1). While for someone like Yáñez (who was serving as secretary of public education in the consequential year of PRI-ist clashes with Mexico's student movement) the pelado (the paradigmatic image of urban poverty) is the figuration of this logic, Rancière develops a variety of figures in his writing for recognizing what he calls "the quality of human beings without qualities" (*Emancipated* 49), or the possibility of glimpsing human beings who claim for themselves what has not been allocated to them. Two of these figures are particularly important for recognizing that the proposal for an an-archival reading of Tlatelolco continues the Mexicanist logic of poverty embraced by figures like Yáñez and Cantinflas three decades earlier and that are incorporated into the PRI-ist apparatus that an an-archival reading seeks to critique. These figures in Rancière's writing are the poor as "the part who have no part" and the "emancipated spectator" who is "at once a performer deploying . . . and a spectator observing" (22).

In the foregoing critique, what is at stake is understanding the limits of both historical understandings of Mexico, 1968 and their recent reassessment in the context of post-1968 French political and cultural thought. Indeed, by revealing what have been relatively unexamined historical resonances between Mexicanist thought and the post-1968 critical tradition that Rancière represents, the present chapter argues that a more nuanced understanding of Mexico's historical navigation of aesthetics and politics can improve our understanding of the historical legacy of the global 1968 as well as how the mistaken notion of poverty as an experience of formlessness interfaces with it.[1] Indeed, if we recognize that the demand for "autogestión" is not so much a demand for "autonomy," which would presume the continued existence of conventionalized forms or norms of social interaction, but instead the demand for a life free of those norms and conventions, it becomes clear that the central idea that an an-archival reading of Mexico, 1968 seeks to recover from the movement is the desire to generalize more fully the logic of poverty developed by the very Mexicanist thinkers these critics and student protestors would seemingly reject. That account of poverty is, as we have seen, synonymous with the experience of formlessness. This would not be the negative experience of the poor as "the part who have no part" but instead its conversion into "politics": the positive experience of the "emancipated spectator" who is "at once a performer deploying . . . and a spectator observing" (*Emancipated* 22), thus making possible a persistent and uncontrollable process of experiential making and unmaking (autogestión).

This is already clear if we note how Steinberg's an-archival reading of Mexico, 1968 turns against the massacre in favor of what he calls the nonplace or nonhappening of 1968. By seeking to "question any demand that we return to the place of repression" (Steinberg, *Photopoetics* 42)—a repression expressed both in the actual state violence that took place in the plaza and in the subsequent naming of the heterogeneous egalitarian projects with the place name of a singular act of state violence—Steinberg suggests that the nonhappening of 1968 can return us to "the movement's possible event, its own opening to what is incalculable, a spontaneous reality" (35). This would be, he says, something that is not "the inscription and policing of any new order of being, but [instead] the experience of . . . the world in its radical opening" (43) to contingency and chance, a notion that shares something with Rancière's account of politics or dissensus as the "action of uncounted capacities that crack open the unity of the visible, in order to sketch out a new topography of the possible" (*Disagreement* 49). Rather than employing Rancière's term, however, Steinberg opts for what might be considered its Latin American variant: the student-popular movement as "posthegemonic practice" (5).

For Steinberg, "posthegemonic practice" (5) is what best expresses the legacy of 1968 because it "cannot serve the reason of the social bond in the way that has usually authorized [Mexicanism]" (*Photopoetics* 140). Unlike the PRI and its bureaucratic, hierarchical, pedagogic, and authoritarian organization, 1968's logic does not articulate, in Steinberg's account, a "consensual claim," a "hegemonic demand," or a "hegemonizing desire." Instead, it affirms "freedom of tendencies" within a "collective consciousness" (4): a persistent and uncontrollable process of experiential making and unmaking (participating and watching participation) through "autogestión." Mexico, 1968's nonhappening, then, is structured by a not-taking-place, a refusal to occupy one's assigned place or, more simply, the assertion that the egalitarian place one already occupies is one that can never be legible within the PRI's hegemonic organization and, as such, has no desire for such a legibility. "Autogestión" in Mexico, 1968, "emancipation" of the spectator in Rancière's thought, and "posthegemonic practice" have clear points of convergence: a politics centered on "the dismantling of the old distribution of what could be seen, thought and done" (*Emancipated* 47).

That political practice hinges on the experience of formlessness as a creative resource. In this way, Steinberg argues that by turning away from litigating the bloody "afterimages" that have structured conversations around Mexico, 1968 that incorporate the student-popular movement and its repression into state-legitimizing narratives, there can be a turning toward the egalitarian practices and forms of life that existed before October 2, 1968: those persistent and uncontrollable processes of experiential making and unmaking (participating and watching participation) through "autogestión." In other words, Steinberg argues that a "posthegemonic" approach to Mexico, 1968, that is, an approach that recovers the horizontalist logic of that era's conceptualization of egalitarianism, is one that can dismantle the hierarchical logic and "partitions" of Mexicanist police logic.

However, as I argued in chapter 1, it is precisely this kind of horizontalist, dehierarchizing project (based, in that era, on the pelado) that failed to critique the historically particular and specific structure of state capitalism that created poverty as an objective relational aspect of that system and that also became essential to both constructing that form of capitalism and sustaining it over time. In chapter 2, I examined Neruda's development of "aesthetic transparency," through which he sought to make his poems politically relevant by transforming them from forms that made an understanding of unequal social relations available via representation into formless materials that could be made useful when they are "activated" by workers who use them in anticapitalist struggle. This aesthetic solution ended up undermining the political critique he sought to achieve with this aesthetic innovation: poverty became an indispensable resource for achieving "aesthetic transparency," thus making the supposed aesthetic solution to the political and economic problem of poverty simply a new iteration of the exclusive aesthetic practices of the "old poets," a term he uses to include his own previous (and insufficient) poetic works. While Neruda did understand poverty as a material problem embedded in capitalist social relations, he continued to struggle with the aesthetic strategies that would enable him to sufficiently achieve a critical relation with them.

However, whereas Neruda discovered and embraced a politics of formlessness within the aesthetics of his poems—that is, in their theatricality or reduction to what Michael Fried calls objecthood—this chapter examines the effects of that impulse. But in this case, rather than serving as a resource for aesthetic creation, the experience of formlessness becomes a resource for political analysis, which subsequently informs arguments, judgments, and conclusions regarding literary, visual, and, in this case, cinematic artworks.

In the first section of the chapter that follows, I examine Steinberg's argument that the recovery of "posthegemonic practice" from the student-popular movement in Mexico, 1968 can produce what he calls an "infrapolitical register" (*Photopoetics* 180) of thought or reflection. As we will see, what he attempts to recover through his posthegemonic-infrapolitical framework is a nonrelation with the political calculations that persistently and permanently remake and reconstruct the nation-state. His analysis of the film *Rojo amanecer* (Jorge Fons, originally released in 1989) provides a cinematic analog for persistent efforts to remake and reconstruct the state. As I argue, however, the experiential horizontalism of the posthegemonic-infrapolitical framework that he seeks to recover did not unmake or create a nonrelation with the PRI-ist state.

As we saw with Yáñez's work years before he was serving as Díaz Ordaz's education minister in 1968, the mistaken notion of poverty as an experience of formlessness was essential to the construction of the PRI-ist state. The critical commitment to the experience of formlessness—the multitude's "posthegemonic practice" of producing life in an "infrapolitical register"—undermines the critical capacities of the "an-archival" politics of Mexico, 1968. In much the same way that an analysis of the aesthetic projects advanced by Yáñez and Neruda made available an understanding of their mistaken account of poverty, so too does an analysis of the an-archival reading of the cinematic aesthetics of Mexico, 1968. However, as we will see, in the visual analysis of *Rojo amanecer*, the an-archival approach does not account for what I argue is the film's use of antitheatrical strategies, which make available a critique of conceptualizations of poverty as an experience of formlessness within the framework of the 1968 massacre.

## Formlessness in What Did Not Take Place

One of Steinberg's most innovative readings (or misreadings) opens his study and sets the stage for connecting Mexico, 1968 to the broader logic of the global 1968. Quoting Mark Kurlansky's *1968: The Year That Rocked the World* (2004), Steinberg summarizes many of the points his book makes through a literalizing gloss of Kurlansky's assertion that "there has never been a year like 1968, and it is unlikely there will be again" (in Steinberg, *Photopoetics* 5). Here, Steinberg insists on reading the consequences of a literalized understanding of the statement "there has never been a year like 1968." At stake here is the notion that not even 1968 itself is a year like "the year that rocked the world." *That* 1968 is a product of the archive: "The thing we call 1968 has until now been bound to reflection in a hegemonic key: finding and discerning points of unity, discussing, cataloguing, and, too often, hastily resolving its contradictions" (4). Against the "Plaza of Sacrifices" archive that seeks to document the "truth" and detail the crimes committed by the state in October 1968, there remains *another* Mexico, 1968, one that is identical to that which refuses to come into view and be confined to a state-legitimizing archive. What Mexico, 1968 was—and, more broadly, what the global 1968 was—instead was "the demarcation of an absence": "Mexico, 1968" was what (was everything that) "did not take [its proper] place" (Steinberg 6). Those who refused to take their place as students or as workers or as peasants or as intellectuals and instead insisted on confusing and reordering those divisions and distributions were Mexico, 1968: the peasant intellectual (in explaining), the studying worker (in planning), the machine-operating student (in filming). But this is the Mexico, 1968 that precisely does not (and cannot) come into view because, as Steinberg points out, the "hegemonic key" of current understandings of Mexico, 1968 hinges on the "instrumentalization of tragedy" and a "sacrificial image" (20).

By taking stock of what "rocked the world" or what contained and demobilized the mass movement that manifested itself in Mexico over the course of multiple months has too often been used to "[suture] Mexican history and [reground] Mexicanism, understood as the ideological proposal of an eternal peoplehood that underwrote the sovereign power of a diffuse Mexican state" (*Photopoetics* 20). Steinberg's an-archival reading of Mexico, 1968 is engaged, then, in "exorcizing" the specter of the massacre, which places at its center archival readings that sustain the policing of the movement's "truth." In its place, Steinberg seeks to situate the life of the student-popular movement. This life or experience would be the potential for a possible politics otherwise through an eternal production of a space in which neither "hegemonic" nor "counterhegemonic" dynamics make sense: it is always located beyond existing configurations of equality, self-management, justice, and so on. Instead of a procedural or methodological "truth" that can be revealed about 1968, Steinberg proposes we turn instead to the idea of a "spontaneous reality": whatever 1968 was, that multitudinous amalgam proposed, in serial, alternative modes of "being-in-common" that were always provisional and always emerging. This effort to "de-instrumentalize" Tlatelolco is in line with "posthegemonic practice": egalitarian experience that never "founds" anything.

Steinberg's "an-archival" 1968 is enabled by his development of "posthegemony as the orienting horizon of [his] book's theoretical operation" (*Photopoetics* 15), and it continues in the vein of frameworks developed by scholars like Gareth Williams. This is a logical step not only since Williams is one of the first in Latin American political and cultural theory to operationalize posthegemony as a "different telos" or an "other thought within thought" but also because he himself develops this logic into a detailed reading of Mexico, 1968. In his book *The Mexican Exception*, Williams produces a connective logic linking his earlier thinking about posthegemony in his book *The Other Side of the Popular* (2002) with the Latin Americanist political and cultural theory that emerged out of the global 1968.

For Williams, posthegemony is a term that refers to "the inherent incompletion of hegemony's social articulations" (*Other* 151), or, more simply, its absences and blank spaces that nevertheless remain there within hegemony, in a kind of nonrelation with it. This incompletion rests on the fact that hegemony is always founded on "the repression of alternative worldings" (151) so that hegemony's notion of completion ("the people") is characterized by an "incompletion" due to unforeseen exclusions and absences that are present within the distributions of hegemony's order. With the notion of incompletion as a starting premise, Williams proposes the notion of "posthegemonic reactivation"—the "affirmation of . . . [the] disjunctive, interruptive, and heterogeneous . . . within hegemonic reflection"—as a way of making unseen or unforeseen or incalculable alternatives available. This presents posthegemony as simply "a question of opening up the present to alternative possibilities and heterogeneous discourses and practices," that is, to alternative modes of being-in-common "that were perhaps open in the past but were discarded or disappeared on the way" (*Other* 151). In this way, Williams's elaboration of posthegemony in *The Other Side of the Popular* maintains deep parallels with his embrace of Rancière's notion of the politics of the part who have no part in *The Mexican Exception*. Like Rancière's rejection of police logic and Steinberg's rejection of archival logic, Williams rejects "the sociological rationalization of 1968" (*Mexican Exception* 152) in favor of "the singular *experience* of the democratic [egalitarian] event called 1968" (130, my emphasis). That democratic and egalitarian experience can be connected to the "posthegemonic practice" Steinberg advocates and is connected to the politics of the poor (the part who have no part) that Williams adopts from Rancière.

Perhaps for this reason, Williams specifically cites Rancière's critique of "the official version of events [in May 1968 in France]" as a model for his own reflection on Mexico, 1968. Rancière rejects the post-1968 efforts by "historians, sociologists, and bestselling novelists who began to regulate the events [of May 1968]" (*Mexican Exception* 130) as a "central episode in the unfolding of mass consumption and capitalist youth culture on an international scale" (131). Instead, May 1968 should have been read as "the eruption of improper words to which no predetermined idea could be attached . . . [and the emergence of] friendship toward the chance experience" (131). In the choice for chance over calculation, nonrelational commonality over national articulation, Williams fuses Rancière's politics of the part who have no part with his own conceptions of posthegemonic practice: an "opening up the present to alternative possibilities . . . that were perhaps open in the past but were discarded or disappeared on the way" (*Other* 151). This unification of his thinking about posthegemony with Rancière's conception of politics provides a clear template for Steinberg's an-archival reading: Mexico, 1968's not-taking-place as the model and legacy for the global 1968.

As we saw in the introduction, the uncapturable experience of egalitarianism is also something that is essential in Jon Beasley-Murray's account of posthegemony. Against understanding politics as a "determinable (representable, reproducible) relation" between a people and their representatives, Beasley-Murray argues that politics only ever operates as an "experience of [an] event" (243). By turning away from the "representable" and toward the open-ended experiences of the multitude that "cracks open" the supposed "unity" of hegemony,

Beasley-Murray argues that we can see how political power becomes "encrusted [and controlled] within the habit of . . . ritualized celebrations organized entirely by the state" (66).

While Beasley-Murray's comments are focused on Argentina and the Peronist rituals so deeply associated with the "balcony effect," it is also the case, as we saw in chapter 1, that Mexicanism mobilizes a similar logic after the Revolution. It took shape through the ways of being, saying, doing, and knowing of the pelado in the 1930s and 1940s, and in the 1960s, that logic attaches to the ways of being, saying, doing, and knowing expressed by the group that scholars of posthegemony would describe as those who "do not take place": the participants in the student-popular movement who make it clear that they do not have and do not desire a place in what Steinberg, citing Roger Bartra, calls the "Mexican Office": the tropes of *lo mexicano* advanced by official nationalist programs that seek to manage and police actions, behaviors, and thoughts. For Steinberg (as for Williams), the posthegemonic legacy of Mexico, 1968 is the assertion of an absence in place of a presence: what (and those who) did not and do not take (their assigned) place.

The unruly processes of life and the experiences of egalitarianism are recovered from what the carefully curated and controlled archive-crypt "discarded or disappeared on the way." The "archival" or "sociological rationalization of" Mexico, 1968 reorganized the country into, on the one hand, a criminal, barbaric state and, on the other hand, innocent students and bystanders as sacrificial victims who would be instrumentalized in the PRI-ist state's process of "democratic" self-reinvention. The problem, however, as Steinberg and Williams see it, is that the students were not taking a pro-state or even anti-corrupt-state position. Instead, they sought to establish a nonrelation with that overdetermined national history by recovering life and experience outside any arc of "national destiny" or "national identity." This is what Steinberg calls post-Mexicanism: a recovery of the movement's spontaneous ways of being, doing, saying, and knowing; or what can also be called the politics of the poor (the part who have no part) and, more simply, posthegemony. I have been arguing in the present study that this logic—the embrace of the experience of formlessness (the logic of poverty)—is what gave rise to and sustained the PRI. But for Steinberg, it is in the reanimation (he calls it the "resurrection") of egalitarian experiences of formlessness that are discovered through the spontaneity of participation (i.e., never set up in advance) that the archival Mexicanist logic can be eroded through a serial process of nonrelation.

Another way to understand the central tension Steinberg sets up, then, is to read the tension of form and formlessness as the tension between Mexicanism (organized by an archival logic) and what he calls post-Mexicanism (organized by an an-archival logic). The failure to put into practice the post-Mexicanist logic of 1968—the choice for a "sociological rationalization of" 1968 in place of the egalitarian experience of 1968—motivates Steinberg's critique of Jorge Fons's 1989 film *Rojo amanecer*. However, rather than following Steinberg's assertion that

*Rojo amanecer* models the kind of archival Mexicanist cinema that brings the need for post-Mexicanist alternatives into relief, what I show is that Fons establishes a critical relation with this pervasive Mexicanist logic. It is through his aesthetic choices, rather than the embrace of a nonrelational experience, that Fons establishes an alternative to the Mexicanist framework.

As Steinberg correctly notes, the student-popular movement rejects the Mexicanist framework. However, as elaborated in previous chapters, the alternative to Mexicanism is not a post-Mexicanist recovery of open-ended experience unconstrained by burdens of nationalist narratives. It is instead the achievement of a critical relation to the experience of formlessness, which is always an appeal to theatricality. An embrace of the experience of formlessness is always the search for an audience's acceptance or compliance or experiential self-recognition through an appeal to the manners, conventions, and tropes that structure existing, or even provisionally proposed alternative, modes of social being (e.g., the peasant intellectual, the studying worker, the machine-operating student). The post-Mexicanist (or posthegemonic) alternative to the Mexicanist framework relies on an embrace of the experience of formlessness, which is to say, the logic of poverty that founds the Mexicanist tradition. The alternative is not an ever firmer adherence to appealing to experiential self-recognition but instead the neutralization or negation of that experiential self-recognition, something demonstrated by Fons in the choices he makes when creating the film. It is this effort to neutralize the direct appeal to the audience's acceptance or compliance or experiential self-recognition that links *Rojo amanecer* to the antitheatrical tradition.

Fons utilizes antitheatrical strategies that place his film in line with works of art that develop a critical relationship with Mexicanist aesthetic and social conventions. As Fried notes, the idea that a work could "detheatricalize beholding and so make it once again a mode of access to truth and conviction, albeit a truth and conviction that cannot be entirely equated with any known or experienced before" (*Absorption* 104) is an idea that is essential to understanding the development of modernist art. Fons's film is marked by his effort to make available a "truth" about inequality in Mexico that is not reducible to anyone's experience of it. Indeed, it is this "truth"—"what really happens," the abstracted real social relations between classes on an international scale that are not reducible to any single national experience of capitalist social relations—that was in play for some elements of the student-popular movement of 1968, and this is what Fons makes available via cinematic form in his film.

## Cinematic Posthegemony: Archive or Resurrection?

At first glance, *Rojo amanecer* would seem to be a film that Steinberg's post-Mexicanist account of Mexico, 1968 could embrace: the Tlatelolco Massacre literally does not take place on screen. Instead, it comes into view through the reactions and on-screen relations between members of a middle-class family who witnesses the massacre from their apartment window, which faces the plaza where the students and bystanders were murdered by the Mexican government. In other words, both the complex set of relations and the sequence of events—the heterogeneous student-popular movement, the state's brutal efforts to control it—appear on screen only as a sort of secondary effect. However, this dynamic is precisely what leads Steinberg to reject the film as a product of the Mexicanist framework rather than the initiation of a post-Mexicanist alternative, free from the state's hierarchical, directed narratives that remain egalitarian only in name:

> In not rendering visible the massacre itself, the film underscores its own documentary nature. . . . It registers both the student movement's rally as well as its destruction on the square below through canned diegetic crowd noises and gunfire, supplemented by the eyes of the characters themselves, who bear witness—for us, in our place—to the action of the plaza. At the same time, in a strangely contradictory turn, the audience will die *in the place* of those students, for the viewer . . . has been placed *in* the plaza by the relation between viewing screen and audience. (*Photopoetics* 134, my emphasis)

This reading—with its option for a confusion of places or the positing of a position or view that does not "take [its] place" within a PRI-endorsed structure—would seemingly realize in cinematic form what Steinberg champions as the optimal approach to Mexico, 1968.

If we were to integrate *Rojo amanecer* into Steinberg's post-Mexicanist (an-archival) framework, it would need to be emphasized that Fons's choices locate "us," the viewing audience, in an unarchivable location with relation to the movement. By dying "*in the place* of those students" and not "taking [their] place" as a passive audience who possesses total knowledge, the viewing public would be transformed into something like an unarchivable student-popular movement: living in the present, it has no place in the past; participating (cinematically) as victims of the violence of the past, they also have no place in the present. The viewing audience makes their own improper location: they both die *in* the plaza at the hands of the government and survive that violence to witness *in* the apartment the government's murder of the middle-class family whose life we've seen unfold on screen.

On this reading, the audience would develop a strange relational position—simultaneously a murder victim and a surviving witness to a murder. Such a position would require them to operate under a unique mode of mobility: being simultaneously in the plaza *and* "under house arrest" in "the apartment [that] never opens onto the square." And it would ultimately require them to reckon with *both* the collective pain registered in the horrified faces of the family that witnessed "our" deaths in the plaza *and* "our" own experience of collective pain when we see those who mourned "us" gunned down by the same state actors who murdered "us" (Steinberg, *Photopoetics* 134). Were this linked to a posthegemonic reading, it would articulate the creation of a being-in-common that has absolutely no relation to any actually existing social group, an open-endedness that the posthegemonic model would seek to recover. This post-Mexicanist account of *Rojo amanecer*, of course, is not the one Steinberg pursues.

As we will see in a moment, Steinberg is right to highlight the strange sets of relations the film achieves with its aesthetic choices, and he is also right to note that *Rojo amanecer* is not a posthegemonic or post-Mexicanist film. However, the reading advanced in his framework is incorrect when it claims that the film harbors an "archival desire" (*Photopoetics* 133) that activates a "melodramatic consciousness" dictating proper and improper ways of making sense of the massacre. In Steinberg's account, the chief concern of *Rojo amanecer* is to "[take] the place of memory" (134) and establish an "archive . . . [with everything] in its place, a place of memorization, of repetition, of reproductions, or of reimpression" (136). In this way, the unruly processes of egalitarian struggle are neatly ordered and organized into an intelligible narrative, which Steinberg argues is ultimately reducible to a logic of substitution: "the film as a whole . . . represents, it takes the place of another. In that place of another, it places itself" (125). And this self-placement, Steinberg suggests, produces a "secret archive of continuity . . . [that] constructs the state's version of 1968, [which is] the archive-origin of its neoliberal transition" (136).

For a model of what a post-Mexicanist cinema or posthegemonic cinema—a cinema of Mexico, 1968—would look like, Steinberg argues that our focus should not be on films that attempt to carefully reconstruct in a step-by-step or hour-by-hour organization something that becomes intelligible only from the negative retrospect mandated by state-sponsored violence. Instead, a cinema of Mexico, 1968 becomes available in films that bring to life alternative modes of being-in-common that have, as Rancière puts it, "no place in [the existing] configuration" (*Disagreement* 29). It becomes available in films that do not participate in what Steinberg calls, citing Roger Bartra, a process of self-inscription through the ritual repetition of the "Mexican Office," or the tropes of mexicanidad, or the postrevolutionary iconology that shaped social, political, and cultural life and came to manage and police actions, behaviors, and thoughts in Mexico. In this way, the posthegemonic legacy of Mexico, 1968 that Steinberg seeks to recover is the assertion of an absence in place of a presence. It is what (and those who) did not (and do not) take (their assigned) place: the unplanned, unruly processes of securing moment by moment a life lived in equality rather than dutifully taking one's place in a predetermined egalitarian order mandated by a carefully curated and controlled national archive-crypt.

As already noted, this reading of Mexico, 1968 as a posthegemonic rejection or nonrelation with the existing Mexicanist order develops a logic that ultimately links the student-popular movement with earlier figurations of egalitarianism, such as the pelado, which, as we saw in chapter 1, was essential to constructing the

Mexicanist state and its structures of inequality. The posthegemonic framework, then, ultimately reproduces the logic it seeks to critique because it does not reckon with how its embrace of the experience of formlessness maintains a problematic shared premise with the existing inegalitarian social order. Indeed, posthegemony's embrace of the unplanned, unruly processes of securing moment by moment a life lived in equality is not unlike Yáñez's account of Periquillo analyzed in chapter 1. And as we saw there, it was formlessness—not following "decorum," engaging in "ill use," not "taking [one's assigned] place"—that emerged as the essence of la mexicanidad as it was constructed in those first decades after the Revolution. Indeed, the posthegemonic formulation of a post-Mexicanism that "always escapes" Mexicanism—"not taking [one's assigned] place"—is actually the foundation of the PRI's Mexicanism: it is, in Yáñez's account of "permanent revolution," that which blurs and makes indistinguishable Porfirio Díaz, Emiliano Zapata, Miguel Hidalgo, and, we can add, Aguilucho and Periquillo.

However, if we acknowledge the strange relations produced by the unique mode of mobility achieved in *Rojo amanecer*, we can recognize that Fons does not reproduce the formlessness that the student-popular movement supposedly took over from the poor, nor does Fons merely repeat the nationalist, archival accounts of the massacre. Instead, this unique mode of mobility—achieved through cinematic technique—enables Fons to enter into critical relation with both aspects of Mexicanism: the "Mexican Office" and the experience of formlessness (the notion of poverty) that provided those nationalist forms their unifying logic. The critical relation Fons develops enables his film to highlight the fissures between the existing social order and "what really happens," that is, capital in its real abstraction and poverty as an objective, relational aspect of it. It is this dynamic that makes *Rojo amanecer* important for recasting our understandings of Mexico, 1968.

## The Meaningfulness of Autonomy

We should return to *Rojo amanecer*, as Steinberg suggests, but we should do so with a revised approach that recognizes how the PRI's logic of poverty extended out into its nationalist ideology, which operated not as an egalitarian resource but instead as permanent process of "state making" by "unmaking." For Steinberg, however, *Rojo amanecer* demonstrates the PRI's operation by the making of a "secret archive of continuity" (*Photopoetics* 134). Through "canned diegetic crowd noises and gunfire" (136) and "the eyes of the characters themselves, who bear witness" (134) rather than the rebellious (political) speech of the student-popular movement, Fons "constructs the state's version of 1968" (134). For Steinberg, this is primarily achieved by Fons's aesthetic decision to close the film off from contingency or spontaneity by centering its action in the apartment: it forever and permanently encloses affective "possibility" under the pedagogical signifier "Tlatelolco."

As already noted above, however, the choice for the apartment actually constructs something quite different from narratives of first-person or experiential historical witnessing. By using the apartment as a visual and narrative device, Fons requires the viewer to reckon with a unique mode of mobility. The viewer is required to understand and contemplate events by being simultaneously in the plaza *and* "under house arrest" in an "the apartment [that] never opens onto the square." The film constructs a view that requires those watching the film to negotiate and understand the relationship between, on the one hand, what seemed possible (or impossible) within the daily life of that particular historical moment (i.e., the mundane routines of the middle class family) and, on the other hand, "what's really happening," which cannot be congealed into a representative on-screen image. This unique mode of mobility that operates simultaneously at the concrete level of everyday activities and at the level of abstract political, economic, and historical processes requires Fons to establish a view that is independent or autonomous from both the "Mexican Office" and the experience of formlessness (the notion of poverty) that provided those nationalist forms their unifying logic.

In this way, Steinberg's assertion that *Rojo amanecer* was "an independent film"—free of state financing—that "nevertheless [was] useful for the regrounding of the state form" (*Photopoetics* 129) does not account for the view of that historical sequence Fons achieves through his cinematic technique. Fons's aesthetic choices are, of course, embedded within the historical dynamics of filmmaking in Latin America in the 1980s. As Ignacio Sánchez-Prado has pointed out, *Rojo amanecer* has a "true importance in the history of recent Mexican cinema" because of "its pivotal spot between 1970s cinema legacies and the emerging paradigms of the late 1980s and early 1990s." As he notes, "*Rojo amanecer* is perhaps the last major Mexican movie that can be productively read from a 'Third Cinema' perspective" (107). What he means by this is that it marks a transition point between two moments in film history. On the one hand, the 1970s saw a cinema that was concerned with a cross-class politics that could effectively critique the "Mexican Office" that sustained Mexico's state-led capitalist development. On the other hand, the late 1980s and 1990s saw the production of a cinema structured by the "politics of a middle class that feels itself in a state of constant siege" (106) because of "the systemic failure of the Mexican State" (108) rather than because of the capitalist system. Sánchez-Prado, then, reads Fons as a filmmaker who can make "films that are able to deal with topics proper to Mexican culture and history . . . without returning to the time when cinema was a vehicle for the advancement of the ideological and political agendas of the State" (214). As he notes with Fons's other films, this takes place, at least in part, because he "recovers a variety of spaces that have been canonized in national film history" and, in making them his own, is able to "emphasize the emerging confrontation between the old social order and a modernizing Mexico" (49).

In this sense, Sánchez-Prado's description of Fons as a filmmaker who sought to make the "spaces that have been canonized national film history" (214) connects with Bruno Bosteels's reading of José Revueltas, the "perceived intellectual architect of the student-popular movement" (Steinberg, *Photopoetics* 4). For Bosteels, against whom Steinberg positions his reading of Revueltas, the goal of Mexico, 1968 was not "to *unmake* what *did* happen, but rather to allow that what *did not* happen to be *made* to happen" (*Marx* 95). In other words, the goal for Revueltas (and the student-popular movement) was not to "unmake" or "undo" the mechanisms of social management that would advance "the ideological and political agendas of the State" (Sánchez-Prado 214) but instead to establish a critical relation with them. In other words, Bosteels's account of Revueltas's "autogestión"—to "allow that what *did not* happen to be *made* to happen" (*Marx* 95)—dovetails with Fons's choice not to "unmake" the massacre but instead to return to the "spaces that have been canonized national film history" (Sánchez-Prado 214) to make them his own, that is, to make them happen on his own terms.

In Steinberg's view, the problem with this kind of approach would be that it would inevitably ascribe to the logic of Mexico, 1968 a "univocal definition": it would be "*a* history"—elements meaningfully organized into a critique, an "archival" principle established by Fons or by Revueltas that locks things into place in retrospect. What Steinberg seeks to recover from the student-popular movement is "action *within* History" (*Photopoetics* 104), which would always be open, unfinished, and never set up in advance. As I have argued above, however, the option for open-ended spontaneity and the moment-by-moment making and unmaking is the articulation of a commitment to formlessness, which, as I have demonstrated, is what provided the PRI's stabilizing nationalist forms their unifying logic. What Fons needed and what I am arguing he achieved is an awareness of how those two dynamics can be organized aesthetically and cinematically so that they may be scrutinized and critiqued.

Steinberg's critique of "archival logic" requires the belief that no critical relation to the Mexicanist tradition can be established: the one and only possibility would be the "an-archival" or post-Mexicanist position that exists in nonrelation with that tradition. As Bosteels helpfully points out, however, this kind of critique in which "any attempt to organize politics . . . cannot but appear 'dogmatic,' 'totalitarian,' 'voluntaristic,' and so on" misunderstands the "challenge" set forward by a thinker like Revueltas (and the events of Mexico, 1968 more generally): "thinking the crimes of communism without converting the inevitability of error into the melodramatic premise for a complex of moral superiority that would deny that anything good might still emerge from Marxism" (*Marx* 72). And similarly, we can read Fons's choice to make the "spaces that have been canonized national film history" his own a parallel effort to think the "crimes of Mexicanism" without "a complex of moral superiority that would deny that anything good might still emerge" from Mexicanism or the Mexican Revolution. In other words, the critical relation established with the art (and thought) of the past opens the possibility of making available "as never before" the real but abstract social relations that, otherwise, might be obscured by social relations as they actually exist. To put this point slightly differently, and as Bosteels does forcefully at a late point in his study, the not-taking-place that is associated with Mexico, 1968 (or, as we saw in chapter 1, with the pelado) is a dynamic that should actually be "made to happen" or made to take place:

> The most important aspect of 1968 in Mexico . . . is not the fact that the repression unmasked [a] blind spot in the seemingly democratic appearance (though it certainly did that), but rather the fact that the students and workers tried to force the situation so as to found a new structure, another frame of reference, or another society (and their failure to do so does not cancel out the attempt). What seems to be at stake for them is not just to occupy the unoccupyable empty place, but to exceed it . . . the task would be to traverse the fantasy. (184)

The point here is not that the experience of formlessness was the essential resource that needs to be recovered but instead that students and workers managed to postulate "a new structure"; they posited new, more egalitarian forms of life that competed with the state's Mexicanist formulas for equality stemming from the legacy of the Revolution. State-led capitalism established the PRI's "monopoly control" over the labor movement, student organization, cultural life, and imagery of the Revolution, and in this way, modes of representing the Revolution as an egalitarian force in Mexican social life stood at an impasse. The legacy of Mexico, 1968, then, would be to make the impossible happen, to "prescribe a sequence to found a new justice" (184).

If something like this notion exists in the everyday lives of the poor, who must use myriad strategies, skills, and relationships to make ends meet, it is also suggested by that all-important concept of 1968: autogestión. Indeed, to the extent that autogestión would be a kind of politics that is "above all a form of practiced thought" (*Marx* 164), it would be a "politics . . . [that] can appear in the least suspected of places, including in art and poetry, many of them considered marginal or unimportant from an external or institutional point of view" (164). This is so because artworks postulate "a specific condition of truth" (187). As Bosteels points out, "Art and poetry can also anticipate some of the consequences that are immanent to a political event—without for this reason becoming confused with it" (164–165). In other words, it is from the self-management or autonomy in social relations achievable within the work of art that political events or dynamics—"what really happens"—might come to be understood without, of course, collapsing that fiction into or confusing it for a clear-eyed view of material political and economic relations.

However, to understand art's role in preparing the ground for "a radical transformation of the structure" (*Marx* 193), we are required to attend to the meaningfulness of the aesthetic choices taken by the artist: How does an internal coherence emerge from the unity of these heterogeneous elements? The answer is not in what is "unmade" or "does not take place" but instead in what is "made to happen." The answer is in how the artist is able to achieve and establish a view that is independent or autonomous from both the existing forms of social relations and from their unmaking in the experience of formlessness. An achieved independence or autonomy of the work of art makes available "as never before" the truth of social relations: the interaction between actually existing social relations (i.e., the mundane routines of the Mexican middle-class family) and "what's really happening," which cannot be congealed into a representative on-screen image because it is not reducible to a view of the Mexican state's crimes on that October day.

As Susana Draper has noted, between 1968 and the emergence in the 1980s of films like *Rojo amanecer*, there emerged a filmic practice in Latin America that was equally concerned with the "exhaustion" of cinematic conventions for representing class conflict. As she notes, these filmmakers came to consider the "militant" nature of "Third Cinema" a "mere instrumentalization of the image" that communicated "the beliefs of the party to which the filmmakers belong" (Draper 122). Seen in this way, the core of what would be a posthegemonic cinematic tradition—Solanas and Getino's notion of "making-ash" or unmaking "as cinema's true object" (Steinberg, *Photopoetics* 141)—seems less plausible as those supposedly open revolutionary structures of unmaking "became more closed" and developed into a "propagandistic cinema . . . converting cinema into a visual pamphlet . . . that offered a prescription for social change" (Draper 122).

Rather than "Third Cinema's" cinematic pamphlets, Draper reads the cinematic dismantling of Mexicanism in the wagers for a "Fourth Cinema" that took place throughout the 1970s with those who continued the struggle in the prisons, in the factories, and in exile. According to Draper, it was "Super 8 filmmaking [that] was used as an essential tool to continue '68 by other means" (124). What she means by this is that the smaller, simpler, and more economical eight-millimeter format enabled the practice of autogestión given that it was possible for "anyone . . . [to] learn to film in small gauge without cinematographic training" as well as "to move easily among sites" (96) enabling the camera to be taken to independent labor union meetings, wildcat strikes, factory floors, and even the Lecumberri prison, where political dissidents were held. Super 8 was important as a legacy for 1968 because it enabled collective production, as with the Cooperative of Marginal Cinema, as well as the filming of "acts of authoritarianism [that] in larger formats" (99) met censorship or repression. These practices, then, opened the door to "autonomy in organization" (autogestión) since, formally, they made it possible to represent scenes that were impossible to create any other way—small, portable cameras made it possible to film clandestinely in the enclosed spaces of the political prison or the factory, for example—and since, economically, this cinema could be disconnected from both the commercial drives of the market and the so-called quality controls of state-financed cinema (120–121).

This cinematic autogestión, in Draper's reading, created alternative modes of education, one modeled on not "imposing a form" or a dogma—a normative

Mexicanism stemming from the "Mexican Office" of the institutionalized revolution—but instead "awakening the gaze to what we do not see when we look, which has to do with a social diagram being both visualized and questioned" (124). This "awakening" was focused not on articulating a singular platform of partisan prescriptions and beliefs but instead on unifying heterogeneous ideas and beliefs into a coherent cooperative or coalition.

Notably, speaking primarily of the Cooperative of Marginal Cinema, she argues that this collective political and aesthetic autonomy (autogestión) is achieved by "a total decentering of the unity and autonomy supposed by the work: the film operates as a bridge that connects experiences and as a trigger for situations (dialogues, discussions, commentaries)" (102). Draper suggests that what is primary here is that the images "seem neither to begin nor to end" (124) and as such create a situation "that generates dialogue" (102). Conceiving film this way led to the "break in the cooperative" because some members wanted "to make more traditional cinema" while the cooperative continued to focus less on aesthetic form and more on the instrumentality of cinema as a political tool (106). This, in turn, led to a de-emphasis on film altogether: "The experience of filmmaking began to be displaced by the experience of truly political militancy" because workers needed "other tools ... [such as] access to lawyers, petitioning to be heard in meetings, instruction on how to use mimeographs for producing leaflets" (106).

What becomes clear is that Super 8 cinema as the politics of 1968 (a not-taking-one's-place) "by other means" met certain limits. While making cinema "[created] a form of trust and connection [that] developed between people who had no other link"—a context in which no one was "in their place" and everyone was constantly moving between roles in the cinematic production process—it is also the case that this connection proved insufficient (106). As Draper reports, citing an interview in which workers' reactions to the students were described, some eventually replied to the cinematic project by saying, "Yes, well, we already saw a bunch of films, and you even filmed us, but we need more help, help us" (115). This leads to an important observation: if these films existed solely as a "trigger for situations," as Draper seems to suggest, then her assertion that this cinematic autogestión "fades without disappearing" becomes difficult to sustain, for it would exist only as long as it actually produced heterogeneous dialogue. If the "collective form of art ... became unnecessary after a time when the artwork and the process of learning was put aside," then in what sense does this cinematic autonomy not disappear as well, especially given that "little remains of the materials produced by the cooperative" (103–105)? Even if more did remain, emphasis would be placed not on the works themselves but instead on the dialogues and discussions (the created situations) that were never meant to be durable, never meant to *not* disappear (103–105).

Draper says that "the logic of the inappropriate"—adapted from Jacques Rancière's concept of politics cited in the preface to her study—"can only last a very short time" (123). While this means that "memory" of this "moment" of autogestión will disappear, she argues that the "fragments [of autogestión] will be reactivated (reactualized) when a new situation comes into contact with this and makes it newly clear in its differentiation" (123). This account of autogestión is clearly in dialogue with Rancière's "emancipated spectator" who is "at once a performer deploying . . . and a spectator observing" (*Emancipated* 22) as well as with Steinberg's account of Revueltas's emphasis on the revolutionary as a theory of the "trace." But the emphasis on situation (and its relation to "emancipation") seems wrong for several reasons.

One of the primary reasons for this is that the notion of the "fragment" awaiting activation—which is simply another way of saying the experience of formlessness (poverty) awaiting its moment to be made useful—stands at odds with other parts of Draper's argument. As Draper notes, the Collective of Marginal Cinema took its commitment to union independence seriously and created in serial fashion what were called *Communiqués of Labor Insurgency*. These were "film[s] [of] the labor uprisings taking place in any part of the country," and they sought "to unify scattered fights for union independence throughout the country through the Super 8 cameras" (102). While Draper tends to privilege the notion of the "situation" created by these "interventions," she also points to how the serial production of the *Communiqués* placed "different struggles" in the same picture plane: "through the image [they were able] both to communicate a situation and to place many situations on a *common plane*" (102). Without the cinematic image, these fights for autogestión remained "scattered." With the image, a unity and coherency began to emerge even when, as was the case with the cooperative, "participants who belonged to diverse movements coexisted . . . [without] imposing one tendency onto the rest" (122): "the image functioned to organize a common language of struggle that was able to trace the polyphonic language of the protests that resisted the union monopolies" (102–103).

Rather than producing for a carefully calculated market niche or to fulfill state-determined ends, the content and organization of these works emerge from the heterogeneous coherency of the collective. But it is a coherency that is "*in the world of the image*." Speaking of the cooperative's films, Draper notes that "the cinema produced in the first years of the seventies . . . [developed] an intense labor of elaborating the meaning of autonomy in the world of the image . . . [by creating] a singular form of relating the autonomous and the political [in a way that was] critical not only of the state and the market but also of the forms of traditional political struggles" (92). While she distinguishes this from traditional modernist autonomy, she also acknowledges that it maintains a relationship with the ways in which "the world of the image"—the strategies available to the medium of a cinema made in eight millimeter and shot clandestinely or in movement—enabled a representation of the "social diagram" that could be not only "visualized" but also "questioned."

This is why some aspects of her reading of *History of a Document*, the film clandestinely made at the Lecumberri prison with Super 8 cameras hidden inside political prisoners' clothing, are so important. They make it possible to understand how the film places at its center not just how to represent the legacy of Mexico, 1968 through a visualization of those who are imprisoned but also how "the world of the image" can be made compelling enough to pose a particular question about the "social diagram." As she argues, a chief strategy of the film is "the pure visual form of the spatialization of power through architecture . . . functioning as a form of expressing control: cells, bars, surveillance tower, guards" (116). Presumably, a prisoner is being watched at all times, and he is, as a result, always normalizing his behavior to prescribed codes of conduct. Or, as Steinberg would have it, he is "taking [his] place." But as these images of "pure visual form" evoke "the drama of how the film was carried out" (114–115) by the prisoners, the film represents spaces that are "the blind spots of the panoptic dream of total control" (119). The "pure visual form" that composes the film's images is made possible by the prisoners not performing for authority (or the market niche of commercial cinema for that matter). Instead, they exercise autonomy, autogestión, something that can take place only by "[showing] us everything at too close a distance" (the only way the image can be made under the conditions of political imprisonment). This places the obstacles of visualization—the challenges to making the "world of the image"—at the center of the film. But because those obstacles are overcome through "pure visual form," the film must engage and overcome a subsequent question, which is how to make "pure visual form" pose the particular questions that would lead to the political critique of the "social diagram." How is it possible to develop "*in the world of the image*" a critique of the Janus-faced appeal to form and formlessness that sustained the PRI's poverty-inspired structures?

Draper argues that *History of a Document* sought to link "pure visual form" to other "struggles from 1957–1970" as a way of "historicizing the prison" as part of a longer political tradition in Mexico, one that is actively "censored and repressed" (117). If this might sound like an appeal to the experience of formlessness, Draper is clear that this structure of serialization (i.e., the longer tradition of political "struggles from 1957–1970" in Mexico) maintains parallels with the work of the Cooperative of Marginal Cinema that had "participants who belonged to diverse movements [but] coexisted . . . [without] imposing one tendency onto the rest" and who also achieved the representation of unity through the creation of a common picture plane in their serialized films. Moreover, Draper explicitly links *History of a Document*'s historicization of "pure visual form" with the cooperative's work "to organize a common language of struggle" (116). In this way, the key was how to make the cohering commonality forming in the autonomous spaces (or spaces of autogestión) within Lecumberri prison or in wildcat strikes into a compelling image, one that poses a question or critique of the "social diagram" through "pure visual form."

The answer in Draper's formulation is to exceed mere visualization by "delving into the possibilities of the medium" (124). The path to the political critique of the "social diagram" is to arrive at the question through "the world of the image," through what the "medium" makes possible. As she notes, visualization is a first step: "When the camera enters Lecumberri Prison, prisoners learn how to use it at first," in much the same way that workers in the cooperative did. The politics, however, which is to say, the move to questioning the "social diagram," emerges in finding aesthetic and formal solutions once the basic technical mechanisms of Super 8 representation are learned: "Later, it is necessary to see what can be done in an everyday carceral space, where not much really happens" (124). In other words, the mere fact of clandestinely filming inside the prison is insufficient for the prisoners making the film, and it is also insufficient for understanding the film. "What can be done" or what can be achieved with the "possibilities of the medium" within a specific historical sequence in which "not much really happens" is essential to the film's politics. "What really happens"—the real but abstracted set of exploitative social relations—comes into view by achieving something within the "possibilities of the medium" and in "the world of the image." "Pure visual form" as an exploration of the medium is called on to do this work when "not much really happens," which is to say, when the structures of exploitation are not readily visibilized in the world of actually constituted or lived social relations.

Taking as an aesthetic problem the creation of a compelling picture that levels a social and economic critique when "not much really happens"—or, when nothing takes place—on screen is precisely the moment when the politics of Mexico, 1968 can come into view. But those politics come into view only by attending to the meaningfulness of the aesthetic choices made to create the "world in the image." In other words, what Draper suggests is that we can see—and we can create—what authority cannot. The inmates perform for the carceral audience of authority (i.e., they go about their everyday tasks in the prison). But the beholder of this documentary can recognize that those actions are not merely recordings of everyday routines but instead meaningful elements deployed to "[delve] into the possibilities of the medium" (124). This, then, gives us a model for better understanding the meaningfulness of Fons's decision to make the Mexicanist "spaces that have been canonized in national film history" his own via the enclosed space of the apartment. As my reinterpretation of Draper's account of *History of a Document* makes clear, the legacy of the politics of Mexico, 1968 requires an engagement with "pure visual form" and "the possibilities of [a] medium" so that the political critique can emerge through the compelling representation of "not much really [happening]."

## Antitheatrical Strategies in the Crisis of Representation

As the above framing of that aesthetic challenge suggests, the politics of Mexico, 1968, particularly as they relate to elements of the workers movement and the wager for independent unions, are politics that dovetail with an antitheatrical aesthetic tradition: enclosed spaces in which "not much really happens" but that nevertheless compel conviction as achievements of "possibilities within the medium" while also communicating the truth of the historical sequence. As with Lizardi's choice for the prison in *El periquillo* as an enclosed space from which to develop his aesthetic project and his political critique (see chapter 1), the prison also is essential to the contrasting aesthetic project in *History of a Document*, which, as Draper notes, "[historicizes] the prison" as part of a longer political tradition in Mexico that has been actively "censored and repressed" (117). That longer political tradition, as Bosteels argues, can be connected to an "actively silenced" revolutionary tradition in Mexico that becomes available through narratives developed and collected within the Lecumberri prison.

That tradition, as Bosteels notes in his reading of Adolfo Gilly's *La revolución interrumpida*, is one in which the revolutionary tradition in Mexico is linked and connected with the 1871 Paris Commune, as Gilly elaborates in his recounting of a conversation he had with a fellow political prisoner at Lecumberri after the Tlatelolco Massacre. This fellow inmate narrates his own family history: his grandfather was a participant in a group of workers in Mexico who actively discussed the experience of the Paris Commune; his mother (born "in the year of the Commune") and grandfather joined the radical *magonista* struggle during the Revolution; and the prisoner (born "in the year of the Mexican Revolution") worked as a union organizer, eventually joining the Communist Party. As Bosteels notes, this intergenerational history demonstrates that "the same utopian ideal comes back again and again, mixing the foreign and the local, the old and the young, peasants and proletarians, men and women, communists and anarcho-syndicalists" (Bosteels, "Mexican Commune" 19). But what he also says is that the Commune, thus formulated within the walls of the Lecumberri prison, constructs an "image of a seamless continuum" that "risks concealing the deeper transformations and discontinuities that the Commune underwent" (19).

What is necessary, then, is understanding this political form that enables the production of a coherent organization of heterogeneous groups, ideas, and beliefs without creating an ahistorical "image" that disconnects it from and makes it impossible to consider the real, material "transformations and discontinuities" that must be overcome if the form is going to be successful in cohering into a functional unity. Art, Bosteels argues, can be essential to this. And, to the extent that the reading I offer of *Rojo amanecer* below argues that Fons's film does just that, it is clear that there is no transhistorical formalist formula for achieving that unity. By meaningfully using the art of the past—making "spaces that have been canonized in national film history" his own—Fons enables the "possibilities of the medium" and the world of the picture to be called upon "as never before" to do important work within this other, "actively silenced" revolutionary tradition in Mexico. In other words, Fons can make "what's really happening," which cannot be congealed into a representative on-screen image, come into view only when it is effectively combined with what seemed possible (or impossible) within the daily life of that particular historical moment: that is, the mundane routines of the middle-class family where "not much really happens."

This "actively silenced" revolutionary tradition and its reappearance in *Rojo amanecer* makes Fons's film legible within the ongoing transformations of the antitheatrical tradition in French painting Michael Fried has studied. As Fried notes in his books on Courbet and Manet, the absorptive or antitheatrical tradition is not a formalist tradition but instead a deeply historical one that is responsive to the historical conditions of beholding. Indeed, important to his arguments is what he calls the "crisis of absorption," which was a sequence beginning in the mid-nineteenth century that saw pictorial innovations stemming from the sense that absorptive scenes were no longer as effective as they once had been for making the painting "hold" as a picture. The antitheatrical tradition—through Courbet and Manet—evolved and incorporated innovations and techniques (including a radicalization of theatricality) in order to establish the fiction that the painting was not made to be beheld (i.e., is not "performing for" or adapting to the demands of an audience). This kind of autonomy or (if we want) "autogestión" underwent additional transformations in the wake of not only the transformations of this tradition as manifested in the works of Courbet and Manet but also in the wake of the Paris Commune. This is made evident in the art of Gustave Caillebotte, whose works, Fried argues, were in deep dialogue with the antitheatrical innovations of both Courbet and Manet. There are, in particular, two paintings that are crucial here.

The first is *The Pont de l'Europe* (1876; currently located in Geneva) and the other a related picture, *On the Pont de l'Europe* (1876–1877, at the Kimbell Art Museum in Fort Worth; figure 3.1). The first painting depicts a street scene in which we see a well-dressed woman strolling with an umbrella, a top-hat-wearing bourgeois figure passing her on her right and gazing to his left, and a worker located on the far right of the canvas contemplating something in the same direction as the gaze of the bourgeois figure. This depicted "site had been the scene of heavy fighting during the Commune" but now, in the moment of the painting's creation, sees "different social classes [come] into daily contact" in a mode of what Julia Sagraves, cited by Fried, calls a "reconciliation of social classes." As Fried notes, Sagraves's reading of this painting hinges on "the moderate Republican agenda for the streets of Paris" (*Another Light* 171), in which the streets are divested of "revolutionary associations" in favor of a peaceable "social space-sharing" (173). Fried disagrees with Sagraves's reading by pointing out that the "political meaning of the painting" is not so much a supposed "compositional and social leveling" but instead what the unification of disunified social classes meant in late nineteenth-century France. This "impossible" unification—what could not take place at that historical moment—is what is represented in the painting's politics: "At that historical moment, [there was an] unnegotiable difference between the two men [the bourgeois and the worker] and the social classes they exemplify *and* in the intimation of a common or rather a converging aim or

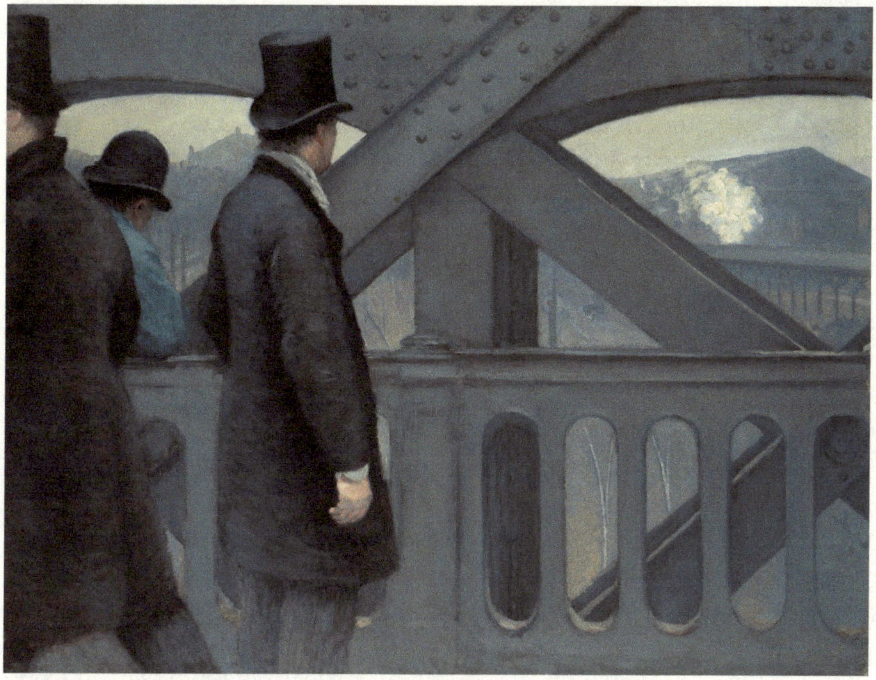

FIGURE 3.1 Gustave Caillebotte, *On the Pont de l'Europe*, 1876–1877. Oil on canvas. Kimbell Art Museum, Fort Worth, TX / Art Resource, NY.

destination [suggested by their gazes unified by an object off-canvas], one that remains at a distance from the present reality and cannot actually be represented but only imagined, wished for, fantasized" (173). This political meaning—a convincing representation of what an impossible political unification might look like—is made possible by "the enterprise of painting as Caillebotte understood it," which itself, in turn, required two modes of absorption to secure its antitheatricality: "*both* mobile looking and prolonged gazing" (173).

The unification of these two modes of absorption, Fried argues, is best on display in Caillebotte's *Paris Street; Rainy Day* (1877). Reading the painting in the context of the pictorial tradition in which Caillebotte worked, Fried notes the ways in which it is not, as Sagraves argues, a "portrait of the modern city just beginning to recover" (*Another Light* 175) after the Paris Commune and its so-called rainy weather. This meteorological notion is evoked, in Sagraves's account, through the prominence of umbrellas, which are wielded by most of the figures in the painting and are said to function as a "defensive arm" that enclosed the figures in a semiprivate, classed space creating "social separation" (in Fried, *Another Light* 175). Contrary to this reading, Fried surveys the ways in which closed spaces—"the theory of the cloister" that created "a world apart" in which the figures could be convincingly depicted as absorbed or unaware of being observed—were essential to the antitheatrical tradition in the 1860s.

The idea of being "enclosed in his or her own absorptive lifeworld" is "elaborated" from the cloister to "a theory of the apartment," where "the modern individual" was "to be found, imprinted, habituated, distracted, absorbed." Fried goes on to note that "the motif of carrying an umbrella to protect oneself from the rain becomes an ingenious device for thematizing a newly mobile and, up to a point, permeable mode of absorptive closure, one that also allows for the sharing or merging of individual life worlds" (176–177). This innovation on "the theory of the apartment" enabled Caillebotte to further the absorptive project but also realize the Impressionist project to "paint the city," in a sort of montage of absorptive fragments that are unified in a common picture plane.

This mobile and impossible (but necessary) commonality that was essential for the coherency of Caillebotte's "enterprise of painting" was also something that marks *History of a Document* as a reflection on "clandestine filming" that unifies the interior spaces of the political prisoners with those of a "population that was also imprisoned, but outside the prison" (Draper 115). Draper's reading of the "image-fragments" filmed by those clandestinely working outside the prison with those clandestinely working inside it creates a unity between prolonged and mobile gazing. It is as if *History of a Document*, at least in Draper's account of it, can function as the mobile cloister or mobile apartment represented by the montage of umbrella portraits in *Paris Street; Rainy Day* but mobilizing as well the "impossibly unified" gaze for a common political project in *The Pont de l'Europe*. This antitheatrical reading of the "pure visual form" of carceral space (perhaps paralleling the "enclosed life worlds" of the cloister or the apartment in French painting) enables us to return to *Rojo amanecer* and Fons's aesthetic decision to place the film, as Steinberg argues, "under house arrest." Rather than enclosing affective "possibility" under the pedagogical signifier "Tlatelolco," the choice in *Rojo amanecer* for the apartment as the space in which he makes "canonized film history" his own can be read in dialogue with the transformation of the antitheatrical tradition in late nineteenth-century France. Caillebotte's innovation of the "cloister" tradition that, in the wake of the Commune, created a common picture plane through the montaging of "mobile looking and prolonged gazing" was one that built off the innovations developed within Manet's enterprise of painting and one that has connections to that "actively silenced" revolutionary tradition in Mexico.

Now, the traditional revolutionary iconographies of the period are undoubtedly present and prominent in *Rojo amanecer*: the students with their Che Guevara poster and demands to go to the streets, the factories, the schools, and the universities; the bureaucratic father of the institutionalized revolution and his reverence for Hidalgo and other independence figures; the grandfather of the era of the 1910 revolution. What is central, however, is not how these varying approaches to the official revolutionary tradition can be made to function together in a kind of consensus. Indeed, the majority of the opening sequences of the film demonstrate the irreconcilable disagreements between these factions as well as their specific demands. In other words, the film can "visualize" the political and social situation by recounting major events from the specific three-month sequence (July, August, and September 1968) that led to Tlatelolco. But the film also wishes to exceed this specific moment by making the "world of the image" pose the question of how Mexico, 1968 and its demands might still resonate: the enclosed world of this apartment spatializes the massacre but also encapsulates the revolutionary tradition itself. Rather than the archival consignation that Steinberg reads into the film, the choice for the "cloistered" or "carceral" or "insular" space of the apartment provides a specific site from which a convincing confrontation with the Mexicanist cinematic tradition might elaborated. This confrontation, I suggest, takes place by thematizing the question of beholding through the use of the antitheatrical strategies of "mobile looking and prolonged gazing" that were central to the painterly critiques Fried analyzes in France and that I have suggested can be linked with Draper's reading of the "pure visual form" of carceral space in *History of a Document.* Indeed, the unique mode of mobility that enables Fons to enter into critical relation with both aspects of Mexicanism (the "Mexican Office" and the experience of formlessness [the notion of poverty] that provided those nationalist forms their unifying logic) is precisely achieved through cinematic parallels to antitheatrical strategies to neutralize the beholder.

In the case of *Rojo amanecer*, the youngest member of the family is crucial to the film's project. In Steinberg's view, the young boy's role in the film is problematic because he operates a politics of substitution: "The child is posited in our place," with his "final emergence from the apartment building" paralleling "the spectator's emergence from the cinema" (*Photopoetics* 137). Both would be "duty-bound" to pay tribute to the total archive of Tlatelolco that the film represents. However, one of the fundamental problems with this reading is that it assumes a complete and full understanding of the student-popular movement and the massacre on the part of the young boy. What is crucial, however, is that he does not hear, witness, or see the totality of what the spectator sees.

For example, while he does witness the debate between his grandfather, father, and brothers regarding the revolutionary tradition in Mexico, that conversation and its airing of some of the day's political debates remains somewhat secondary to the end of the Beatles song he hears on the radio. More importantly, the young boy is absent from the following scene in which the student activists narrate to their mother the main events of the student-popular movement that would seemingly function as a required archival instruction. The boy is, instead, in school where he was in history class learning about Mexico's nineteenth-century struggle for independence. And when he comes home, he can tell his grandfather that in what he understood from the debate from earlier that morning—whether the independence hero Hidalgo had long hair like the student activists and the Beatles—could be settled with a picture in his history book: his brothers were right. The students were right, not the institutionalized revolution (embodied by his father and expressed in his history classroom) nor the veterans of the Mexican Revolution (like his grandfather).

It is in this context of attempting to work out the relationship between the irreconcilable traditions in conflict in the enclosed space of the apartment that he begins to hear fragments of the speeches being given in the plaza below his window as the student-popular protest begins. However, unlike the viewer of this film, it cannot be said that, as a consequence of what he has seen and heard in his home and in his school, the boy would consequently understand the violence he witnessed against the students. Because of this lack of understanding—his inability to properly take his place in the "archive"—it is all the more shocking for him to come out of the bedroom where he was hiding to find that his entire family had been murdered.

The boy's situation, like everyone else in the film, is as a figure who is confronted with fragments of image, text, and sound that he must piece together into a coherent understanding of the narrated events. His fragmentary understanding of Mexico, 1968 cannot possibly be the same as the one possessed by the viewers, who are separated not only by history but also, and more importantly, by their position solely within the enclosed world of the apartment. If the boy, as most of the other characters, leaves the apartment to, presumably, walk through the plaza to another destination, the viewer never leaves the space of the apartment building. In this way, while the boy does not possess Steinberg's total archive of Tlatelolco, given that he does not see and hear everything the viewer does, neither does the viewer possess this total archive, given that the boy possesses access to images, texts, and sounds that he never reveals to the viewer (e.g., the sounds he hears in the darkness [with no image] as his family is being murdered).

What the viewer possesses instead is the way in which Fons utilizes what can be described only as absorptive scenes as a primary strategy of representing the narrative sequence constituting the young boy's experience of Tlatelolco. These absorptive scenes encompass both the "prolonged gazing" and "mobile viewing" that were essential for constructing the "impossible" unity represented by the unrepresented "common" or "converging aim or destination." As examples, we can point to two related sequences.

In the first (figure 3.2), toward the beginning of the film, we see an image of the young boy, who is on a balcony playing toy soldiers with his grandfather, absorbed in thought as he begins to process the fact that he's seen armed, plainclothes members of the military or police setting up surveillance. We later see a domestic scene in which the mother is knitting, the grandfather is reading, and the young boy is writing or drawing. These are classic scenes of absorption, which exclude the viewer from the enclosed world of these figures lost in thought. We do not have access to what it is that they see or what they can contemplate as they stitch together fragments of this day—and the political sequence—in

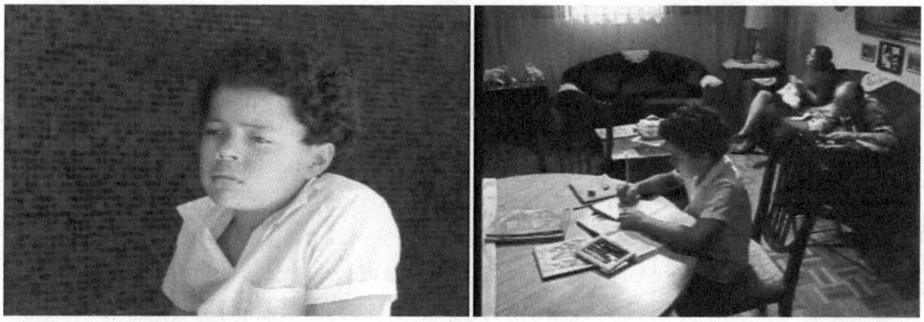

FIGURE 3.2 Still images from *Rojo amanecer* (dir. Jorge Fons, 1989).

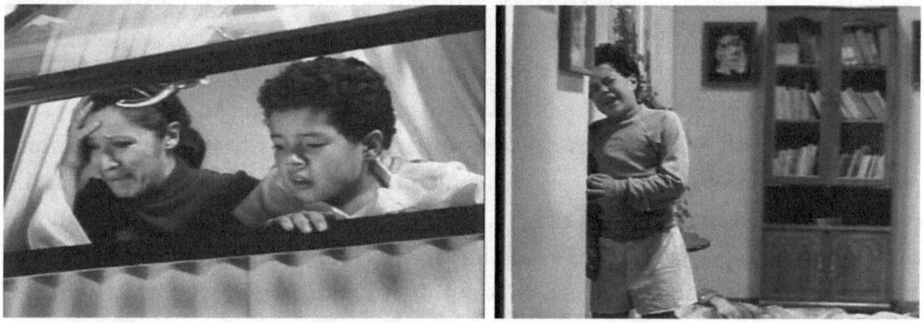

FIGURE 3.3 Still images from *Rojo amanecer* (dir. Jorge Fons, 1989).

progress. We do know, however, that reflection on their fragmentary understanding of politics is taking place as the grandfather advocates the experience of political imprisonment for his activist grandsons while the mother expresses fear. The young boy is revealed to be drawing a violent confrontation. While this gives us access to a particular moment before the massacre, it does not give us access to an archive of the massacre itself. Instead, these related scenes represent a process of coming to terms with the competing claims and disagreements without coming to a resolution that is meant to be instructed in didactic fashion.

Similarly, toward the end of the film, we see absorbed scenes (figure 3.3) of the young boy coming to terms with the violence that takes place on this day. In one, he is watching from his apartment as the massacre unfolds in the plaza. His is a look of incomplete understanding, while his mother gazes in horror. In another scene, in the final sequence of the film, the young boy emerges from his hiding place to see the second massacre that has taken place, this time inside his apartment. Here we see full anguish on his face, though this is perhaps also accompanied by incomplete understanding since he did not witness the sequence that led to his family's murder and since he is also aware of (though does not fully understand) the deep political disagreements between those whose slain bodies he is now seeing.

What we have in the first antitheatrical sequence is a visualization of the politics of Mexico, 1968 through an incomplete understanding of the ways the "social diagram" functions. In the second antitheatrical sequence, we see a representation of what it would mean to question the "social diagram" by demonstrating the insufficiency of that diagram as an explanation of what the young boy sees. Importantly, the boy's visualization and questioning are not the viewer's, who is removed by distance of history and the formal choice to locate the beholder within the closed space of the apartment. The viewer must come to terms with the young boy's visualization and critique by recognizing that it is not interchangeable with their own, just as those who clandestinely film outside Lecumberri are not interchangeable with those who film clandestinely within it, and these not interchangeable with those who would view the film in the "carceral space" outside the prison.

This visualization that poses a question via the strategies of antitheatricality cannot produce the common political space, the "converging aim or destination" that would resolve the economic and political divisions that are represented. Instead, by acknowledging the ways in which the camera finds a way to be mobile within prolonged gazing created within the enclosed space of the apartment, we can see how the film functions as a solution to representing what it looks like to not take place. At the same time, that mobility cannot be activated without the prolonged gazing that encloses the space and produces the necessary visualization and questioning. In this sense, Fried's account of the historically specific transformations of the antitheatrical tradition in artistic representation converges with Larsen's assertion that the "crisis in representation"—the coming apart of the abstractions of capital and the particularities of individual class experience—is a fundamental aspect of "*reality* [which is] a continual movement through identity to nonidentity" (*Modernism* xxxiii). Representation is necessary in Larsen's model since the only other option would be an evasion of representation paralleling what I have been describing as posthegemony and Rancière's emancipated spectator.

What has become clear, then, is that if we are to discuss a political legacy for Mexico, 1968, it is something that requires not the posthegemonic an-archival opening but instead the antitheatrical aesthetic of closure and separation. For if, as Bosteels argues, "the task [for those coming after Mexico, 1968] would be to traverse the fantasy" of being able to "prescribe a sequence to found a new justice," we should simply remember what Fried pointed out in Caillebotte's *The Pont de l'Europe*, depicting the years following the Paris Commune: the desired political model is "one that remains at a distance from the present reality and cannot actually be represented but only imagined, wished for, fantasized." This is articulated in a double gesture of "visualization" and "questioning," that in turn are made possible by the double absorptive strategies of mobile looking and prolonged gazing that enables an overcoming of the obstacles internal to the "world of the image."

While *Rojo amanecer* cannot construct the common political space, its antitheatrical strategies locate it within a specific historical moment in which it is responding to its political, economic, and aesthetic contexts in order to articulate a meaning, in order to "visualize and question the social diagram." Rather than insist on "many deaths and resurrections of the Commune" through an insistence on "the image of a seamless continuum" of radical struggle, we should instead draw attention to the antitheatrical strategies of closure and separation as approaches to confronting and overcoming the "crisis in representation." Fons's film demonstrates his ability to establish, through antitheatrical cinematic technique, a view that is independent or autonomous from both the "Mexican Office" and the experience of formlessness (the notion of poverty) that provided those nationalist forms their unifying logic. It is, thus, in opening the tradition of representing "not much happening" or nothing "taking place"—that is, the antitheatrical tradition of absorption—to new innovations that the legacy of Mexico, 1968 might emerge as a representation of our "converging aim or destination" in a "radical emancipatory politics" based in an understanding of the objective relational aspects of our historically specific economic, political, and social systems.

# 4

# Photography and Borges's Landscapes of Poverty

This chapter examines Borges's relation to the documentary photographic tradition and its importance for examining the political consequences of valorizing the experience of formlessness that emerged as coterminous with poverty in twentieth-century art, politics, and economics in Latin America. I begin with what is probably an unlikely candidate for this kind of analysis: the famous short narrative "Borges and I" (1960). While poverty is barely mentioned in this text (though it is mentioned in a way that is very important, as I will show in a moment), it is possible that it is relatively uncontroversial to say that it is a reflection on problems of realist representation since the text, in essence, is a self-portrait. The narrator, the "historical" or actually existing Borges, explores his relationship with the "public" or internationally recognized *image* of "Borges" created by readers.[1] The problem at the center of this exploration is how to make that "historical" Borges register or become visible in what is the increasing dominance of the "public" Borges. In other words, the question is how Borges can demonstrate that he is still engaged in working out a series of concrete aesthetic and political problems when readers respond not to what they read—not to his meaning—but instead to their interaction with the "public" Borges, to an image of Borges that corresponds to their needs or desires. What's more, Borges is aware that the "public" or "the reader's" Borges is increasingly creeping into his own conceptualization of his fiction. That he identifies this as a problem is clear enough given that knowing how to read this text is made quite difficult: "I do not know which of us is writing this page" (*OC* 221).

What is also clear, however, is that Borges recognizes that this situation is not new and that his earlier attempts to solve the problem have not been (or no longer are) successful. More specifically, he states that he cannot approach this dilemma at the level of content of alone. As the narrator notes, he and the "public" Borges have the same preferences. The difference is that while the "historical" Borges has them as a central concern for his artistic production, the "public" Borges possesses them only "in a conceited, self-conscious way and turns them into the attributes of an actor" (*OC* 221). The problem, then, is that the actual preferences that sustain Borges as a person and an artist—maps, hourglasses, etymologies—have become linked to the "public" Borges that a literary marketplace demands. To put this another way, the difficulty at the center of his art—at the center of this self-portrait—is to create an artwork that cannot be collapsed into the public performances readers demand. The challenge is to turn away from his readers without turning away from himself, which would simply be another way of turning toward them, of performing (or not performing) "Borgesian" narrative puzzles based on reader expectations. What "Borges and I" explores, then, is the problem of theatricality: the structures, images, topics, and formulas that seem to be placed there for readers and their responses rather than emerging as convincing solutions the artist developed to an aesthetic problem he decided to address.

Borges describes this shift in preferences, which took place in the late 1930s and 1940s, in the following way: "Years ago I attempted to free myself from [the 'public' Borges] and I turned from mythologies of the slums to games with time and the infinite, but those games belong to Borges now, and I will have to dream up something else" (*OC* 221). What Borges says here is very interesting: the move from the "slums" (a significant feature of his literary production of the late 1920s and early 1930s) to "games with time and the infinite" (in the late 1930s and 1940s) should be understood as a textual strategy. They should be read as an effort to "free" himself from external demands like those being called forth by rising (and, for Borges, troubling) modes of nationalism in an era marked by a "crisis in representation" (e.g., European totalitarianism and Peronism). But their persistence in his work within a new historical sequence like that of the late 1950s and early 1960s was seen (at least by Borges himself) negatively. They were taken as a kind of "falsification and exaggeration" and as an effort to appeal to readers or play to the crowd rather than to himself: "I am certain of his bad habit of falsification and exaggeration . . . I recognize myself less in his books" (221). That notion of "falsification" (a key strategy in works like "Pierre Menard, Author of the *Quixote*" [1939]) is seen in this subsequent sequence as productive of the "falsity" that calls forth the crisis he identifies: "those games [with time and the infinite] belong to Borges now, and I will have to dream up something else" (221).

For Borges, then, something like Neruda's "palpable objects" and aesthetically transparent poems that can be used by readers as they wish are not only unsatisfactory but also indicative of the identified problem (i.e., what, following Fried,

I am calling the issue of theatricality, or, more broadly, the experience of formlessness viewed as essential resource). Indeed, the task as it is formulated in "Borges and I" is to neutralize "the conceited, self-conscious manner of the actor": to write a text that is not "Borgesian" but instead "good" (*OC* 221). This would be one that successfully produces the fiction that it "belongs to no one, not even to the other, but rather to language or tradition" (221) (or, as Neruda might have it, to "everyone").

This is increasingly difficult to achieve because if Borges turns away from his preferences, he is responding fully to readers and their demands: *he* becomes the actor. However, if he does not turn away from his interests, the results will inevitably be read as "Borgesian": "[they will] belong to Borges" and whatever it is readers create in their interactions with the works. In other words, the problem is that theatricality leaves Borges with few options to overcome his situation: "the stone," Borges says, "forever wants to be a stone and the tiger a tiger" (*OC* 221). The representation communicating meaning (a "rock" or a "tiger") tends to collapse into the circulating object that needs no understanding but instead should be only experienced and used. But the narrator of "Borges and I" (unlike Neruda's "Invisible Man") does not accept this collapse. "I will have to dream up something else," he says, a statement in which we can see that Borges is reformulating his approach to this problem.

One way to read the task of "dreaming up something else" as Borges formulates it in this famous text is to consider how one might build into the artwork itself—its form—the necessary historical context that would prevent its collapse into pure materiality and reader experience. As we have seen in previous chapters, this dynamic existed in historically different ways in different countries throughout the 1940s, 1950s, and 1960s and has been tied to varying conceptualizations of poverty. And as we just saw, some of Borges's most famous textual strategies—the "games with time and the infinite"—emerged from his engagement with poverty: "I turned from [the] mythologies of the slums" that characterized earlier works to "[those games as attempts] to free myself from [the 'reader's' Borges]." Borges's development of his interest in time and the infinite is not always read as relating to his understanding and representation of poverty. But once we recognize that this shift in content is oriented toward developing a strategic approach to aesthetic form—one where content and form are fully unified—so as to secure meaning within sequences of crisis, the role of poverty in his aesthetic project more broadly becomes clearer.

For example, we can reexamine the dilemma of theatricality from "Borges and I" by considering its structural parallels with earlier works. There is a clear parallel between the two Borges in "Borges and I" (they have the same preferences but nevertheless remain separate and distinct from each other) and the authors he imagines in "Pierre Menard, Author of the *Quixote*." In that story, what appear to be two identical passages from *Don Quixote* are actually two different passages, written in two differing historical sequences by two different writers (Cervantes and the fictional French Symbolist poet Pierre Menard). As Charles Hatfield has argued, the difference between the two *Quixotes* (that of Menard and that of Cervantes) is "invisible" (59). That invisibility is of a piece with the different meanings each of the texts has, each drawn from the particular artistic and aesthetic sequence in which those authors compose (e.g., Cervantes interfacing with the tradition of chivalric literature and the broader socioeconomic crisis of his time; Menard interfacing with the tradition of modernism, the *Quixote* itself, and Menard's own socioeconomic milieu). But we might say that Borges's return to this issue in the 1960s with "Borges and I" marks a moment when he is reconsidering it under changed historical circumstances. In this later historical period, highlighting or thematizing the invisibility of historical context, at least in Borges's view, is no longer enough to secure the text's ability to defeat its tendency to be collapsed into reader expectations and demands. In other words, if the framework of the narrating literary critic in "Pierre Menard" could secure the "invisibility" of distinct meanings, "Borges and I" ends with uncertainty about whether securing the meaning of a text would even be possible within this new historical sequence: "I do not know which of us is writing this page" (*OC* 221).

This topic—the invisibility but necessity of history to make an artwork understandable as an artwork—also appears in "Mutations," a text that accompanies "Borges and I" in *El hacedor*. Here, Borges specifically foregrounds the question of the meaningfulness of objects in history, expanding out beyond his autobiographical experience with fame. It makes the self-portrait that is "Borges and I" parallel similar visual objects he analyzes in the very short "Mutations." The narrator of this story reflects on having seen an arrow hung on a wall in a building, which provided him with the near-automatic understanding that it was directing him to his destination. But he also reflects on how that "inoffensive symbol" (*OC* 211) would have been understood as a threat in another context, such as medieval Europe, when the arrow was a deadly weapon of war. He similarly reflects on seeing a photograph featuring a rider twirling a lasso and conjures up images of rounding up steer, only to learn that the photo was nothing more than a showy demonstration produced during Sunday leisure. A similar contrast emerges in his shifting contextual reading of a tombstone shaped like a cross in a cemetery: "Cross, lasso, arrow, ancient tools of man, now degenerated or elevated to symbols . . . there is no object on earth that forgetting does not erase or that memory does not alter and no one knows into what image that object will be translated in the future" (211).

Unlike Neruda's embrace of the infinite uses for the "palpable objects" he created in his odes, which envisioned "the unity of the earth, / the water, / human beings" in an endless landscape of plenty, Borges has considerable trepidation regarding use and the experience of formlessness. Indeed, the "degeneration" and "forgetting" of the meaning embedded in the arrow, the lasso, and the cross-shaped tombstone—their return to a status of raw material or useable objects—do not suggest revolutionary or egalitarian results, nor even a basic awareness of the means and relations of production. For example, how could what lays "beyond the form" of the arrow—that is, medieval Europe's landscape stratified and shaped by a feudalist structure of land ownership and the forced labor of peasants—become available if, as an object, the arrow is almost automatically experienced as an "inoffensive [directional] symbol" (*OC* 211)?

This dissolution of historical context into presentist experience, or meaningful artwork into useable object, of course, also organizes the dilemma in "Borges and I." The dissolution of form—the dynamic of theatricality or valorization of the experience of formlessness—threatens to render the "historical" Borges indistinguishable from the manufactured image of "Borges" created by readers, something that, as the narrator makes clear, presents real dilemmas for the "historical" Borges's own self-conception. In this sense, we can see how Borges is confronting this new historical sequence through an exploration of aesthetic resources he developed in the past. Indeed, to the extent that Borges's work is informed by his experience with Peronism and his observations of European totalitarianism, we can understand "Borges and I" as a reworking of his critiques of those systems and their valorization of the experience of formlessness. Those societies came into being in response to the words and gestures of those on the "balcony." This "balcony effect" manufactured an image of "workers" or the "people," which, like the effects of the "public" Borges on the "historical" Borges, can increasingly creep into workers' own self-conceptualization without the possibility of recognizing it or criticizing it.

As we saw in chapter 2, Neruda understood a similar dynamic as the tension between light and shadow: the *hacerlo para todos* and the *no hacer nada para nadie* that compose his "terrible obligation." As we also saw, he did not look to the internal resources of the aesthetic as a solution to this dilemma but instead viewed aesthetic form as the obstacle he needed to eliminate on the path to the utopian embrace of objecthood and theatricality. Borges, however, faces the crisis prompted by the dilemma of theatricality by returning to what is possible within the artwork itself. Indeed, he concerns himself with developing strategies to circumvent the erosion of the necessary context that would make possible both the understanding of an artwork's meaning and the critique of existing forms of social organization.

While in 1960 (as demonstrated in works like "Borges and I" or "Mutations") Borges seems to express real concern that the paradox is irresolvable, by 1970, with the publication of his short story collection *El informe de Brodie*, which is the primary focus on this chapter, Borges had identified solutions by returning to his past artistic practice as a resource for his contemporary production. More specifically, he returns to the landscape of the "slum" and, more generally, to poverty, which he understood as a specific *form* of socioeconomic life embedded in a specific community of social relations. In the landscapes of poverty he created in the late 1960s and early 1970s, Borges developed a kind of an antitheatrical solution to the dilemma presented by the dynamic of theatricality emergent from the "crisis in representation." This is made all the more evident when we note that part of Borges's prologue to *El informe de Brodie*—a passage from its embryonic version, which appeared in a speech Borges gave in Chicago in 1968—became the epigraph for the catalogue essay accompanying the seminal photographic exhibition *New Topographics: Photographs of a Man-Altered Landscape* (1975). In much the same way that those photographers' interrogation of aesthetic form in photography provided resources and strategies utilized by contemporary photographers who are both responsive to the antitheatrical tradition and critical of contemporary capitalism,[2] so too can Borges's engagement with what I am arguing is his own variant of an antitheatrical aesthetic tradition provide resources and strategies for thinking and developing a politics of the left in our own "crisis in representation." To understand this argument, I first interrogate the relation between the "new form of documentary" discernible in the dialogue between the artistic practices of the New Topographics photographers and Borges's work in the late 1960s. I then turn to an analysis of poverty and the antitheatrical aesthetics Borges develops in *El informe de Brodie*.

## "A New Form of Documentary"

In his catalogue essay accompanying the seminal photography exhibition *New Topographics: Photographs of a Man-Altered Landscape* (1975), curator William Jenkins famously asserted that the images he selected for display, depicting urban sprawl, office parks, and industrial constructions set against broader natural landscapes, "postulate, at least for the time being, what it means to make a documentary photograph" (7). Jenkins postulates this "new form of documentary" (Rohrbach xviii), however, not simply by foregrounding the participating photographers' "statement[s] about their own work or the exhibition in general" (Jenkins et al. 7), which he solicited and distributed throughout the essay as support for his claims, but rather by placing "at the center" of the exhibition the "problem" (5) posed by the following passage by Borges, which Jenkins chose as an epigraph: "I should try to tell in a straightforward way, plain stories, so that I will try to get away from mazes, from mirrors, from daggers, from tigers, because all of those things now grow a bit of a bore to me. So that I will try to write a book, a book so good that nobody will think I have written it. I would write a book—I won't say in somebody else's style—but in the style of *anybody* else" (5). The passage is drawn from a discussion Borges had with the audience after a speech he gave on Walt Whitman at the University of Chicago in 1968. This quote, like Jenkins's essay as a whole, has been "submitted to disproportionate scrutiny" (Salvesen, "New Topographics" 49) over the years as the influence of the exhibition has grown. And it is this continued scrutiny, of course, that led Britt Salvesen to point out that the "parallels" between Borges and the New Topographics photographers tend to "break down" (Salvesen 50) after acknowledging their common appeal to "anonymity" (Jenkins 5). Indeed, in linking this anonymity to Borges's efforts to "avoid contemporary subjects" and "go back to [his] childhood" ("Post-Lecture" 719), Salvesen draws a direct contrast between his fiction and the images of new suburban constructions by photographers such as Joe Deal, Robert Adams, and Lewis Baltz, which "forestalled nostalgia and prevented an escape to the past" by requiring "viewers to remain in the present and think about the future" (Salvesen 58). In other words, whatever continuity Jenkins sought to highlight between fiction and photography by choosing the quote, Salvesen sees only distance between Borges's interest in the past, and the "'contemporary subjects' the New Topographics photographers embraced" (50), which mandate a focus on the world coming into being through "development."

At one level, it is hard to argue with Salvesen that there is a certain incongruity in comparing what Borges says in response to audience questions in Chicago and the practice of photographers like Deal, Adams, and Baltz. Borges's evocation of long-disappeared unplastered brick houses in the suburban Palermo neighborhood of early twentieth-century Buenos Aires has, on its face, very little in common with the depiction of the booming construction of tract houses, office parks, and mobile homes in the U.S. Mountain West and Southwest of the 1960s. However, despite Salvesen's dismissal of Jenkins's pairing of these bodies of work, I nevertheless belabor this connection by making two suggestions that build my arguments above:

1 Borges's temporal orientation toward the past should be understood not as an "escape" from "contemporary subjects" but rather, as we saw with "Borges and I," as a formal technique he uses to comment on them. The return to narrativizing the landscapes of impoverished, semirural neighborhoods of early twentieth-century Buenos Aires operates as an aesthetic strategy deployed to overcome in a new historical sequence a theatricality that Borges had previously sought to defeat with his turn away from "the slums to games with time and the infinite."
2 This aesthetic strategy or formal technique, which is premised on temporal distancing but also on simplicity and "straightforwardness," parallels the camerawork of New Topographics photographers.

I develop each of these in turn, beginning with the "straightforward" aesthetic of the stories and the photographs.

Borges's comments made in Chicago, which he would eventually develop into the prologue to the collection of short stories executing that artistic vision (*El informe de Brodie*), should be read in relation to the needed response to the crisis produced by the theatricalizing impulses of readers described in "Borges and I." As he notes there, he abandons not only the tiresome "Borgesian" tropes of labyrinths or mirrors but also what he has come to perceive as the ineffective formal flourishes readers identify with his fiction: the "surprise ending" or "unexpected finale" (*OC* 458). At the same time, he also rejects efforts to recover a specific version of the Argentina from the past through the trappings of local color or geographical specificity: "If I set out to describe a particular cafe in a particular quarter of Buenos Aires," Borges told the audience in Chicago, "then people will find I'm making all sorts of mistakes. . . . I don't have to become a historian or newspaperman [to write these stories]" ("Post-Lecture" 719). By locating his stories in "the slums of Palermo" in nineteenth-century Buenos Aires (*OC* 459), he creates a spatial and temporal distancing that provides him with the space—the "literary elbow room" ("Post-Lecture" 719) or "freedom of imagination" (*OC* 459)—to defeat not only the "Borgesian" but also other theatrical appeals to the reader, like what he calls the "literary joke" that is "lunfardo" (459), which is the term used to describe, for example, the vocabulary and language structures embedded in the omnipresent mass-media musical commodities of tango lyrics. His strategy is to make art out of "facts [that] are essentially true" ("Post-Lecture" 719) by narrating them with invented circumstances. In so doing, he does not appeal to the reader: his stories don't appear to be "Borgesian" or seek to evoke particular partisan political sentiment in Argentina. Instead, he is focused on making stories that are "so good" they produce the fiction that they could have been written by "anyone" or "no one" at all. Or, alternatively, with no surprise ending, inventive narrative structure or revelation of specialized knowledge, these commonplace, everyday, straightforward stories seem to have been created by everyone as part of a shared "language or tradition."

A similar dynamic exists in the camerawork of the New Topographics photographers. Their pictures were oriented by an awareness of the practice of landscape photography in the United States and the need to "[break] substantially from the outlook of Ansel Adams and Eliot Porter" (Rohrbach xvii) or "Wynn Bullock, Minor White, and Paul Caponigro" (Jurovics 1). The practice of earlier landscape photographers such as Ansel Adams was marked by the appeal to "monumental grandiosity" (Salvesen, "Real Estate" 80) as well as to "lyricism" and "sentimentality" (Jurovics 12). And like the commodified sentimental tango lyric Borges rejects along with the surprise ending readers expect and demand, Ansel Adams's landscape photographs converted the "land into landscape, into [an] aesthetic object" that circulated as "a commodity" (Giblett and Tolonen 73).[3] In other words, Borges's effort to turn away from the "Borgesian" (that is, his desire to return to landscapes of the "slums") can clearly be related to the New Topographics photographers who were turning away from the iconized "landscape photography" viewers had come to expect and demand.

What the New Topographics photographers sought was to establish the pictorial qualities of their photographs, that is, to achieve their status as art by asserting the difference between "what a photograph is *of* and what a photograph is *about*" (Jurovics 2). This fact is highlighted by the emphasis many of them placed on the quality of the prints they made of their photographs. Michael Fried, for example, has noted observations made by James Welling as well as by Tod Papageorge regarding the way Robert Adams sought to use his technique in print making to create a particular quality of light in his pictures. Salvesen similarly notes of Lewis Baltz that the prints "had to be well made—to give [the work] authority, it had to be high-definition, it couldn't have shake or blur" ("Real Estate" 81). The "perfection" of these prints—or at least the importance of their status as "well made" prints—of what otherwise were "dull" pictures (80) was essential to the ability of these photographs to assert themselves as art in the context of a theatrical "landscape photography" that dominated in their era as the face of a "capitalist politics of land use" (Giblett and Tolonen 70).

This is why Jenkins insists that the New Topographics approach to "what it means to make a documentary photograph" holds only "for the time being" (7). It is in the specific context of the theatricality as a value in landscape photography and its status as a useful commodity that the "objective" or "neutral" or "anonymous" style these photographers pursued possesses the importance it does. Notably, the photographers did not appeal to a contemporary "vernacular practice [such as snapshot photography]" but instead "looked at nineteenth-century precedents" (Salvesen, "Real Estate" 80) in order to secure their approach "as a move *within* photography rather than one seeking to escape it" (80–81). "The salient historical dialog" the New Topographics photographers developed to comment on the contemporary was "with the nineteenth century" (Jurovics 9) and its photographic catalogues. As it turns out, then, these photographers looked to the art of the past as a resource to critique the contemporary and achieve the status of their work as art (rather than only useable object) in much the same way that Borges's literary return to the narration of early twentieth-century landscapes of impoverished neighborhoods can be properly understood as a way neutralize the "Borgesian." In both cases, central to commenting on the contemporary is an appeal to strategies from the past that enable a reimagining of expected artistic conventions so that theatricality might be neutralized from "*within* photography" or from within Borges's own conception of literature rather than attempting the impossible, which would be to evade or "escape" them.

These parallels follow into the formal execution of these artworks. The "well made" print that would give "authority" to these otherwise "dull" photographs with their "objective" or "neutral" or "anonymous" style obviously has parallels with Borges's desire to create "plain" stories that appear to have been written by "anyone" or "no one" or everyone but exist as they do only because the author's renderings of them (i.e., Borges's stories, like the photographers' "well made" prints) are "good." Moreover, just as the New Topographics photographers do not, as Juha Tolonen notes, "proselytize or preach" (Giblett and Tolonen 166) through their photographs, so too does Borges assert in his prologue to *El informe* that he is not a "writer of fables" or a "politically-engaged writer" (*OC* 457). He notes that he's never shied away from making his (anti-Peronist) political positions known, but he also asserts that "I have not let them interfere with my literary work" (457). In other words, those political positions—his views on the poor and Peronism—are present but are not reader-addressing interferences with the realization of these stories as "plain," "straightforward," and "non-Borgesian."

This is achieved, in part, through the strategy of temporal distancing, which Annick Louis has called Borges's "*oblique* strategy" (332), or "non-thematic way" (332), of speaking "about the real and the contemporary" (332). This hinges, Louis argues, on Borges's "critical rereading of his own aesthetic from the 1930s and 1940s" (332), and as I have been arguing, it is prefigured in "Borges and I."

Of course, as we saw above with "Borges and I," Borges confronts the question of theatricality on changed grounds in the 1960s. Simply put, the "Borgesian"—the "public Borges" or "reader's Borges"—was a problem in the late 1960s that it simply wasn't in the late 1930s and 1940s when he was composing works like "Pierre Menard." The relationship between him and his readers must be confronted within the confines of his own art. As he says in Chicago, "I can't get away from myself. I wish I could," almost reproducing his reflection from "Borges and I": "a stone forever wants to be a stone and the tiger a tiger" (221). Indeed, in the prologue to *El informe*, he would refine that reflection into a similarly clear statement: "My already-advanced age has taught me that I must resign myself to being Borges" (*OC* 458). And yet, being collapsed into the "public" Borges is not sufficient for "being Borges": there is a "historical" Borges who, like his own readers, must interact with that "public" Borges and work through the dilemmas it presents for creating and understanding art.

In this way, Borges accepts the literalist fact of objecthood as an inescapable premise for creating art: a tiger *is* a tiger; a stone *is* a stone; paint and canvas *are* paint and canvas; paper and ink *are* paper and ink; Borges *is* inescapably Borges with his preferences and experiences. But even if "a stone forever wants to be a stone and the tiger a tiger" (*OC* 221), even if the "mazes, . . . mirrors . . . [and] daggers" (in Jenkins 5) are transformed by readers into objects that "[the 'public'] Borges now" uses (*OC* 221), the "historical" Borges can still "dream up something else" (221).

As Salvesen notes, it was that ability of creating "something else" that presented visitors to the original New Topographics exhibition in 1975 with "trouble interpreting [the photographs]" ("Real Estate" 84). As she notes, many viewers saw them as the product of something the photographers "were just paid to [do]" as part of "their job," as pictures of "progress" or as pictures of environmental devastation (84–85). In some sense, this may seem understandable. Lewis Baltz took photographs of Park City, Utah's "piles of dirt and debris . . . rather than [its] resort[s]" (Jurovics 7). Robert Adams took photographs of mobile homes and tract houses. Bernd and Hilla Becher took pictures of blast furnaces and water towers. As a literal or indexical fact of making the photograph, they needed to have piles of dirt, mobile homes, and water towers in front of the camera. But the photographs are not *about* those objects: "what a photograph is *of* and what a photograph is *about*" are not necessarily identical (Jurovics 2).[4] That difference, however, between mere encountered object and an object made meaningful or expressive of the community of social relations it represents is not a happenstance of a reader's experience or reaction. It is one that is *achieved* or *established* by the artist in the "well made" print (or via other resources that, within other historical sequences, were [or will be] necessary for doing so as a practical matter) in relation to the viewer.

Thus, when Borges presents himself as the literary problem of the "public" Borges, which parallels the possibility of his works being "mutated" into "inoffensive symbols" like the "cross, lasso, arrow, [and other] ancient tools of man" in "Mutations," he is presenting himself with the dilemma of achieving art and securing meaning amid the intense social pressures for artworks to be made useful objects, whether those be understood as him "doing his job" to create narrative puzzles and surprise endings for readers in an expanding international literary market or as a version of the "politically-engaged writer" creating some kind of alternative to the aesthetically transparent object. In this way, Borges acknowledges the inevitability of objecthood, but in seeing it along the lines paralleling indexicality in photography, he creates pathways for himself to neutralize the pressures to which his work is responding. While this may explain the importance Jenkins intuited from the "Post-Lecture Discussion" he read and the relations he draws between the New Topographics photographers and Borges, it most certainly explains Borges's decision in *El informe* to return to *el paisaje arrabalero* (the semirural landscapes of early twentieth-century Buenos Aires slums).

The decision to "set [the] stories some distance off in time and in space" (*OC* 457) and avoid direct commentary on "contemporary subjects" is not an escapist gesture but instead an antitheatrical strategy: an attempt to neutralize the "degeneration" of a meaningful, specific critique (one with which we might agree or disagree) into a mere object that can be circulated, used, commodified, and rendered an "inoffensive symbol" that, perhaps, could be utilized to support the very structures the author set out to critique. Borges's understanding of poverty through landscape in these stories enables him to comment (indirectly) on the contemporary. The importance is not so much that landscapes of poverty are *in* these stories—though that is important—but instead that they are used as an aesthetic strategy to secure what his stories are *about*: the ability for "anyone" and everyone to assert meaningful critique even when a "crisis in representation" threatens to dissolve objective, relational aspects of a social system into the vortex of a valorized experience of formlessness.

## Against the "Balcony Effect": Antitheatrical Aesthetics and Poverty

As we turn to an examination of the "straightforward" style of these stories, it is important to note first a productive tension enabled by Borges's turn to the poverty of the past, setting his stories "some distance off in time and space." On the one hand, this strategy is what makes it possible to assert meaning, providing the required "literary elbow room" that remains outside (but also within) the sets of symbols that constitute the "Borgesian." On the other hand, that distance in time and space can exist only because of a generalized "forgetting" that produces the anxiety at the heart of "Mutations": the creative "elbow room" exists because of the erosion of historical context. In other words, the key to understanding these stories is to note how Borges appeals to what was of little account at the time—"what happened in a northern or a southern slum of Buenos Aires some sixty years ago [is something] nobody would care [about] or remember" ("Post-Lecture" 719)—a resource for his art comment on the contemporary political and economic situation.

For example, in one of the more widely read stories from the collection, "Juan Muraña," Borges is confronted with a former classmate, Emilio Trápani, who criticizes Borges's work from the 1930s on Evaristo Carriego's poetry, which focused on Buenos Aires's slums: "Someone loaned me your book on Carriego. There you talk all about *malevos* [neighborhood toughs]; tell me, Borges, what could you possibly know about *malevos*" (*OC* 483). Borges says that his is a work about literature, about literary uses of the city's slums: "I have documented myself" (483), he says, and conducted research. Trápani responds to Borges's assertion by saying, "I don't need documents; I know those people" (483), and he proceeds to narrate to Borges his childhood experience with poverty and violence. What emerges here is a distinction between what Buenos Aires slums mean: one developed from Borges's analysis of their literary function in Carriego's poetry and another from Trápani's critique of Borges's analysis, which he sees as having little to do with what the slums mean, especially given the fact that it is *Borges* who is making the statements: "Tell me, Borges, what could *you* possibly know . . . ?" (my emphasis).

What we see here is Borges's evocation of readers' tendency to degenerate his artworks into "Borgesian" objects. Implied in Trápani's statements is that Borges's fiction is populated by mirrors and mazes, the infinite and time: it has nothing to do with poverty or the lived conditions of violence and inequality in a slum. This appeal to the problem of the "Borgesian"—the "degeneration" of his artworks into "inoffensive symbols" distanced from critiques of socioeconomic realities—repeats several times in *El informe*. For example, in "Historia de Rosendo Juárez," a character, who had appeared in one of Borges's earliest stories, makes a reappearance in this collection when he encounters Borges late one night and tells him that there is a difference between Borges's artwork and the life of the poor: "You, sir, have placed these events in a novel, which my [lack of] knowledge [about art] makes me unable to appreciate, but I want you to know the truth about those vicious lies" (*OC* 471). In "El indigno," the bookseller Santiago Fischbein tells Borges that what he is going to narrate "[might serve you] for a story, which you, without a doubt, will fill up with daggers" (*OC* 465). This dynamic indicates the ways in which Borges is foregrounding the problem he had identified in "Borges and I."

The "public" Borges—the figure created by readers—does not have concern with the needs and experiences of the poor and distances himself from the political through his appeal to literature rather than experience: "I don't need documents" like you do in order to talk about poverty, Trápani says, "I know those people." That "public" Borges has a focus on far-off, hard-to-pronounce places and makes obscure literary references that are uninterpretable by the poor and working class: "My [lack of] knowledge [about art] makes me unable to appreciate [your fiction]." The "public" Borges has a series of preferences and narrative structures that make any response to or relation with the needs of the contemporary moment impossible: "You, without a doubt, will fill up [any story] with daggers" or mirrors or labyrinths.

However, these are stories that the "historical" Borges writes in order to confront the dilemma presented by the dynamics of theatricality and open-ended experience of objects. And that solution, as it emerges in these stories, is to defeat the "Borgesian" by writing stories that appear to be by "anybody" or everybody but *not* Borges. Indeed, all of these stories depart from the premise that are antagonistic to Borges's own fictional universe. They are generally written as if they were concentrated oral narratives related from one person (often someone who experienced poverty) to another (usually Borges himself). Though these narratives are (and even this specific narrative structure is) firmly rooted within Borges's fictional universe, its effect is that the meaning of these narratives—the childhood stories of poverty and life in impoverished neighborhoods shared by Trápani, Juárez, and Fischbein—cannot be collapsed into the "Borgesian."

Whatever the "Borgesian" is taken to be (e.g., "games with time and the infinite," "mirrors, mazes, daggers, tigers") it cannot be what those narrators produce in those stories: they are presented as the product of what Borges could not possibly know, or what lays outside the old books and fragmentary manuscripts that are often the source of the narratives we read in many of his most famous works (e.g., "Pierre Menard," "Tlön, Uqbar, Orbis Tertius," etc.). In attempting to meet the challenge of neutralizing the collapse of meaning into experience—the degeneration of artwork into object—Borges foregrounds the extent to which his previous strategies to defeat theatricality are no longer sufficient and must be reconceived. The question, then, is why narrated experiences of poverty from early twentieth-century Buenos Aires became such an important aesthetic strategy for Borges. Why are poverty and the "slum," rather than any other object or experience he might draw on from that earlier era, the key narrative strategy?

For an answer we can turn to a story like "La señora mayor," where Borges makes clear how poverty is the optimal figuration for preventing the degeneration of meaning into experience. "La señora mayor" narrates the story of María Justina Rubio de Jáuregui, the last surviving daughter of a colonel who fought for independence. The family's estate was confiscated and redistributed in the nineteenth century, leaving the family living "modestly in Palermo" (*OC* 489), a situation that left them "in a somewhat false situation. They felt a belonging to the aristocracy, but the movers and shakers ignored them" (491). It is this impoverished state, which remains at a distance from others living in poverty in the

Palermo of late nineteenth- and early twentieth-century Buenos Aires, that enables them to narrate the landscapes of poverty they saw and that were of interest to Borges in his earliest fiction. Relating an episode shared with the narrator by doña María Justina's son, Mariano, we learn of the contours of life in the impoverished neighborhoods of the early twentieth century, which was distanced in time and space from the contemporary moment of 1960s Argentina: "[He] remembered having seen, from the Gran Nacional street car, a lagoon around which were scattered several small homes marked by their lack of plaster rather than by their use of sheet metal; the poverty of yesteryear was less poor than the poverty that industrialism now provides to us. The fortunes amassed [by the wealthy] were smaller as well" (489). What is interesting here is that "the slum"—"the poverty of yesteryear"—and "the shantytown"—"the poverty that industrialism now provides to us"—are placed in relation to each other, much like "ancient tools of man" in "Mutations" or the "historical" Borges and the "public" Borges. However, while "Borges and I" demonstrates that it is difficult to distinguish Borges from the "Borgesian"—an aesthetic problem that Borges must solve—and the narrator of "Mutations" demonstrates concern that it is unsolvable because "no one knows into what image that object will be translated in the future" (*OC* 211), what becomes evident in "La señora mayor" is that this representation of poverty—Mariano's narrative description of a long disappeared Palermo—has something that Borges and the "cross, lasso and arrow" do not. There is a meaningful and objective difference between "the lack of plaster" and the "use of sheet metal" in the poor's construction of their homes.

The point brought out in the cited passage above is that this difference is not simply the mere availability of or preference for certain kinds of materials over others during the half decade or so separating the "slum" Mariano recalls from his childhood and the "shantytown" that is familiar to the narrator in the 1960s. This difference is the objective difference between two economic systems and their related distributions of wealth: the agro-exporting oligarchic model stemming from the nineteenth century and the Peronist and post-Peronist industrial models that came into being during the late 1940s, 1950s, and 1960s (discussed in the introduction). The "slum," as evoked here, was "less poor" and had less economic inequality (given that fortunes of the wealthy were not as distanced from the poor) than is the case with the "shantytown," which is presented as its contrast.

Thus, while an "arrow" or the "Borgesian" tends toward objecthood—problematically open to the "degeneration" of meaning and the open-ended uses that could transform it into its opposite—the appeal to poverty—at least in Borges's attempt here—is understood (or made) not to function this way. An arrow on the wall in a twentieth-century hallway could evoke medieval warfare or directional guidance: those possibilities are interchangeable and manifest as the product of the viewer's experience. In contrast, the poverty produced by industrialism is not successfully interchangeable with its nineteenth-century antecedents. Or put slightly differently, poverty after Peronism cannot be collapsed into poverty before Peronism. And whether one is a Peronist or anti-Peronist, the notion that there is a separation between those modes of poverty is likely to be a point of agreement even if there is not agreement in the interpretation of that separation between those advocating an agro-exporting economy, or those in favor of a nationalized, industrial economy, or those envisioning another economic organization altogether. There is an objective difference that is not produced by or explicable through an appeal to the experience of the reader or viewer.

It should be noted that Borges does not idealize or make picturesque the poverty of Palermo's nineteenth-century neighborhoods. Indeed, various texts in *El informe* make clear that those "rudimentary lives of the poor" (*OC* 500) cannot produce nostalgia nor are they oriented toward a direct political stance. For example, "El otro duelo" features the story of two impoverished *gaucho* soldiers who, after various altercations in their rural community that had economic consequences, became rivals and enemies. Both were conscripted into the army and were captured in battle. For the entertainment of the victorious soldiers, the official holding the two impoverished rivals as prisoners (who himself hailed from an oligarchic family) decided to hold a race between them, allowing his soldiers to gamble on the outcome. He then had their throats slashed and forced them to race each other until they each died. The status of these two men is never presented as preferable to the significantly more impoverished life in the "shantytowns" of the 1960s. As the narrator notes, "The life of the soldier was not more difficult than the life of a cattle worker [*gaucho*]" (500), and that life was one in which those men "possessed nothing but their sheer hatred for each other, which they continuously accumulated. Without suspecting it, each became a slave to the other" (500).

This accumulation of hatred under the singular face of his rival leads to a complete nonrelation with the historical context conditioning what is ultimately these men's experience of poverty and exploitation. For example, what might it have looked like to see those two men, along with others, recognize their shared situation and refuse conscription or, alternatively, to see them work with the other impoverished soldiers gambling on the spectacle of their death to rebel against the sadistic oligarch? The point in narrating the story, which is built from the narrator's stitching together of a variety of oral narratives he collected, is to "recuperate, [after the passage of] an entire century, the obscured history of these two men's lives, who had no other claim to fame than the death they met in their final duel" (*OC* 499). What is recovered is not only the difficulties faced by the rural poor, though these are featured prominently in the story: for example, economic disputes created by unmarked animals, claims of misbehavior in low-stakes card games, the hard manual labor involved in the lives of both impoverished cattle workers and military conscripts, the likelihood of violent death for the rural poor, among others. What is also recovered is the need to insist on something other than the primacy of these experiences of poverty. In other words, Borges insists that readers come to terms with the meaning of their poverty.

If every instance of dispossession is ascribed the face of the rival, the story of these men and their poverty can only ever be relegated to their infamous duel: the image of them emerging from the "fame . . . [of] the death they met in their final duel." They would be rendered only objects of entertainment: first of those gambling on their fate and later as narrative objects traded amid the smoke of cattle workers' campfires or that of cigar-chomping oligarchs guffawing in their parlors. Borges's goal in the story is to "*recuperate*, [after the passage of] an entire century, *the obscured history* of these two men's lives," not as a nostalgic appeal to what, in Borges's view, are even worse conditions for the poor in the late 1960s, but instead as a way to return these men to their status as full human beings acting (with complicated human fullness) within a specific socioeconomic system. In that sense, his "recuperation" of the historical life of these impoverished cattle workers who had been converted into uncomplicated images or objects used for the enjoyment of readers and viewers provides a model of the solution he seeks for the dilemma of theatricality he previously identified in "Borges and I," which is also the problem of meaning "degenerating" into experience. He achieves this "recuperation" through his focus on creating art: a "good," "straightforward" story.

This is also what is foregrounded by the narrator of "La señora mayor" through his juxtaposition of Mariano's view of the turn-of-the-century "slum" and his own view of the 1960s "shantytown." There is an insistence on differentiating between two very different manifestations of poverty that have the tendency to be collapsed under the singular, homogenized, presentist image of the poor existing in a continuous, uninterrupted line stemming from the past. As we saw above, "El otro duelo" makes possible the positing of alternative pathways, of considering courses of action for those impoverished workers that would operate as alternatives to the "sheer hatred" for the "face of the rival." Their poverty and violent fate, Borges seems to be saying, was not inevitable even though there's nothing we could do to change their fate. Similarly, by emphasizing the contrasting poverties—Mariano's recollection of the "slum" and the narrator's contrasting description of the "shantytown"—Borges is seeking to crack open an understanding of the present.

It enables the possibility of imagining a socioeconomic sequence alternative to one completely circumscribed by Peronism and its effects even if there is nothing that can be done to change the ultimate roles that Peronism (and reactions to it) have played in national history. In this way, poverty becomes a model for Borges's narrative interests more generally. Whether it is what is named by the difference between Pierre Menard and Cervantes or the "historical" Borges and the "public" Borges, the point is to insist on attending to meaning in spite of the fact that there is a readerly tendency to "degenerate" that meaning into presentist experience.

The point in placing landscapes of poverty from *El informe de Brodie* into relation with examples from stories from Borges's previous volumes is not to assert that Borges and his work is unchanged over time. The argument is not to say that all of these examples are interchangeable and exactly the same. Instead, I am arguing that Borges appeals to various kinds of solutions to the problem of theatricality as he understands it in the varying historical and socioeconomic sequences he inhabits over the course of his artistic production.

Stories such as "El otro duelo" and "La señora mayor" provide evidence that landscapes of poverty from the early twentieth century emerged as a key resource in Borges's rereading and reworking of the needed aesthetic solutions to the degeneration of meaning into experience, art into object. However, the story providing the clearest view of how his antitheatrical aesthetics provide a mode of access to the truth of reigning economic conditions of inequality is the previously mentioned "Juan Muraña," which immediately precedes "La señora mayor" in *El informe* and maintains clear parallels with the contrasting the "slum" and the "shantytown" in that story as well as the tensions between the "obscured history" and "fame [of] . . . [the] final duel" in "El otro duelo."

As noted above, "Juan Muraña" begins with Emilio Trápani, a former classmate of Borges's, questioning his interest in the poor and placing his own experience in a place of importance that Borges's art could never aspire to achieve. This, however, is preceded by a singular paragraph in which Borges reminds the reader of his earlier book, *Evaristo Carriego* (1930). This paragraph serves, Louis argues, as "a new version of the prologue to the 1955 edition of *Evaristo Carriego*" (345) in which Borges relates a now-famous anecdote describing how he grew up not in the Palermo of impoverished, knife-wielding street toughs but instead in a library of English-language books. If, as Louis suggests, Borges posits "[an] opposition between the library and practical knowledge of the neighborhood" (345), there is also a way that there is an emphasis on the literary nature of each of those poles: Trápani "[confesses] that he has no memories of [Juan Muraña]" (345) and that, in essence, he does not, as he had asserted, "know those people."

In this way, Trápani's narrative rests on his own collection of documents: his understanding of the narratives shared by people who knew Juan Muraña and the life of the nineteenth-century "slum." These, of course, parallel Borges's collection of documents in *Evaristo Carriego*: his understanding of Carriego's poetry and the life of the "slum" that was its origin. As Trápani says of Juan Muraña's fearsome reputation as a knife-wielding thug, "I do not know if the stories [about him] are true; what is important now is the fact that they have been narrated and believed" (*OC* 485). This also, I suggest, functions as a kind of rewriting of the 1955 prologue in which Borges asserts that *Evaristo Carriego* is "less documentary and more imaginative" (*OC* 113), an impulse that is also not so different from the desired "literary elbow room" he evokes in Chicago in 1968 and built into the prologue for *El informe*. The "straightforward" story of nineteenth-century "slums" that indirectly comments on the contemporary situation of "shantytowns" emerges from what Trápani narrates and that Borges must believe. The "authority" of that narrative rests on Trápani's account of his experience of poverty. Borges's juxtaposition of Trápani's narrative and his own writing on poverty is an attempt to assert the centrality of the literary form—the antitheatrical aesthetic practice Borges develops—to overcome the "degeneration" of meaning into experience. If Trápani's assertion of meaning were dissolved into Borges's presentist experience (or, for that matter, the presentist experience of any other reader or listener) it would eliminate what Trápani's narrative makes available: the "obscure history" of poverty that lies outside Borges's documents.

At the center of Trápani's narrative was his family's desperate economic situation. Living with his aunt, who was Juan Muraña's widow, and his mother, a home-based garment worker who existed in relation to the larger textile industry (*una costurera de cargazón*), the family "was in dire straits" and was faced with the significant threat of "eviction because of their inability to pay rent" (*OC* 484). Trápani's elderly aunt told him that she knew that the landlord, "some man named Luchessi," would not make good on a threat to evict them because "Juan will not allow that *gringo* to throw us out" (484). Trápani says that he and his mother were less convinced of the legacy of Muraña's fearsome reputation, and as he notes, "My mother made me go with her to talk with Luchessi. . . . She was going to request an extension; without a doubt, she took me along so that the person making decisions about her outstanding debts [*su acreedor*] could see her helplessness" (485).

This sentimental scheme, however, was not needed because when they arrived, they found police attending to the crime scene of Luchessi's murder. It is revealed toward the end of the story that his aunt had named her own dagger "Juan Muraña" and that she had murdered Luchessi to avoid the eviction. Trápani explains that he is uncertain if his mother ever knew the story but notes that his aunt "died not long before they were evicted" (*OC* 487). What is clear here is that like in "El otro duelo," "Juan Muraña" is a text in which the experience of poverty is ascribed an all-encompassing face: Luchessi, in this case. Equally so, the "accumulation of hatred" for the rival amid the experience of economic insecurity and exploitation stemming from poverty does not resolve what is ultimately a structural economic and political problem. The eviction still takes place; his mother is still poorly remunerated as a garment worker; Borges's classmate still was required to face the fear (and perhaps reality) he described to Borges: the threat of having to sleep "on doorsteps along Serrano street or [to beg] for spare change or [spend the day] with a basket of peaches [selling on one street corner or another]" (485). More to the point, making the rich (or anyone else for that matter) see "[the poor's] helplessness" has very little or no effect on undermining the broader economic and political underpinnings that make that unequal and exploitative system operate.

The narrative strategy of the impoverished garment worker, like Borges's own narrative strategy, cannot prevent the operation of the political and economic systems in place. To be sure, the garment worker's appeal may be more effective at achieving the short-term extension. But if the target is the broader structural transformation of economics and politics so that no one faces the fear (or reality) of homelessness, poverty, and child labor, a different narrative strategy is necessary. In this sense, it is important to highlight the separation between those two narrative strategies, one on which Trápani and Borges himself insist at the outset of the story. While Trápani's mother, with her intimate knowledge and experience of poverty and exploitation, seeks a direct effect by foregrounding "helplessness" or victimization as she seeks "an extension," Borges seeks to defeat the direct political effect to instead focus on making a "straightforward" artwork. In this way, "Juan Muraña" contains within it Borges's interpretation of those systems that Trápani, his mother, and his aunt experienced. And as with "El otro duelo," Borges demonstrates that one particular act cannot resolve what is actually a structural problem. This is why Borges's literary alternative—with its insistence on interpreting the system and on revealing the dynamics by which meaning tends to "degenerate" into experience—is important for understanding and recognizing the limits of any model that would place primacy on the experience of poverty. As "Juan Muraña" ends, the narrator (Borges) speaks again to say that the figure of this knife-wielding street tough functions like "a symbol or many symbols" (*OC* 487), not unlike "ancient tools of men" in "Mutations." In this case, as Borges says, "Juan Muraña was a man who walked the streets I knew, who found out what it is that men know, who came to know and taste death itself and afterward became a dagger and now a memory of a dagger, and tomorrow not even that: the common material of forgotten history" (487).

While Muraña passes through not just Borges's neighborhood but also his poetry and narrative, he nevertheless was a man with a certain body of rooted historical knowledge connected to a particular configuration of economics and politics, which, when it disappears, problematically becomes absorbed into similar dynamics like that of Peronism, which remains distinct from this earlier era. As Daniel Balderston points out, "Muraña served as thug to the local political boss [in Palermo] Nicolás Paredes" ("Evocation" 326).[5] That political system in which Muraña—a favorite figure for Borges—was an "electoral thug" (Balderston, "Evocation" 326) was distinguished from a subsequent Peronism with its own local muscle. As Louis notes, while there was an effort to approach the former, the latter was an object of derision. Much as there is a fundamental difference between "the slum" (*el arrabal*) and "the shantytown" (*la villa miseria*)—a difference that has the tendency to be eliminated as poverty undergoes its process of symbolization—so too is there a difference between figures like Juan Muraña and his Peronist counterparts. That difference, of course, is clearly articulated in *Evaristo Carriego*.

In this book, Borges analyzes poetry by Carriego and describes the social, political, and economic context of the slums of turn-of-the-century Palermo, which gave rise to Carriego's poetry of poverty. It is also where Borges identifies an aesthetic problem that will become increasingly important for him in the 1960s. That problem stems from the double conceptualization of poverty he identifies in the analysis: its social aspects and its aesthetic aspects. Regarding the former, and no doubt a reference point for his distinction between "slum" and "the shantytown" some four decades later in "La señora mayor," Borges explains that poverty in Carriego's poetry is distinct from that of the European peasantry that had become canonical in the nineteenth-century literary tradition:

> Poverty [in Carriego] is not the desperate or congenital poverty of European peasantry . . . but rather the poverty of those believing in the lottery, in the committee, in a network of connections and influences, in the luck of the draw, which produces its own mysteries, in the *quiniela* [sports gambling] with its modest possibilities, in the structure of recommendations or, in lieu of any well- or poorly-reasoned alternative, in pure hope. [Carriego depicts] [a] poverty that is comfortable within hierarchies . . . which are pleasant due to their appeal to the structure of mysterious [inner] workings. (*OC* 154)

In a word, poverty in Carriego's Palermo was "carefree" ("despreocupada") (120) in the sense that hopes and understandable hierarchies structured social life.

The problem, however, is that while the area became more densely populated but was still characterized by "dirt roads and handpumped water" (*OC* 154), the modes of social life and organization that gave shape to the neighborhood came to be displaced by the proliferation of mass media distribution of the tango, in which "the phonograph" and "the radio" distribute what Borges calls "the jargon of actors" ("[una] jerigonza de actor") (152). Certain listener-addressed accounts of the life of the poor came to dominate society, including the emergence of "el lunfardo," which Borges critiqued once again four decades later in the prologue to *El informe*. Borges sees the emergence of a certain kind of representation of poverty—the reader-, beholder-, or listener-addressing tango, for example—as responding to the forms of life as they emerged not from the poor's lived experiences but instead from a series of reader-pleasing formulas that come to direct the development of the modes of sociality the poor subsequently live and experience.

It would be easy to criticize Borges's distaste for the poor's enjoyment, use, and appropriation of popular culture as reactionary, but it is important to recognize what is taking place here. What Borges dislikes about tango (in this particular context) is that its very popular but also very exaggerated representations of life in poor neighborhoods became increasingly formulaic and consequently easier to control. What had been, in his account, heterogeneous neighborhood-level modes of sociality with particular figures (e.g., Juan Muraña) responding to and shaping the rhythms of daily life, now, in the post-tango (and, later, post-Peronist) context, begins to be organized and homogenized under a singular mode of national social organization. What is at the heart of his interest here is an insistence on distinguishing the forms of life emerging from those coping with the agro-exporting economy from the forms of life that are of a piece with the emerging urban-industrial economy. And just as he is interested in distinguishing Borges from the "Borgesian" or Pierre Menard from Cervantes, this distinction between modes of poverty and their rootedness in a particular historical moment are of a piece with his interest in separating meaning from a reader or beholder's experience.

This is a dynamic that is derivable from Borges's interest in that book from 1930 in what he considers "the true virtues of [Carriego's] posthumous work" in contrast with what many readers had considered "the virtue of Carriego's poetry" (*OC* 156). What most readers considered "virtue" in Carriego's poetry was that his verses were premised on "provoking pity" in the reader (156):

> A poetry sustained by domestic oppositions and that hooks [its readers] by pursuing trivial matters, imagining or registering [images] incompatible [with that world] so that the reader will react and deplore them, seems to me like [the poet] has thrown in the towel, a self-inflicted wound. The story line seeks the bruised emotion, discomfort; the style seeks to produce scandal [es chismoso], with all the interjections, discussions, false pieties and pre-prepared suspicions characteristic of women in the neighborhood [las comadres]. The contorted logic of general consensus (which I have the decency not to understand) affirms that showing the misery of others implies a generous act of kindness. It is more a complete lack of tact. (156)

What Borges explicitly says here is that despite some excellent works like "El alma del suburbio," "El guapo," or "En el barrio," Carriego's worst poems—such as "El otoño, muchachos," "Hay que cuidarla mucho, hermana, mucho," or "El nene está enfermo"—are those that directly appeal to a reader so that he or she will reject of the miseries of poverty. These latter poems, in Borges's assessment, "do not pertain to the literary" but instead to "the criminal" (156). What he means by this is that this reader-addressing tendency in Carriego is "a deliberate sentimental blackmail, reducible to this formula: I present you with [an image of] pain and suffering; if you are not moved by it, you are heartless" (156).

In contrast, Borges views Carriego's best poems as those that are so rooted in their historical moment that the appeal to unity and meaning are required to make them intelligible. For example, Borges cites a twenty-verse passage of Carriego's that insists that the woman described in the poem be understood through her non-interchangeability: her uniqueness made intelligible by her existence within a particular series of historical events. More importantly for Borges, however, was that the expression of this idea was carried out "all at once as if it were a single, extensive word" (*OC* 157). Borges admires the near-instantaneousness of this poem as an attempt to prevent its conversion into "the common material of forgotten history."

This attempt to prevent the loss of the necessary historical context—to insist on interpreting meaning of an artistic work within the context of its production—is also articulated in what might very well be described as Borges's interest in the deeply absorptive scenes Carriego develops in other poems. Borges expresses admiration for one of Carriego's poems in which a figure is described as occupying a domestic space while absorbed in the task of attending to the presence of loved ones who have departed. Similarly, he admires another poem focusing on the deep intimacy of a relationship that could not be produced were it to take place in front of a beholder: "You are familiar to us like something / that was ours: only ours" (in Borges, *OC* 157).

While these examples seem far afield from Borges's interest in poverty and indeed contrast with the explicit representations of poverty Borges critiques in Carriego's worst poems, his characterization of Carriego's absorptive or antitheatrical verses as his best are related to what he considers the best aspects of Palermo's landscapes of poverty and underscores his reassessment of his poverty aesthetics in *El informe*. In a footnote expanding on his description of the "slum," Borges says the following: "On the outskirts are the involuntary beauties of Buenos Aires, which are also its only beauties—its easy-to-navigate street, Blanco Encalada; the vulnerable corners of Villa Crespo, of San Cristóbal Sur, of Barracas, the miserable majesty of the edges of the depot where cargo trains arrive in La Paternal and in Puente Alsina—these, I believe, are better expressions [of beauty] than those works deliberately made to be beautiful" (*OC* 154). As with the figure absorbed in contemplating or interpreting what their loved ones left behind or the familiarity that results from a relationship that develops with no concern for a beholder, Borges sees in "vulnerable corners" and "miserable majesty" what he characterizes as "the involuntary beauties of Buenos Aires."

What the rhythms of the daily life of the poor produce is not the tourist-oriented postcard images of the city—"works deliberately made to be beautiful"—but instead the landscapes emerging from life absorbed within the social structures and forms of life that emerged as a way to cope with and navigate the poverty produced by the agro-exporting economy. This question of absorption is important because, as the contrast between Mariano's nineteenth-century view of the "slum" and the narrator's view of the 1960s "shantytown" in "La señora mayor" makes clear, there is the seeming impossibility of something like absorption within "the poverty that industrialism now provides to us," that is, the transformations of the life of the poor through Peronist populism's cocreating participants and reader-addressing tango lyrics structured by a "sentimental blackmail."

## The Intuited Revelation of an Antitheatrical Aesthetics

To say that Borges's writing is interested in poverty and, moreover, that his interest in poverty is oriented toward securing the artwork's meaning against the "degenerating" effect of reader experience not only is a less common conclusion but also, in fact, goes against a widely accepted understanding of Borges's account of the aesthetic. I end this chapter by looking at some of the works that might be cited as evidence that the role of poverty I have identified in *El informe* and elsewhere is contradicted by those "primary" works where he lays out his aesthetics. One such "primary" work is the opening text in his volume of essays, *Otras inquisiciones* (1952): "La muralla y los libros." In this essay, which he drafted in 1950, Borges discusses two emblematic actions taken by Shih Huang Ti, the first emperor of China: the construction of the Great Wall (an act of creation) and the burning of books that predate him (an act of destruction). Borges postulates that these acts are foundational not only because they establish Shih Huang Ti as both a beginning (symbolized by the wall) and an ending (symbolized by the destroyed books) but also because the meaning of subsequent acts will exist in relation to him: "There will be a man who feels, as do I, and he will destroy my memory and he will be my shadow and my mirror and he will not know it" (*OC* 15). Obviously, this repeats the main conviction at the center of some of Borges's most famous texts (e.g., "Las ruinas circulares," to name just one), but the durability of the critical reference to "La muralla y los libros" comes in the relation that is drawn between these commonalities and the closing clause of the essay, which is said to encapsulate Borges's account of the aesthetic: "This imminence of a revelation, that is not produced, is, perhaps, the aesthetic act" (15).

This formulation of the aesthetic hinges on an account of form that Borges develops by generalizing the premises at the heart of Shih Huang Ti's actions: "Generalizing the previous case, we could infer that *all* forms have their virtues in themselves and not in their speculative 'content'" (15). As examples of forms that contain within themselves their meaning, Borges mentions "music, states of happiness, mythology, faces worn down by time, certain moments at dusk and certain places" (15). What all of these maintain is that they are intelligible only within a particular historical sequence: the moment when "a place" become "a certain place" or the series of events that culminate in "a state of happiness." These sequences of events are contained within the image that we see even though they are not made explicit and even if one might not be fully aware of the totality of the events leading to its production. For example, the portrait of someone existing in full "happiness" contains within it the series of events producing it, whether they be a certain art-historical sequence or a series of personal satisfactions. What Borges says is that these meaning-bearing forms "are trying to tell us something, or told us something that we should not have lost, or they are about to tell us something" (15). What they want to say is intelligible only if we are able to account for the unity of form and content, the ways in which content and form are inextricably tied together. If content is separated from form as something purely "speculative"—a reader-driven transformation of the text—then we enter a situation in which we have lost something we should not have lost: meaning that is drawn from—or "revealed" through an understanding of—the unity of form and content.

This is not how this passage is usually interpreted. A number of scholars have long drawn attention to the aesthetic as "a revelation, *that is not produced*": the revelation that "does not take place" or "never comes." In other words, the emphasis in traditional understandings of Borges's aesthetics has been the idea of deferral of meaning and the foregrounding of a reader's experience of the text, which is never complete or never fully produced. In an early reading of *El informe*, for example, Carter Wheelock asserts that "for Borges . . . the only true value or 'meaning' of literature, lies precisely in the reader's awareness that 'art' . . . has occurred . . . particularly when it comes as an intuition without conceptual form" (153), and he then cites the famous "revelation" passage as evidence. Some thirty years later, this same emphasis on "reader awareness" or the reader's experience of an "intuition" that "art has occurred" is repeated in Andrés Camilo Torres Estrada's Rancière-inspired reading of Borges: "This revelation, 'that does not take place,' does not remain in the text . . . [but rather] in the way in which the subject is interpellated directly, in the way in which [the subject] experiences aesthetically its perceptible context" (137). As we have seen, this kind of reading runs into difficulties if we examine Borges's interest in solving the dilemma of the "public" Borges and, more to the point, his appeal to poverty as a strategy to avoid the "degeneration" of meaning into the experience of the object.

One way to approach this critical impasse is to consider Patrick Dove's work on these issues in Borges's work as well as in Borges's relation to the contemporary literary production of authors like Sergio Chejfec. In Dove's reading of Borges's construction of the aesthetic in "La muralla y los libros," which he links directly to Chejfec's conception of literary form, he also privileges reader awareness of what "does not take place," of what exists as a "disruption [that] occurs in or as an experience of temporalization" (189). He calls this disruptive poetics that unifies Borges and Chejfec "[el] contratiempo literario" (190). In developing this term, Dove is more careful and nuanced in his assessment of Borges's account of the aesthetic than the critics mentioned above, focusing on how literature might avoid collapse into a "hegemonic liberal interpretation" (191) and the reproduction or re-creation of capitalist logic. In Dove's reading, the idea of "contratiempo" is geared toward disrupting a self-evident logic to make visible that which had been unperceived: "Disruptive effects generated by [el contratiempo literario] open up new possibilities for rhythmic variation" (189). Put another way, Dove sees "el contratiempo," which he associates with "the peculiar silence . . . [of] the working class" (189) in Chejfec's novels, emerge as a different kind of solution to the dilemma of theatricality than what I have argued for above. However, Dove's exploration of the concept runs into several difficulties, which I briefly outline before returning to the concept of antitheatricality as an alternative and better explanation of the tradition of poverty aesthetics Borges developed.

For Dove, at the center of Borges's formulation in "La muralla y los libros" is an "aesthetic of distancing" (181), which should obviously remind us of Borges's comments in the prologue of *El informe* where he says distancing narrative events in time and space is central to his "straightforward" style. In Dove's account, however, this distancing is premised on the concept of "withdrawal" (180), which would be something like "systematically erasing formal relations in order to arrive back at their beginning" (182). An example of this would be Borges's account of Shih Huang Ti, who erases all forms (the destructive act) so as to establish himself as a beginning (as others before and after him have done and will do). In this way, the point of focus would never be what is created (e.g., the meaning of any particular book, the actually existing social relations a particular order creates) but instead (1) the fact that there has been an erasure (e.g., the books Shih Huang Ti destroys, the forms of socioeconomic organization destroyed by an emergent new order) and (2) the fact that there will be erasure in the future (e.g., the destruction of what Shih Huang Ti has created, the emergence of a new socioeconomic order). To put this point another way, Dove says that this account of the aesthetic assigns primacy to "the indeterminacy of what remains formless in or alongside the presentation of what is" (184). In other words, "what does not take place," which could literally be anything, is where the aesthetic resides. Dove points out how for Chejfec the emblem (if such a word can be used) for this would be the silence of the working poor who point not to a utopian world beyond neoliberal capitalism but instead to the fundamental incompleteness of history (the erasures "to come"). This is what Dove understands as the centrality of withdrawal and distance: they are the "possibilities waiting to be unleashed" (174) by the disruptions of the rhythms that govern life under capitalism. For this reason, Dove arrives at the conclusion that "literary language" is "something other than a conduit for meaning" (190) and instead functions as an architecture for "the loosening of the ties (linguistic, epistemological, social) that constitute meaning" (190). This "something other than meaning" for Dove opens onto the possibility of avoiding the homogenization and efficient organization of life under the regime of capitalist production processes and the exploitation that stems from it: "it highlights a thought of heterogeneity at the heart of totality" (191).

It is logical for Dove to arrive at these conclusions, not least because Borges's rejection of Peronist politics and Europe's totalitarian regimes led him to be skeptical of these kinds of homogenizing processes. However, as we have seen above, Dove's option for the "loosening" of a relationship between historical context and artwork essentially restates the dynamic of "degeneration" and the pressures of theatricality that Borges appeals to an aesthetics of poverty to solve. If the notion of "contratiempo literario" is an attempt to come to terms with an aesthetic that can successfully turn away from "the prevailing social logic" (189), it is helpful to recognize that the privileging of "what remains formless in or alongside the presentation of [the prevailing social forms]" cannot be associated with Borges's assertion that "the aesthetic act" is "a revelation that does not take place."

This is clear in "La muralla y los libros" if we consider the fact that "the aesthetic act" is a generalization of a specific dynamic Borges develops in his reading of the meaning of Shih Huang Ti's creations. The specific "revelation that does not take place" is the hypothetical man in the future who will destroy Shih Huang Ti's wall but does not recognize—does not have the "revelation"—that his actions parallel those taken by Shih Huang Ti when he destroyed the libraries and built the wall. In other words, for Borges, "the aesthetic act" is the successful production of a fiction in a given historical sequence that one's works have no relation to the past. That fiction is that they make their meaning autonomously in the present historical sequence even though they are a specific response to the past. That nameless future man, in seeking to establish himself as a foundation for history, turns to the act of destruction. While his destructive act comes after Shih Huang Ti and is defined against the legacy of his regime, the similarity of form produces an unknowing relation to Shih Huang Ti: "he will be my shadow and my mirror and he will not know it."

It is not difficult to see the relationship here between the argument in "La muralla y los libros" (1950) and "Pierre Menard" (1939) or "Borges and I" (1960). However, when he writes "La muralla y los libros" in the midst of Peronism and in the wake of the Second World War, he foregrounds the extent to which the specificities of historical context—"what we will not know about the past," to paraphrase the description of Shih Huang Ti's future rival—will tend to (or will be made to) fade, which will make it difficult or impossible to achieve an understanding of a particular work's meaning. This status, Borges says, does not render the past formless, indeterminate, and without meaning, but instead he insists that "the aesthetic act" lies in understanding that artworks are constituted by meaning: "[They] are trying to tell us something, or told us something that we should not have lost, or they are about to tell us something" (*OC* 15). This point, which is present in "Pierre Menard," "La muralla y los libros," "Borges and I," and numerous other texts, is what Borges is seeking to secure in his return to landscapes of poverty in *El informe*.

As we saw in "La señora mayor," the juxtaposition of Mariano's view of the "slum" and the narrator's view of the "shantytown" produces a distinction or difference between poverty before Perón and after. This difference—the building materials used, the location and organization of the neighborhoods, the social relations organizing them, and so on—is recovered by each character (Mariano, the narrator) and assigned a meaning: "The poverty of yesteryear was less poor than the poverty that industrialism now provides to us. The fortunes amassed [by the wealthy] were smaller as well." That there is a difference between these modes of poverty is a point on which most everyone would agree, just as everyone would agree that Shih Huang Ti is not interchangeable with the rival who seeks to destroy him, or that Cervantes is not interchangeable with Menard. The "historical" Borges is noncollapsible into the "public" Borges; the directional sign remains distinct from the weapon of medieval warfare; and the "famed" image of the murdered cattle workers and their duel is not interchangeable with the "obscured history" of their lives.

If there are any doubts about the relation between Borges's account of the aesthetic in "La muralla" and his turn to the aesthetics of poverty as a resource for resolving the dilemmas posed by theatricality and the valorization of the experience of formlessness, we need turn only to the prologue to his anthology, *Las poesías completas de Evaristo Carriego*, which he drafted in 1950 within just weeks or months of writing "La muralla y los libros." In this text (unlike the more famous 1955 prologue to the reissue of *Evaristo Carriego*), Borges traces out an image of Carriego—"young, proud, timid and poor" (*OC* 182)—wandering the city feeling himself "exiled from life" (182), given that he could not live in France (the center of the art world) but instead found himself required to live in "a mediocre South American slum" (182). Borges then emphasizes something like a momentary spark that revealed to Carriego that art could be made from that impoverished landscape: "Something happened.... Something that we will never be able to recover, something whose meaning we will know but whose form, something from the everyday and trivial but not perceived until just then, which revealed to Carriego that the universe (which is available in full in every moment, in every place, and not only in works by Dumas) was also there, in the mere present, in Palermo, in 1904" (183). That significant "revelation"—"the universe... is available in full... in every place, and not only in works by Dumas"—has an origin point in "something from the everyday and trivial." Whatever that "everyday thing" might have been—"the uneven line of small houses seen through the window" or "the moon on the rectangular patio" (183)—what is key is not to recover the *biographical* origin point of Carriego's poetry (the causal life details [the literal series of objects] they were made *of*) but instead to attend to the meaning of his artworks (the aesthetic details key to understanding what they are *about*).

The aesthetic that Borges takes from Carriego is one that emphasizes that revelation can and does take place, and that revelation is a meaning that is drawn from both what a landscape of poverty is attempting to tell Carriego as well as what he interprets and ultimately transforms into the artwork. Borges puts it this way in the 1950 prologue: "Any human life, as intricate and vast as it might be, in truth is comprised of one moment in which the person knows forever who he or she is. From the moment of that difficult-to-pinpoint revelation that I have tried to intuit [Desde la imprecisable revelación que he tratado de intuir], Carriego is Carriego" (183). Borges cannot definitely say whether it was "the uneven line of small houses seen through the window" or "the moon on the rectangular patio" that led to Carriego's revelation and his ability to produce his meaning-bearing artworks that, like those emerging from nineteenth- and early twentieth-century France, have a claim on the universal. But his point is that there is a historical sequence—"something happened," "a moment," "the difficult-to-pinpoint revelation"—that produces the context in which the artwork emerges. In the case of Borges's *El informe*, we see something similar emerge when the mere "use of sheet metal" in the 1960s "shantytown" is, in a sense, destroyed when the narrator re-creates it in the meaningful historical contrast that becomes available with Mariano's recollection of the "lack of plaster" representing the "poverty of yesteryear." And this, of course, also parallels what he says in "La muralla y los libros," when he provides an account of forms that contain within themselves their meaning, such as the moment when a generic place is, so to speak, destroyed as a "*certain* place" is created. It is the destruction of the object as mere object with variable and infinite uses that secures the possibility that the artwork can emerge.

Something like this point is made in Michael Fried's account of antitheatrical photography that had its origin point in the same late 1960s and early 1970s moment in which Borges was consolidating his navigation of antitheatrical aesthetics in *El informe*. Of particular interest is his reading of Thomas Struth's cityscapes made between the 1970s and the 1990s. As Fried notes, Struth's black-and-white photographs of neighborhoods in New York, Düsseldorf, and other European cities featured scenes that, like the "involuntary beauty" Borges admires in Buenos Aires's slums, were "never intended by anyone to be precisely what it strikes the viewer of the photograph as being" (*Photography* 277). What Fried means here is that Struth, like Borges, was interested not in "works deliberately made to be beautiful" but instead in "a collaging together of traces of multiple intentions, traces laid down at different, even widely disparate moments, thereby modifying, covering, or effacing the traces of previous intentions, so that the scene as a whole presents itself as everywhere stamped by intention albeit (with a few exceptions) not by a single or collective intention to produce the scene, the place, the milieu as it appears to the viewer" (277). These photographs produce images of the rhythms of daily life and the trivial or banal comings and goings that make up a large part of the lives of the inhabitants who live in those neighborhoods. For this reason, Fried notes that they produce "an effect of heightened meaningfulness—at once global and minutely detailed—that at the same time refuses to be pinned down, reduced to sociological or psychological commonplaces" (278). Rather than producing a directly political reading of these spaces, Struth is attempting to produce a visual account of the meanings of these places. Or to put it as Borges does in "La muralla y los libros," he is attempting to show within the picture itself what it is that makes this a "*certain* place," which is at the intersection of both formal and historical considerations.

Struth's photographs—and their parallel to Borges's "straightforward" style—are important to note because Struth trained under Bernd and Hilla Becher, who were included in the New Topographics exhibition. In Fried's reading of the Bechers' work, there is something paralleling Borges's interest in the historical specificity of poverty as a figuration of insisting on meaning more broadly. The Bechers were known for their "typologies" of industrial landscapes, photographing and placing into relation with each other images of similar groups of industrial objects (e.g., blast furnaces, cooling towers, water towers, gasometers).

As Fried notes, these photographs often isolate the building from its surrounding context, leading some to incorrectly associate the Bechers with minimalist (or literalist) art. But what Fried notes is that "the object in question, as the Bechers put it, is not moveable like a cup or a sewing machine but rather is 'strictly connected to the ground'" (*Photography* 323). This is not a minimalist commitment to situation or "site-specific" artworks in which the object depended on the space of its display and the embodied subject viewing it but instead on "the fact that each belongs to a particular spot of earth (also to a particular economic and social network) and not another" (323). The meaning they have comes from their status as the result of a particular sequence of historical events and the decision of the Bechers to photograph dozens of similar objects in contexts across the United States and Europe. As they note, "One just has to select the right objects and fit them into the picture precisely, then they tell their own story all by themselves. In other words, we did not want to change anything about the object we were photographing" (in Fried, *Photography* 323).

This is what Borges is approaching in *El informe* when juxtaposing accounts of poverty: Mariano's "slum" and the narrator's "shantytown"; Borges's Juan Muraña and Trápani's Juan Muraña; the circulating image of the dueling impoverished cattle workers and the "obscured history" of their lives. In much the same way the Bechers attempt to produce their pictures "without any composition," so too is Borges attempting to produce in his "straightforward" style an avoidance of "composition"—the "Borgesian" surprise ending, for example—in an effort to produce the fiction that these stories were written by "anybody" or "nobody" or everybody or that they are something like "typologies" that parallel the "involuntary beauties" of the Palermo he once admired.

The point here, as with Struth's cityscapes and the Bechers' typologies, is that Borges's *El informe* possesses a tendency to "[collage] together . . . traces of multiple intentions" that appear to "never [be] intended by anyone to be precisely what it strikes the [reader] of the [text] as being." This antitheatrical strategy of reducing composition so as to foreground meaningfulness demonstrates that the insistence on meaning does not homogenize the rhythms of life under a capitalist organization of production, as Dove fears in his attempt to "loosen the ties that constitute meaning." Instead, meaning and the aesthetic decisions that were made to produce it function as a central component in formulating a critique that would otherwise be evacuated by formlessness.

Borges's "straightforward" style and interest in the everyday landscapes created by the poor emerged in the 1960s as a key resource for addressing the problem of the theatrical (reader-addressing) mode of fiction Borges associated with the image of the "public" Borges. Just as he was interested in how to secure readers' meaningful engagement with the stories he was actually writing (rather than their own manufactured image of "Borges" created to serve their own uses), so too was he interested in how to return those living in poverty to their status as full human beings acting (with complicated human fullness) within a specific socioeconomic system. This stems from his broader concerns about the effects of Peronism and other political systems that valorized the experience of formlessness as a political resource. He shared a sensibility with the New Topographics photographers who sought strategies to "postulate, *at least for the time being*, what it means to make a documentary photograph" (Jenkins et al. 7, my emphasis), with that "time" referring to the an increasingly theatricalized art-historical tradition of landscape photography. By insisting on developing strategies to secure within the artwork the resources for interpreting its meaning—i.e., by crafting an antitheatrical aesthetics of poverty—Borges was also gesturing toward a different way of conceptualizing poverty and politics in the 1960s. Just as the New Topographics photographers worked against the charismatic nature of a commodified landscape photography marked by "monumental grandiosity" in favor of the "well made" print of the "dull," mundane, everyday processes of "development," so too does Borges work against the charismatic figures casting shadows over his own art: both the "public" Borges and the political figures on the "balcony" whose words and gestures built an image of the poor that elicited the open-ended responses experienced by those in the plaza. Borges's antitheatrical aesthetics appeal, in contrast, to the mundane realities and structural fact of poverty that the reader should confront. In other words, the point is to recognize that the conditions producing the "eviction" of someone like Trápani are dynamics that neither a sentimental appeal to a particular landlord nor violence against that particular landlord (or against a particular *caudillo*, for that matter) can change. In reading Borges's antitheatrical aesthetics of poverty, then, we are turning to Borges not to search for an antipoverty program or politics but instead to develop an understanding of an aesthetic model that might enable us to think poverty and art against the "balcony effect" and against their reduction to "sheer hatred" for the "face of the rival."

# Conclusion

Throughout this book, I have examined the various and related political and aesthetic projects that flow from the commitment to understanding poverty as an experience of formlessness. As we saw, diverse historical experiences like Peronism in Argentina, Mexicanism in Mexico, and the variant social and aesthetic models emerging from Chile's political left developed in a context of maintaining that commitment to poverty as an experience of formlessness within what Larsen calls a "crisis in representation." In this way, poverty is understood not as a problem to be solved with behavioral, sociological, or political interventions nor as a "necessary obstacle" that must be endured within the positive process of modernization (as was the case in both capitalist and social modernities). Instead, poverty emerges as a necessary resource amid the crisis of necessary norms and conventions: experiences of formlessness and nonnormativity were understood as productive of alternative norms and conventions (alternative modernities). A phenomenon like populism (as well as the post-Marxist or cultural studies concepts like "articulation" it inspired) is in line with this framework: those political and analytical models utilize the experience of formlessness as a resource to manage or steer the crisis.

However, as scholars of posthegemony like Beasley-Murray, Steinberg, and Williams have correctly observed, these strategies of social management bring us no closer to the equality of social relations and no closer to bringing poverty to an end. Yet however correct theorists of posthegemony might be in their rejection of "articulation," populism, and cultural studies, posthegemony nevertheless has tended to carry forward a commitment to the experience of formlessness as a necessary resource for politics and aesthetics and therefore, also, I have argued, a commitment to maintaining, as a logical necessity, the experiential account of poverty that has been the primary target of critique in this study.

In this way, their models of analysis do not address the objective nature of classes as they are, classes as they are coming into being and the fissure between them.

A corollary phenomenon in the posthegemonic model is that the work of art is also set aside as the objective, normative bearer of meaning that it is. Works of art are understood not as communicating something (a meaning) that transcends any individual subjective experience of it but instead as an object that produces effects *for* and *through* a subject. By demonstrating that the posthegemonic (and hegemonic ["articulation"]) account of what artworks are and how they operate is incorrect, I have been able to demonstrate how the corollary commitments to understandings of poverty and politics also fail to meet the analytical and political challenges posited by poverty. In this way, I have made the case for understanding the kind of problem the work of art is as a needed strategy for understanding the kind of problem poverty is. And that understanding comes most clearly into view through what I have been calling, following Michael Fried and Walter Benn Michaels, a kind of antitheatrical tradition in Latin America, one that has been examined by scholars such as Di Stefano and Sauri. That tradition has been underexamined for the variety of reasons that these and other scholars have elaborated in their work. But aside from the implications that this lack of attention has had for political and aesthetic theory in the field, there are also more practical kinds of oversights that have emerged as a consequence of how the field's critical frameworks have developed. More specifically, some significant artists who more closely align with the kinds of strategies and approaches I have examined as part of the antitheatrical tradition have not received needed analysis and attention. One particularly emblematic case is Mexican film director Marcela Fernández Violante, whose work is helpful in clarifying the arguments I have developed in this book as well as what is at stake in those arguments.

## Outside the "Existing Parameters"

Having released her award-winning film short *Azul* in 1967, Mexican film director Marcela Fernández Violante began 1968 slated to be the director of the first feature-length film for the newly founded University Center for Cinematographic Studies (CUEC) at the national flagship institution, the UNAM. However, the events of that year led the CUEC to turn away from works of fiction to focus on the events of the day. More specifically, the CUEC shifted its activities to documenting how the single-party state—the PRI (or Institutional Revolutionary Party)—was utilizing authoritarian tactics to repress the student movement, including the infamous massacre of unarmed protestors in Tlatelolco in October 1968. As Elissa Rashkin notes, the result was that the CUEC's first feature was not Fernández Violante's planned fiction film but instead Leobardo López Arretche's *El grito*, a feature-length documentary on the student movement and the massacre. As Fernández Violante noted in an interview she gave to Julianne Burton in 1986, "With the country in such turmoil, nobody wanted to work on a fiction film. Everybody went out to *participate and film what was happening*" (in Rashkin 78, my emphasis).

While Fernández Violante's planned fiction film from 1968 was never made, she did go on to make a number of (mostly) fiction films. After making one of the first feminist recoveries of Frida Kahlo's art in her 1970 documentary short (shown at the 1974 New Mexican Cinema exhibition at the Museum of Modern Art in New York), she made the historical fiction feature *De todos modos Juan te llamas* (translated as *The General's Daughter*, 1974). She followed that with her second feature: another historical fiction film, *Cananea* (1976), which is the main work I analyze here. The film centers on an infamous episode in Mexican history when, in 1906, William Cornell Greene, the U.S. capitalist owner of a copper mine in northern Mexico, called in the Arizona Rangers to suppress striking workers, which resulted in their massacre.

A film like *Cananea*—with its narrative featuring an exploitative U.S. capitalist, sovereignty-breeching paramilitaries, and violent repression of a popular mobilization—would seem to be in line with the kinds of interests that were motivating both the creative activity of Latin American filmmakers in the late 1960s and early 1970s (as with directors engaged with "Third Cinema") and critical interest in their works. But Fernández Violante's films have, for the most part, remained little studied and unexamined. Her films (as far as I can tell) are not regularly considered as part of the Mexican film canon of this era. As Niamh Thornton notes in her study of *The General's Daughter* and Fernández's Violante's 1980 film *Mystery*, there is "a paucity of critical analysis of her work" (198) mostly due to the fact that Fernández Violante "is difficult to fit into the existing parameters" (198) of scholarship on Mexican film: "She does not belong to the first wave of pioneering women" (197) in the industry, but "her work [cannot] be described as 'feminist,' as that term was defined to describe the work of the 1980s generation" (197).

What I argue is that part of the lack of critical interest in Fernández Violante's films is linked to her political and aesthetic choices, which did not align with existing political and aesthetic agendas of that era. More specifically, *Cananea* deploys representational strategies that compel the viewer to set aside as irrelevant identitarian claims or appeals to the experiences of workers and the poor in favor of understanding a critique of transnational economic systems of exploitation. She does so, I argue, by rejecting the dominant cultural logic of Mexicanism that, as a set of aesthetic conventions and political strategies, required the literal depiction of workers and peasants as components of a justifying populist, identitarian, anti-imperial (and, I want to say, beholder-addressing) logic that sustained the single-party state of the PRI. My claim about Fernández Violante's aesthetic project in this film, then, is that she achieves this critical approach by appealing to the ability of fiction (through the use of antitheatrical devices) to represent and compel understanding of an exploitative, transnational economic system that does not neatly map onto the populist, anti-imperialist narratives that sustained the capitalist state in Mexico.

## Understanding *Cananea*

*Cananea* was made within the state-run film industry and its structures. As such, it would seem that the choice for the repressive, cross-border incursion at the mine would place the film in line with the PRI's traditional narratives of the state as the leftist defender of the gains peasants and workers made during the Revolution, a legacy that was formalized in the 1917 Constitution. As the single-party state emerged in the 1940s and 1950s from the variety of Revolution-securing strategies of the 1920s and 1930s, the PRI gradually but persistently abandoned the radical class politics of the Revolution in favor of a "culturalist legacy" of the Revolution as the moment when the country became itself by (finally) reckoning with its long history of colonialism. But Fernández Violante is not interested in struggles for national identity despite her film's complete focus on an infamous episode that often stokes exactly those kinds of identifications. Instead of beginning the film with, say, the drudgery experienced by working miners or scenes of managerial oppression/harassment (as, for example, in muralist art), the first forty minutes or so of the two-hour film are in English, focusing almost exclusively on the actions taken by the U.S. capitalist (played by Steve Wilensky) to establish a successful mining operation in Mexico. As Fernández Violante complains in a 1983 interview, she was "attacked" by Mexican critics for this decision because, as with her previous film, *The General's Daughter*, where she "didn't talk about the peasants," they saw that "with *Cananea* I didn't talk about the worker. I talked about the rich American" (Mosler and González 16).

What is so important about this decision, however, is that Fernández Violante is asserting her interest in representing how capitalism actually operates in Mexico rather than creating a film that appeals to or falls within the Mexicanist cinematic formulas. She does not play to the expectations of domestic audiences accustomed to celebrations of joyous or heroic peasants and workers or, alternatively, to transnational audiences seeking encounters with "life itself" in works of "Third Cinema." Instead, she represents the social relations of a transnational economic system, which means foregrounding not only processes of "primitive accumulation" (staking a claim to the mine) and financialization but also the means by which labor can be organized and compelled to enter into the social relations set into motion by the actions we see take place on screen. In other words, Fernández Violante is interested not only in how a capitalist like Greene gets the land and money needed to begin his operation but also in the strategies he uses to keep operations humming. This includes the contributions of Mexican politicians, managers, and capitalists but also, importantly, the knowledge he gains about the social relations of Mexican workers. In this sense, Fernández Violante sought cinematic strategies that would compel audiences to set aside desires to participate in "struggles for liberation" or in so-called authentic expressions of a national essence to attend, instead, to how systems of exploitation are created and how they operate.

Early in the film, we see Greene meet the woman he will make his first wife, Priscilla Johnson (Beatriz Sheridan). Johnson is a widow from the United States who had immigrated to Mexico with her first husband, who had been involved in labor organizing in Chicago and fled the country amid the violent crackdowns and blacklisting of the 1890s. Greene's first words in Spanish were learned from and through his engagement with this immigrant woman and the milieu of radicalized workers who populated her life. He learns the important word "compadre," which essentially evokes an idea of mutualist solidarity and friendship. But as he develops an understanding of alternative social relations learned through his acquisition of Spanish, he uses the knowledge embedded in the language of Mexican workers to establish the working conditions that submit them to structures of exploitation.

By focusing on Greene, Fernández Violante is able make this "story [that] is about the rich American" a compelling and critical representation of *capitalism* in Mexico, a representation that would require a viewer to set aside nationalist narratives that organize standard identitarian understandings of Mexican history and postrevolutionary social relations. As Fernández Violante asserted in an interview in 1983, "[Greene's] property [remained untouched during the Revolution] . . . if he lost Cananea, it was not because of the Mexican Revolution; it was because of a movement on Wall Street . . . [by the] Anaconda Copper Company . . . the Mexican Revolution did nothing to him" (Mosler and González 16).[1] The film, then, is a critique of the social relations of postrevolutionary Mexico, which are framed within the PRI's Mexicanist revolutionary nationalism, a populist logic that often operates via the "balcony effect." This phenomenon, which has been examined throughout this book, is, again, the production of a seemingly "authentic" experience of egalitarian encounter that nevertheless leaves economic structures of inequality untouched. Fernández Violante utilizes this "balcony" structure within the film as a tool to develop a critical relation with Mexicanist cinematic production. This is clear if we analyze two key scenes.

At the center of one of them (figure C.1) is a bilingual Mexican accountant and office worker, Esteban Baca (Carlos Bracho), who has begun to follow the anarcho-syndicalist writings of the Flores Magón brothers and emerges as a labor organizer in the mining camp. The other (figure C.2) has Greene at its center. As each man takes his place "on the balcony," he uses the words of workers to reorganize workers' experiences of social relations in the mining camp. For Fernández Violante, the positions Greene and Baca take on the "balcony" serve to secure their role as figures that mobilize the Janus-faced logic of the PRI's beholder-addressing populism, which is her object of critique. In figure C.1, Baca arrives on the scene after newly established work processes left a significant number of miners without work for the day. He begins speaking to the workers

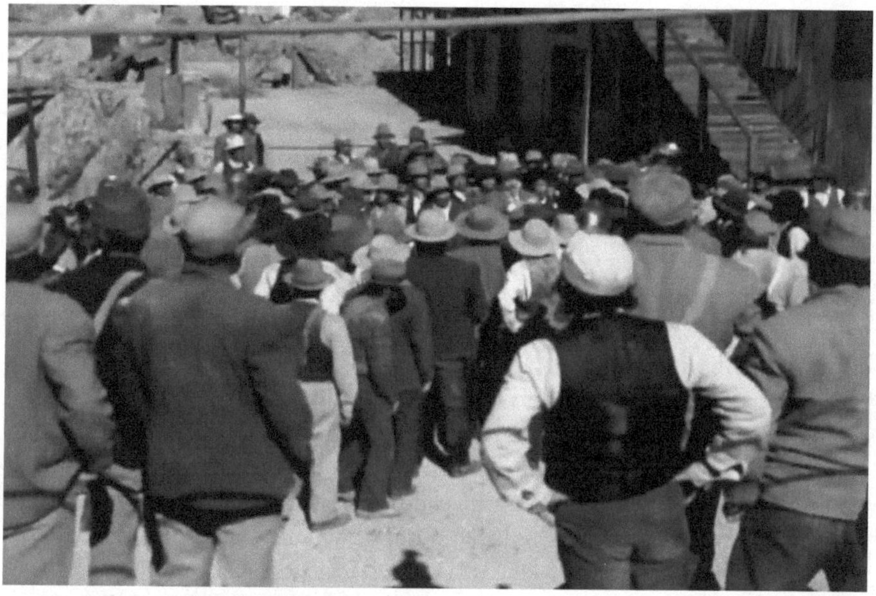

FIGURE C.1 Still image from *Cananea* (dir. Marcela Fernández Violante, 1978). A group of gathered miners seen from behind as they listen to a labor organizer.

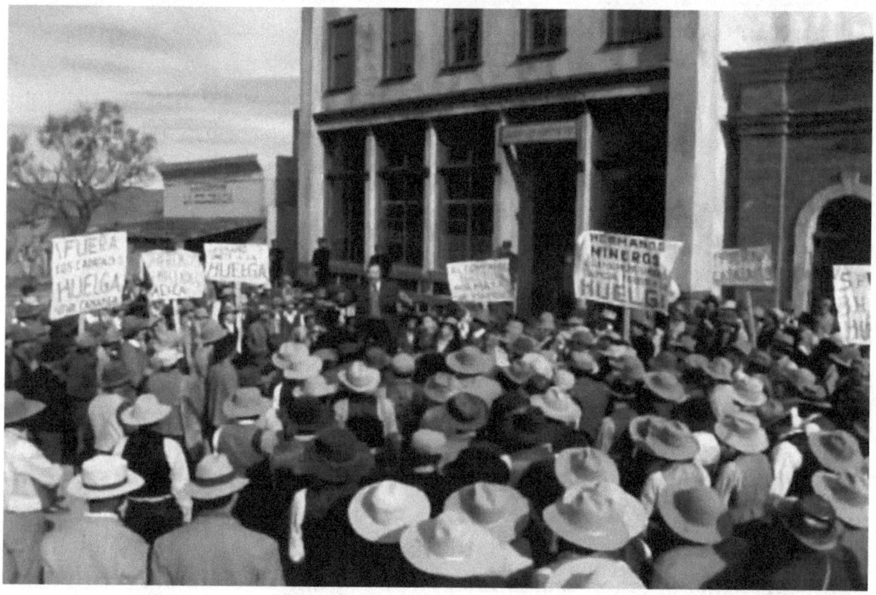


FIGURE C.2 Still image from *Cananea* (dir. Marcela Fernández Violante, 1978). A group of striking miners seen from behind as they hold placards and listen to a speech from the mine owner.

by interpreting the changes in process through the lens of the Flores Magón brothers as the camera begins to pan back and more and more sidelined workers move into the frame to surround Baca and listen to him speak. However, the engagement between Baca and the workers is conflictual. Many interrupt him and heckle him, and in an instance that recalls an earlier moment in the film, one worker shouts a homophobic slur at him, referring to Baca's status as an intellectual (though an intellectual who, like the miners, is subjected to the structures of segregation Greene set up in the camp). However, unlike the previous moment, where Baca ignores the slur and returns to the boarding house where he lives, Baca uses the slur (the words of that milieu of workers) in an effort to highlight how Greene uses the words of workers against them. The slur is contrasted with the word that Greene uses to address all of his workers: "compadre." This term, referring to mutualist solidarity, is contrasted with the slur, connected to violence and the exploitative structures of capitalism and segregation that organize everyday life in the camp.

What this scene depicts is an interaction between the figure on the balcony (Baca) and those in the plaza (the workers). Baca's goal is to use the juxtaposition of the homophobic slur and "compadre" as a strategy that would make available knowledge of Greene's practices of exploitation and prevent the collapse of that knowledge into the everyday experiences of work in the camp: for example, divisions between miners and office workers that are demarcated through language and cultural practice, divisions between Mexican workers and U.S. workers that are demarcated by formal systems of segregation established by Greene, Greene's efforts to manipulate and manage those experiences through his populist egalitarian rhetoric, and so on. Baca's goal in the balcony scene is not to produce experiences of the realities of the working class that are more or less "authentic" via a more or less "realistic" use of their words. Instead, the scene is concerned with how to generate knowledge about how their words are used against them (perhaps especially when they appear to be "authentic"). The problem, however, is that Baca remains uninterested in acquiring knowledge of the concrete, material working conditions of the miners and is committed to the mine as an example of an a priori set of conclusions. While the result of this "balcony effect" here is collective action in the form of a strike, Baca's approach to the labor struggle (i.e., his insistence on concept over material conflict) leads him to abandon an interest in acquiring knowledge in favor of applying predetermined formulas. As we will see in a moment, this ultimately leads him to a kind of "left-formalist" position that sees the goal of knowledge creation obliviated by the experience of conceptual formulas that map only imprecisely onto the concrete situation at hand (i.e., are ultimately unconvincing).

The scene featuring Greene at the center (figure C.2) is a response to the strike. As Greene arrives by car and ascends to a platform to address, in Spanish, the striking workers, it becomes clear that he needs to remobilize experience to obscure the knowledge revealed by the juxtaposition Baca created in his balcony scene. Indeed, Greene speaks of brotherhood and the dynamics of working as a "compadre," a caring equal with the miners, in an effort to justify the fairness of a low wage that, if raised, he suggests, would force a closure of the mine. When Baca interrupts Greene's speech with an appeal to what the accounts in the office show (i.e., the vast profits Greene is making), Greene descends from the platform and develops his own juxtaposition of terms. Calling Baca a "stranger" or "outsider" ("un desconocido") who is unfamiliar with the needs and struggles of the workers, he presents himself as a "friend" to workers ("su amigo") who has provided them with jobs and wages for years. The strike begins to break as fear begins to sweep through the group in the wake of what appears to be the loss of Greene's egalitarian "embrace." It is important to note that the result of these competing balcony scenes is violence: Baca sabotages the mine; Greene calls the Rangers; Baca sabotages Greene's carriage; and Greene dies just before text appears on the screen to link the events to national revolutionary history. However, it would be incorrect to read the film as only the story of how two men are able to climb onto a balcony and use workers' words to pursue competing models of modernity (capitalist in the case of Greene and left syndicalist in the case of Baca), and it would be a mistake to conclude that the film opts for the models advocated by Greene or Baca.

Part of the deftness of Fernández Violante's film is the way it rejects populist theatricalities that are presented as the only available political options, which, equally, in the nationalist-Mexicanist and "Third Cinema" models were generally understood as the only cinematic options. The film is focused on producing a knowledge of how capitalist production flows across borders and confounds straightforward national narratives of anti-imperialism. Indeed, one way to read the on-screen text at the end of the film is not as encapsulating this transnational story of capital and poverty within the nationalist, institutional narratives of Mexico's Revolution but instead as a way to demonstrate the myopia that officialist narratives of postrevolutionary mexicanidad produced. In this way, the film does not pursue an anti-Greene position, a pro-Baca position, or a position paralleling a kind of nationalist "mestizaje" that has tended to dominate understandings of postrevolutionary Mexico. Instead, the film focuses on producing knowledge about transnational economic structures by neutralizing or overcoming the beholder-addressing strategies of Mexicanist cinema, on the one hand, and anti-imperialist "Third Cinema," on the other, both of which evoke aspects of the PRI's governing logic.

Fernández Violante's strategy is to demonstrate the failure of the PRI's Janus-faced balconies in which both Greene and Baca "perform for" and seek the compliance of the workers they address. In very practical ways, her film establishes an *anti*theatrical position, critiquing Baca's strategy of foregrounding anarcho-syndicalist formulas that excise experiential knowledge (a kind of "left formalism") and Greene's strategy that foregrounds workers' feelings and experience in an effort to excise knowledge of exploitative economic structures through populist address. This antitheatrical critique is developed through the representation of a balcony that emerges in a way that parallels the absorptive enclosure of what Fried calls the "theory of the apartment" in 1860s French painting. Two related images demonstrate what I mean and allow me to bring this study to an end.

These images (figures C.3, C.4) are improvised balcony scenes that prefigure the two we have already analyzed. These balconies are staged inside Baca's room (or "apartment") at the boarding house when he receives a visit from a miner named Manuel Diéguez after their brief encounter waiting in line at the segregated cashier's window. In the apartment, Baca begins to explain to Diéguez his

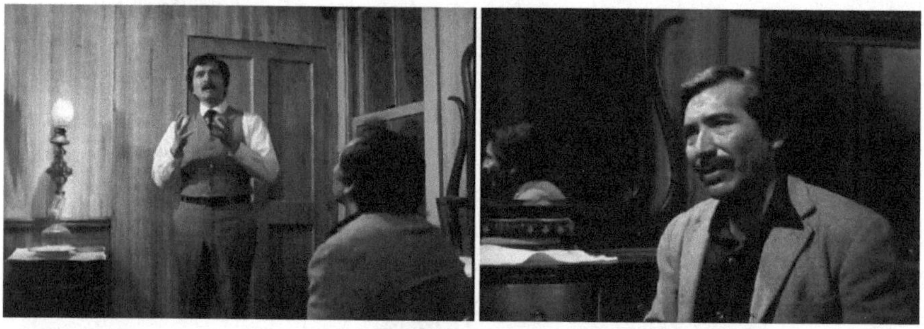

FIGURE C.3 Still image from *Cananea* (dir. Marcela Fernández Violante, 1978). An improvised "balcony" scene in the room of a boarding house.

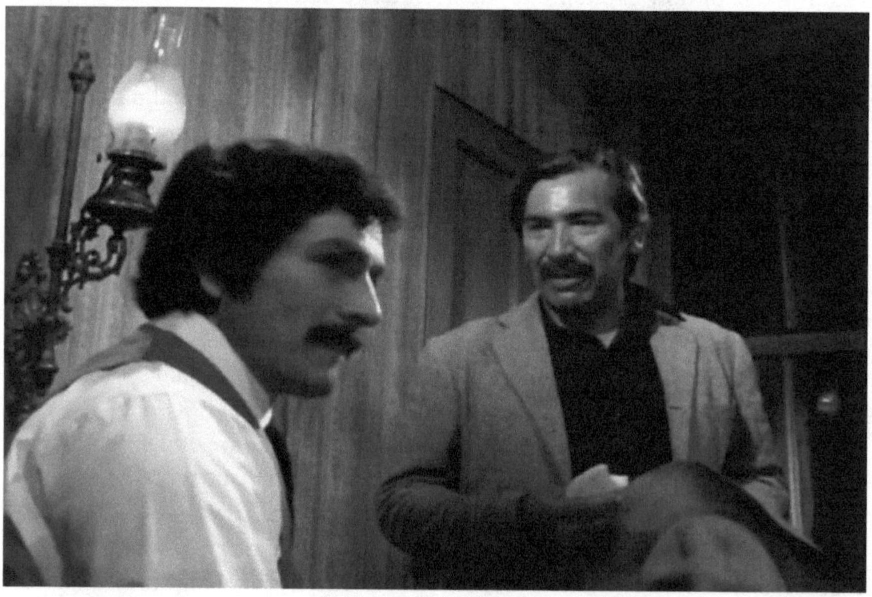

FIGURE C.4 Still image from *Cananea* (dir. Marcela Fernández Violante, 1978). Diéguez calls for an end to politics driven by calculated effects: "¡Dilas así no más!"

affinity for the writings of the Flores Magón brothers. He contrasts the egalitarianism advocated by the Flores Magón with the stilted speeches of the ruling dictator Porfirio Díaz. As we see in the shot, reverse shot structure of figure C.3, Baca imitates Díaz giving a speech, uttering the typical platitudes of Porfirian ideals. As Baca's parody of Díaz continues, the camera cuts to Diéguez, who is intently listening, and then back to Baca, who, after finishing, asks Diéguez if he understood. Diéguez ultimately responds in the negative, which is the point Baca wishes to make: Porfirian language obfuscates Porfirian structures of capitalism.

It is at this point that Fernández Violante begins to set up the critique of the "balcony effect." Baca's problems reside in his misdiagnosis of the situation: he is concerned with how to produce an effect on a beholder, to make people listen, to "open their eyes." The beholder of *Cananea*, however, is in a position to recognize this mistake through Fernández Violante's construction of a narrative that is unified with the composition of the cinematic image in this "apartment." As a preamble to a crucial shot in the film (figure C.4), Diéguez responds to Baca's Porfirian parody by reflecting on what he understands as Baca's struggles with language: "I don't know what's going on with you, but if your problem is how to say things, well, you just have to say them, plain and simple [dilas así no más]." This, I am arguing, is advice that articulates Fernández Violante's absorptive, antitheatrical critique: the challenge is to compel the conviction one is expressing oneself without calculated "authenticity," without concern for audience reaction. Baca rejects Diéguez's advice out of hand, suggesting that, while Diéguez's approach "is fine for negotiating prices with sellers at the market," his own task is different: "to open people's eyes to what is going on, a person needs to choose his words very carefully and know the precise moment when to say them." The basic distinction elaborated here is one between truth and effect. Because Baca is completely committed to a notion of meaning embedded in the effects an utterance produces (that is, whether action follows utterance), he very easily discards Diéguez's appeal to truth in favor of an appeal to "manners and conventions" as if they were or could be independent of the truth he wished to communicate.

It is at this moment that, in compositional contrast to the shot, reverse shot structure of Baca's staging of the Porfirio Díaz speech just a moment earlier, the camera joins the two men in a single shot but is positioned at an angle that makes Diéguez appear to be slightly elevated in relation to the seated Baca, who is shown first from behind and, at the end of the sequence, in profile (as in figure C.4). Following his own antitheatrical advice, Diéguez plainly narrates an anecdote from his romantic life as a young man in his village. Having spent time hatching a plan to make an elaborate marriage proposal to a love interest, he finally arrives at the decision to declare his love for her at the village dance. However, when he arrives, he finds that a rival had already proposed marriage to his love interest after the rival simply said, "We're getting married," while the young woman was plucking the feathers from a chicken she was preparing for a meal. Reflecting on that sequence of events, he shares the knowledge he gained from living and then (after representing it to himself through narrative reconstruction) understanding that experience, which is that, what he understood himself to want and what he actually wanted were nonidentical to each other, a notion he expressed via the jocular quality of an often-told anecdote shared between workers during a lunch break: "Afterward, I thought about it a lot and what I think it was, was that, well, I really just wanted to keep playing the field."

As his expression in figure C.4 suggests, Baca did not share Diéguez's amusement, nor did he seem to understand the knowledge embedded within that narrative: the nonidentity between what one thinks one wants and what one actually wants. Baca persists in his conviction that abstract theorizations alone—diatribes on surplus value expressed in journalistic detail or laid out in the company ledgers smuggled from the office—would bring an understanding of and solution to the poverty that the miners experience. Indeed, after Diéguez tells him that they are going "to die for nothing" when they are being led to a prisoner transport train after the massacre and the breaking of the strike, Baca again rejects Diéguez's assertions by saying that they have won because the workers now have knowledge of who Greene is: "We weren't staging a strike; we were opening the eyes of our comrades to what is really going on." For his part, Greene persists in his conviction that the production of experience alone would solve the problem of poverty by keeping the processes of work flowing uninterruptedly.

However, Diéguez is neither seduced by the "rags-to-riches" platitudes of Greene's "capital fictions" nor does he accept Baca's self-satisfied martyrdom from the left. Indeed, his reaction to Baca makes it clear that he stands against an account of poverty as a negative experience that can be transformed into the positive experience of the process of equality instead. As Diéguez repeatedly makes clear, he wants not a "consciousness-raising campaign" but instead a life lived in brotherhood, freedom, and equality. Grabbing Baca by the shirt collar as they walk, shackled, to the prison transport, he straightforwardly critiques Baca's effects-driven plan: "¡Hijo de la chingada! It's your fault they killed twelve of our comrades! . . . Was it really necessary for so many to die?" The implied answer, of course, is no. Diéguez recognizes and knows that Greene's mining operation does not produce a mutual "compadrazgo," but at the same time, he recognizes that Baca's effects-driven sacrifice of himself and striking workers doesn't make Greene any less an oligarch. Diéguez's call for straightforward, noncalculated expression of the state of things—"¡dilas así no más!"—is an antitheatrical call for narratives to express the truth of those moments of crisis in which there is a nonidentity between what a self (or a class) in its real abstraction wants and what an actually constituted self (or class) wants. This is achieved not through experiential encounters with "the real" or formulas for the programmatic or "authentic" but instead through successful representations of the true: compelling works of art that make available "as never before" the nature of poverty as an objective relational aspect of a modernizing economic system, an objective relation that is subjectively experienced by millions around the world each and every day.

We all aspire to move beyond the modest and ultimately defeatist notion that an end to poverty only ever exists as a dream or a fiction and that antipoverty initiatives can only ever work to ensure that no one *experience* the exploitation and dispossession they actually live. As I have demonstrated in this book, the best way to make progress toward achieving that aspiration requires approaching the problem of poverty—the specific problem of recognizing how the "crisis in representation" both has shaped the tendency to develop an experiential account of poverty *and* reveals poverty's status as an objective relational aspect of a historically particular economic sequence—through indirect analysis: through an analysis of debates about the work of art and the kind of problem *it* is. Indeed, the work of art—with the specific historical developments and visual strategies making a work of art entails—has the possibility of enabling us to intuit the desired political model "that remains at a distance from the present reality and cannot actually be represented but only imagined, wished for, fantasized." But as what is needed in the moment can be embedded in the "world of the image," those undertaking the challenge to analyze, interpret, and cognize the crisis and its potential solutions will be able "to traverse the fantasy" and bring into reality an egalitarian social order that responds to the objective relational nature of everyday exploitation.

# Acknowledgments

The path to writing and publishing this book has been long and winding. As my first single-authored scholarly book, its existence owes so much to just about every person I've ever interacted with over the course of my life. Whether they have been my teachers, students, classmates, friends, family members, colleagues, acquaintances, or even strangers whose names I will never know, the interactions and conversations I had with them have shaped my understanding of the world: how socioeconomic phenomena like poverty and inequality manifest in daily lived experience; how art might be able to approach those phenomena and help us keep the nature of the problem in view as we engage in efforts to bring poverty to an end. I want to acknowledge with gratitude everything I've learned from each of you.

There have been continued and sustained interactions with a number of people over the years who gave me opportunities and provided me their feedback, their guidance, and their time. They have helped me learn how to transform observations about the world and about works of art into the sustained arguments I've made across my research and in this book. A simple thank-you does not seem sufficient to recognize the support, guidance, feedback, time, and opportunities Dianna C. Niebylski has given me over the years. I am indebted to her for what I have learned through her individual guidance before, during, and after the process of completing my PhD as well as for what I learned in the courses I took with her over the years. I will forever be grateful for the opportunity to have read Ricardo Piglia, Borges, Julio Cortázar, Valenzuela, and others with her as an undergraduate; to have taken her graduate seminars on nineteenth-century Latin American literature, on the poetry of Vallejo, Neruda, and Paz, on the Gothic and Baroque traditions in Latin American literature, on Borges and his legacy, and on poverty in film and literature. I participated in reading groups with her on *The Exhaustion of Difference*, *The Other Side of the Popular*, *The Art of Transition*, and *The Philosopher and His Poor*, and we worked together on our coedited volume. Dianna introduced me to the work of Sergio Chejfec, and through his work to a wide array of the debates in our field. My hope is that this book can serve as my thanks for all she has given me. Patrick O'Connor, who has read seemingly everything, gave me the gift of his time and his feedback. His ability to concisely synthesize references and ideas pointed me in the direction of the next thing to read and led me to a fuller understanding of connections across works, languages, and genres.

This book is heavily indebted to the work and thought of Walter Benn Michaels. I have been lucky to have had his feedback and suggestions at various points along the path to this book. He introduced me to the work of Michael Fried, which is obviously essential to the arguments of this book. But Michaels's ability to read across painting, photography, sculpture, legal issues, literary theory, economics, political theory, and literature to create a cohesive, singular argument that, nevertheless, takes each work or body of scholarship on its own terms, is an aspirational model. While I do not reach the bar his books set out, his example of a holistic approach to analysis has been important for me, and I am indebted to it throughout this book.

I want to thank my professors at UIC: Margarita Saona, Nena Torres, Cristián Roa, Ellen Baird, Klaus Müller-Bergh, Leon Fink, Ralph Cintron, Matthew Marr, and Rosilie Hernández. My thanks also to Nicholas Brown: his lectures, his scholarship, and conversations with him following campus events have been important for me in the course of developing my work.

Michael Fried's work is essential to the arguments of this book. My thanks to him not only for his scholarship but also for accepting an invitation to give a lecture on my campus in Fort Wayne.

It is not an exaggeration to say that this book would not have been possible without the friendship and support of some amazing scholars, whose influence is present throughout the book. Eugenio Di Stefano has given constant and consistent feedback, encouragement, support, and friendship. Emilio Sauri has always asked questions that helped me see how my arguments could make their fullest claims with precision and clarity, and his understanding friendship has been an important source of support. Eduardo Ledesma has been generous with his time, his feedback, and his friendship. I am a better scholar and writer because of them, and without their friendship and support, I never would have been able to write this book.

The anonymous reviewers of this book provided ample feedback on its arguments. I am pleased with how I was able to respond productively to those critiques to produce the present text. My thanks to Kim Guinta, Emma Downer, Nicole Solano, Vincent Nordhaus, Evelyn Orvaez, and everyone at Rutgers for the opportunity to publish with the press, for their support through the process, and for a wonderful book design. My thanks also to Brian Ostrander at Westchester

Publishing Services and Joseph Dahm for their work in copyediting the manuscript. As with this book, comments and feedback from editors and peer reviewers at the venues where I have published my research over the years have been essential as I have worked to clarify and hone the arguments that have sustained my research. Thank you for the time you spent with my work and for your support.

In recent years, an important source of support and feedback for my work has come through collaborations between *nonsite.org* and *FORMA: A Journal of Latin American Criticism & Theory* (for which I am now editor-in-chief). Many thanks to Jennifer Ashton, Todd Cronan, Charles Palermo, Lisa Siraganian, Davis Smith-Brecheisen, Ken Warren, Rachel Watson, and Daniel Zamora. Conversations with Todd, Charles, and Lisa have been particularly helpful, and I am thankful for their scholarship.

Charles Hatfield organized symposiums that have been important venues where I presented research. *FORMA* began as a conversation between Charles, Emilio, Eugenio, and myself after one of the symposiums Charles organized. Many thanks to Charles for his scholarship and for his support.

I want to extend my thanks to those on the *FORMA* Editorial Board: Bram Acosta, Ericka Beckman, Ignacio M. Sánchez-Prado, Salomé Skvirsky, Irmgard Emmelhainz, and Susana Domingo Amestoy.

I also would like to thank those who helped me early on the path to this book, particularly professors at the University of Kentucky where I completed my undergraduate and master's degrees. Susan Larson recruited me into the Hispanic Studies program at UK when I was deciding on a path after graduating from undergrad. My thanks to her for seeing possibilities for me and suggesting I pursue them. My thanks to Edward Stanton for teaching me how to approach poetry in Spanish with rigor, for connecting me with the work of a wide variety of poets writing in Spanish, and for teaching my first class on literary theory. My thanks also to Aníbal Biglieri, who not only taught me the history of the Spanish language as a graduate student but also was my first contact with the UK Spanish program, sitting with me and my parents when we visited during my senior year in high school as he emphasized study abroad. My thanks also to Sherry Velasco, who gave me a solid foundation in Peninsular literature, and Ana Rueda, who helped me develop an appreciation for eighteenth-century literature. My thanks also go to the faculty in the UK Social Theory program, which was an impactful educational experience for me (e.g., the cotaught graduate seminar, the graduate student journal). Working with Herb Reid and Betsy Taylor was an impactful early experience with political and cultural theory. As an undergraduate, my first experience presenting at a literature conference was under the direction of Brenda Weber, and I will always be grateful for her guidance and the opportunities she gave me. In my very first year of college, Dr. Joe Jones and Dr. Margaret Jones showed me what it meant to take literature and the study of the Spanish language seriously. One of the alumni of the UK Hispanic Studies program, Mary Ann Naser-Hall, was my high school Spanish teacher and helped me acquire my first skills in the language and gave me my first access to some of the authors I would go on to write about in this book and elsewhere. Thank you to all of you.

In 2009 I was able to complete a graduate seminar offered by Boston University in Buenos Aires. My thanks to Alicia Borinsky, Julio Crespo, and the artists who participated in the seminar sessions. While in Buenos Aires, I had the opportunity to meet Marcela Croce, who was generous and took time to meet with me. Thanks to Luis and Marcela Provenzani who hosted me in their home. And my thanks to my fellow students in that seminar, especially Arlene Ovalle-Child and Jill Gonzalez.

My thanks to my students over the years, particularly those students completing research projects under my direction: Cristal Galicia, Nicole Kroetz, Cydney Bridges, Rabia Ibrahim.

I am lucky to have many amazing colleagues and friends in Fort Wayne, and I want to acknowledge and thank them for their support. Rick Weiner and I have regularly discussed our research together in great conversations. I am thankful for the support of Ana Benito, Farah Combs, Maria Conforti, Mike Wolf, and other PFW/IPFW colleagues in ILCS, COLA, COAS, and elsewhere. Many thanks to my library liaisons at the Helmke Library over the years: Margit Codispoti, Susan Anderson, Ann Marshall, and Emily Tock. Special thanks also go to Graham Fredrick and other library staff working with Document Delivery. Thank you to Yvonne Zubovic and others in FACET for providing community on campus to think seriously about good teaching. I also want to express my thanks to Noor O'Neill, David Schuster, and others in the Indiana AAUP. Thanks especially go to Steve Carr, who, in addition to his friendship, has shared with me his knowledge in the areas of governance and academic freedom as well as his knowledge in the areas he teaches and researches. Thank you to all of you.

Nancy Virtue has made working at the university more fun and less stressful over the years. The times we've spent laughing together have been some of the best parts of the time spent writing this book. I am lucky to have her as a friend.

I want to give a big thank-you to the Roberts family: Lee, Suin, Lilly. Lee and Suin, your work across languages and cultures is inspirational, and I have benefitted so much from you as colleagues and friends. Chatting with Lee over lunch, coffee, and cards is something I always look forward to.

Thank you to my family: Paul, Stephanie, Elizabeth, Lilly; Laura, Johnny, John, Angie, Jeremy, Robbie, Joseph; Aunt Carol; Aunt Judy and Ron; Tammy, David, Jenna; Kelci, Anthony, Emmy; Dawn, Jared, Jake. All the time we've spent with each other has helped sustain me, and your love has kept me going in the toughest of times. I love you.

Thank you to Steve and Kathie Eggers and to Erin, Tom, Evelyn, and Arden Hayes. Your support helped me write this book, and I am thankful for all the fun times we've shared.

A huge thank-you to the Malanson family: Jeff, Katie, Sam, and Drew. You've been there for me during the hard times, during celebrations, during everyday challenges and worries, during weekend hikes and evening dinners, and during long, winding conversations and emoji-filled text threads. You have made our life better, and this book was easier to complete because of your friendship.

I have dedicated this book to my parents: Tony and Connie Buttes. I will forever be indebted to them for their unconditional love, for their sacrifices, and for their willingness to do everything in their power to ensure that I received a good education. I have been able to achieve things like this book because of what you made possible for me. I love you.

Most of all, I want to say thank you to Jessica and to Olivia. Thank you for loving me, for laughing with me, and for making the world better every day just by being in it. Completing this book would not have been possible without your support. I love you both so very much.

I want to end with one final acknowledgment: Sergio Chejfec. Some twenty years ago when I first read his work and saw what it made available, my understanding of both art and the world changed. Thank you. May you rest in peace with the knowledge that I and others have learned so much from you. *Más claro se lo ve cuando se lo ve borroso.*

Some material from chapter 3 is included in another essay, "Autogestión and Autonomy: Mexicanism, Cinematic Form and the Legacy of 1968," to appear in Joan C. Hawkins and Joseph Roskos, eds., *Wounded Galaxies, 1968*, vol. 1, *Geopolitics and Culture Wars* (Bloomington: Indiana University Press, forthcoming).

# Notes

## Introduction

1 For several reasons, I am focusing on the common term "poverty" rather than specialized alternative conceptualizations developed by sociologists: for example, Loïc Wacquant's "advanced marginality" and "urban outcasts," Pierre Bourdieu's logic of "disenchantment," Zygmunt Bauman's "outcasts" or "wasted lives," Saskia Sassen's "expulsion," among others. The goal of this book is not to replace the precise sociological analysis of "advanced marginality" or other historical socioeconomic systems of impoverishment with an analysis of literary or artistic approaches to poverty. However correct a specific sociological analysis might be in describing the *forms* that the state and the economic system take in a specific historical sequence, defenders of that unequal system make use of the existence of "poverty" from preceding, more egalitarian historical sequences (however different they might be) as a tool to short-circuit diagnosis of inequality and displace critique. One way to describe what my book is interested in exploring is to say that its interrogation of "poverty" makes available an understanding of how a sophisticated analysis of specific historical *forms* of exploitation and dispossession can so easily slip into a discussion of the transhistorical presence of "poverty" across space and time. That slippage is built, as I argue, on what I describe as a transhistorical experiential account of poverty, which I generally reference as "formlessness" throughout the study. For more on Wacquant's work, see "Penal State," *Punishing the Poor*, and *Urban Outcasts*. See also Bourdieu's *The Weight of the World* and *The Social Structures of the Economy*; Bauman's *Wasted Lives* and *Liquid Times*; Sassen's *Expulsions*. Dianna Niebylski and I provide a survey of a wide range of approaches to poverty in the introduction to our edited volume: *Pobreza y precariedad en el imaginario latinoamericano del siglo XXI*. This volume features essays written by scholars working in Latin America, the United States, and elsewhere. The essays in the volume provide a wide array of approaches to the phenomena of poverty, precarity, and marginality (including some of the sociological and anthropological approaches mentioned above).

2 For a general history of these modes of thinking about poverty, including what has been termed the "First Poverty Enlightenment" (at the end of the eighteenth

century) and the "Second Poverty Enlightenment" (in the 1960s and 1970s), see Ravallion. For a critique of the world emergent from the "Second Poverty Enlightenment," or approaches they term "welfare for markets," see Jäger and Zamora, *Welfare for Markets*.

3 This summary extrapolates what I argue is the common ground that cuts across the three specific country-based sequences I analyze in this book (Mexico, Argentina, Chile). See Ravallion's *The Economics of Poverty* for a more general survey of those arguments as they appear in philosophy and economics.

4 The present study presumes a general familiarity with the twentieth-century political, economic, and aesthetic histories of Latin America generally and Mexico, Argentina, and Chile more specifically. Some sources to fill in details about these phenomena include the following. For a general history of Peronism and its broader context, see Brennan and Rougier, *Politics*; James; Pizzorno; Pozzi; Romero, *Breve Historia*; Sarlo and Altamirano; Tcach. For a history of the Mexican Revolution and its institutionalization in the PRI, see Gauss; Knight; Knight and Pansters; Knight and Rodriguez; Loaeza; Garcíadiego Dantán; Gilly; Páez Varela and Delgado. For an overview and critique of the Mexicanist logic emergent from the PRI, see Bartra, *La jaula*, or my article "Partition of the Pelado." For a general history of Chile's political experience with poverty, see Barr-Melej; Sater and Collier; Frazier. For a recent historical survey of Latin American worker movements in Argentina, Mexico, Chile, and elsewhere, see Bravo Vargas and Mastrángelo. For a general history of twentieth-century political parties and their governments, see Di Tella.

5 In *Urban Outcasts*, Wacquant contrasts "specific forms" with "generic mechanisms." Wacquant's "generic mechanisms" are not synonymous with "formlessness" as I treat it in this study. "Generic mechanisms" instead are, I believe, closer to what Neil Larsen calls social relations in their real abstraction.

6 For more on how experiences of poverty such as unwanted hunger factor into questions of art and politics, see my essay "Para una literatura chorra" in my coedited volume with Niebylski.

7 Amartya Sen's famous work on poverty and famines in the 1980s long ago demonstrated that famines are not unavoidable phenomena of the natural world but instead human-made phenomena. As he notes in a recent article summarizing his previous work, "I have argued . . . that hunger is best seen in terms of failure of 'entitlements' of people, that is, the failure to establish command over an adequate amount of food and other necessities. A person may have few means of commanding enough food if he or she has no job, no other sources of income, and no social security; the hunger that will result can coexist with a plentiful supply of food in the economy and the markets. Famines have, in fact, occurred in situations of high food availability—sometimes even peak food availability" (Sen, "Political Economy of Hunger," 351). The point he has highlighted and continues to highlight is that poverty and famines are the product of social relations (politics and economics). To acknowledge this point is not to accept whole-cloth and uncritically the prescriptions and solutions that emerge from Sen's analysis. That debate would be separate but would productively begin with, for example, Jäger and Zamora's *Welfare for Markets* and Wacquant's *Urban Outcasts* and *Punishing the Poor*. But it is important to cite Sen's insight on the manmade nature of poverty and to say that he is correct in noting that it is a "decisively solvable" problem and that "it is [not] a tragedy that is essentially unpreventable (in the way ancient Greek tragedies were)" (*Development as Freedom* 204). For more on Sen's views, see "The Political Economy of Hunger" (2019), the expanded edition of *Collective Choice*

*and Social Welfare* (2017), *Development as Freedom* (1999), and his classic study *Poverty and Famines* (1981).

8 For the accounts of modernism informing my approach in this study, see Michaels, *Our America*; Siraganian, *Modernism's Other Work* and *Modernism and the Meaning of Corporate Persons*; Pippin, *Persistence of Subjectivity*; and Fried, *Manet's Modernism*. Fried utilizes the metaphor of the "hinge"—the linking of concrete pictorial strategies of the past with subsequent historical sequences—as what ultimately establishes antitheatricality as a "tradition" within the development of modernism. That "hinge" structure is similarly helpful for me in elaborating the tradition of poverty aesthetics I analyze in this study.

9 For a general economic history of Latin America, see Bulmer-Thomas. For an overview of social relations on haciendas, see Newman. The "culture of poverty" was a term developed in Oscar Lewis's study of Mexican families, *Five Families: Mexican Case Studies in the Culture of Poverty* (1959). The term later migrated to debates about poverty in the United States. For an analysis of that term and the role it played in the United States, see Jäger and Zamora (60–62).

10 For an extended explanation of the term "structures of feeling," see Raymond Williams (128–135).

11 For a discussion of the crisis of 1956 in the context of Pablo Neruda's poetry, see Greg Dawes, *Multiforme y comprometido* and chapter 2 of this book. For more on socialist realism in Latin America, see Fierro, Kite, and Lewin.

12 Fidel, of course, refers to Fidel Castro (1926–2016), who led a leftist guerrilla war (the Cuban Revolution [1956–1959] against the Fulgencio Batista dictatorship [1952–1959]). Following success in the revolution on January 1, 1959, Fidel ruled Cuba with an authoritarian and anti-imperialist bent from 1959 to 2008. Omar Torrijos (1929–1981) came to power in a military coup that ended civilian rule in Panama in 1968. Torrijos was a nationalist, perhaps best known for securing the treaties that brought an end to the Canal Zone and eventual Panamanian sovereignty over the Panama Canal. While Torrijos was friendly with Fidel and, for example, provided refuge for leftist Sandinista rebels fighting against the Somoza dictatorship in Nicaragua, he also provided refuge for the military authoritarian Shah of Iran in the wake of the Iranian Revolution. As one reference source puts it, "[Torrijos] was condemned as a Marxist stooge in the United States and as Uncle Sam's puppet by critics in his own country" ("Omar Torrijos" in *Encyclopedia of World Biography*). Perón, as explored in more detail later in this introduction, was also a military man and developed his own eclectic brand of nationalism (Justicialism), which became a hallmark of working-class politics in the country throughout the twentieth century.

13 For a discussion of the limits of projects valorizing regional or national identity, which have been a cornerstone of politics, culture, and art in Latin America since the late nineteenth century, see Charles Hatfield's *The Limits of Identity*. One of many important components of Hatfield's study is his critique of the underlying logic of José Martí's influential essay "Nuestra América" as well as that of Roberto Fernández Retamar's *Calibán*. Both works were important in the anti-imperialist intellectual framework of the Cuban Revolution and Fidel's government. See also Beckman's *Capital Fictions*, which shows how a defense of "free commerce" was also derivable from (and, at times, explicitly stated) in Martí's writing (23–28). For an account of the problems embedded in projects valorizing an anti-imperialist regional or national identity in the United States, see Michaels, *Our America*.

14 In this introduction, I usually refer to the phenomenon as Justicialism rather than Peronism so as to avoid having my analysis bleed over into the broad array of

political groups that adopted the label of "Peronism" but had vastly different programs or dynamics than those I critique here. For a description and analysis of the Justicialist economic and political program, see, for example, Brennan and Rougier, *Politics*; Romero, *Breve Historia*.

15 *La fuerza es el derecho de las bestias*, or *Strength Is the Law of Beasts*, is a collection of heterogeneous texts (newspaper interviews, speeches from his time in power, memoir-like narrative accounts of his life in exile) published in 1956. Perón sought to produce an "accessible" and "[panoramic]" take on "Argentina's situation" after the 1955 coup that toppled his government (known as the Revolución Libertadora [Liberating Revolution]).

16 "Ningún justicialista debe sentirse más de lo que es ni menos de lo que debe ser. Cuando un justicialista comienza a sentirse más de lo que es, empieza a convertirse en oligarca" (Perón 14).

17 The "Day of Peronist Loyalty," or Día de la Lealtad Peronista, was an annual celebration that took place on October 17. It commemorated October 17, 1945, when "thousands of protestors gathered in the Plaza de Mayo and demanded Perón's freedom" from the military junta's imprisonment of him and his reinstatement as the secretary of labor. They also demanded that the junta hold elections. Perón was eventually released, "spoke to the crowd," and set into motion the events that would carry him to elected power and secure his reelection in 1951 (Romero, *History* 97). This annual event is paradigmatic of the dialogue between the words of the leader and the joyous responses of the crowds gathered in the plazas and streets of the country in regular public gatherings organized by Perón's government.

18 As Paul Bowman notes, "What something is and what it does is always a matter of articulation: 'effects' are matters of connections, relations, reticulations, interruptions. In fact, articulation is to be construed as the central concept of both cultural studies and post-Marxism. The same can be said for deconstruction" (181–182). See *Post-Marxism versus Cultural Studies: Theory, Politics and Intervention*. For an important critique of cultural studies and articulation, see Jon Beasley-Murray's *Posthegemony*, esp. 15–67 (more on Beasley-Murray's critique follows in this introduction).

19 The term "hegemony" has varying historical and theoretical traditions and trajectories. In the field of Latin American cultural and political theory since the 1990s, the work of Italian Marxist Antonio Gramsci has been central. As Beasley-Murray notes in *Posthegemony*, taking on the Gramscian framework as a target of his critique, hegemony is "the notion . . . that the state maintains its dominance (and that of social and economic elites) thanks to the consent of those it dominates. Where it does not win consent, this theory suggests, the state resorts to coercion" (x). Beasley-Murray argues for an alternative to "hegemony theory" in his book and directly critiques (as I do here) the framework developed by Laclau and Mouffe. However, I also part ways with Beasley-Murray in my critique of his "posthegemony theory." Larsen's *Modernism and Hegemony* has detailed the history of the development of the concept of hegemony and acknowledges the "general ideological and intellectual import" (Larsen, *Modernism* xxvii) of Laclau and Mouffe's work in *Hegemony and Socialist Strategy*, given its status as something like the "culmination of the postmodernist road to 'politics' via Lyotard [and] of a self-referential series of poststructuralist attempts to trace the route from deconstruction and the critique of the sign into some new Marxian/post-Marxian vision of revolutionary strategy" (xxvii–xxviii). Larsen draws careful and clear parallels between Jean-François Lyotard's concept of "paralogy"—internal elements within the interplay of language continually produce modifications, variations, and thus new rules that subvert or destabilize at a local level any

overarching claim by a state to dominate the social whole—and the operation of articulation in Laclau and Mouffe (see xxvi–xxviii). For related critiques of Lyotard, Gilles Deleuze, Michel Foucault, and Susan Sontag, see Lash, *Sociology of Postmodernism* (100–113 and 172–180). For an additional critique of posthegemony, see Di Stefano and Sauri, "Making It Visible." For an important account of the history of hegemony and posthegemony in the field of Latin American studies and what he has called "a methodological impasse" or "deadlock of resistance" in the field's approaches and procedures, see Acosta, *Thresholds of Illiteracy* and "The Posthegemonic Turn."

20 In scholarship around the notion of the "culturally" or locally "appropriate" in Latin America, the key term utilized since at least the 1990s has been "autochthony": for example, the wager for an "autochthonous modernity" or the utilization of "autochthonous materials" in the writing of literary works. For early examples of this, see Julio Ramos's *Divergent Modernities* (1989, translated in 2001) or Alonso's *The Spanish American Regional Novel* (1990). For more recent examples, see Dalton's *Mestizo Modernity* (2021) or Khan's "Chimera" (2022).

21 The "not-yet-fully-articulated" element, or those who cannot "speak" via the readily available forms in existing modes of social organization, are explicitly related to the conceptualization of the "subaltern" as that figure was analyzed in postcolonial criticism since the late 1980s. The Latin American Subaltern Studies Group (roughly 1992–1998) structured the development of some of the most significant works of scholarship in the field of the late twentieth century as well as innovative approaches to the intersections of politics and art. For an overview from the period, see Rodríguez, *Latin American Subaltern Studies Reader* (2001). See also Moreiras, *Exhaustion of Difference* and Williams, *Other Side of the Popular*. For developments over the past two decades, see Beverley, *Latinamericanism after 9/11*; Acosta, *Thresholds of Illiteracy*; Hatfield, *Limits of Identity*; Di Stefano, *Vanishing Frame*; Williams in Poblete, *New Approaches to Latin American Studies*.

22 Laclau actually acknowledges a version of this assertion in his essay "The Impossibility of Society." In that essay, Laclau argues that "society tries to institute itself as such on the basis of closure, of the fixation of meaning, of the non-recognition of the infinite play of differences" (92). However, because there is "the impossibility of any ultimate suture" (92), such an effort would be directed at constructing an "impossible object: society" (92).

23 For an account of the competing theories of affect and a critique of affect theory more generally, see the essential volume *The Ascent of Affect* by Ruth Leys. See Di Stefano, *Vanishing Frame*, Hatfield, *Limits of Identity*, and Di Stefano and Sauri, "Making It Visible" for critiques of affect theory in Latin American studies. For additional perspectives, see Moraña and Sánchez Prado, Reber, and Laura Podalsky's chapter in Poblete, *New Approaches*.

24 Beasley-Murray engages Hardt and Negri's writing on the multitude at length in his book and develops his own critical approach to the term. I discuss Beasley-Murray's and others' account of the multitude in chapter 3 of this book. See also my article "Re-fictionalizing the Argentine Dream" (2017) for a more direct critique of Hardt and Negri and their transhistorical account of poverty.

## Chapter 1 Managing to Get By

1 For an overview of Monterde's work through the 1950s, see Zelson.

2 As Yáñez tells Carballo, the "silence" that characterized his literary and intellectual production between 1930 and 1940 is the collapse of the availability of publication

outlets for intellectual and literary production. Nevertheless, as he claims, he did write the first essay in Mexico engaging in substantial ways with Heidegger's thought ("La nada en Martín Heidegger") as well as an additional essay pairing the work of Heidegger and Kierkegaard ("Kirkegaard y Heidegger"). While he does not mention his work for Monterde's series in the interview, it is clear that his work on Heidegger was simultaneous with the work he completed for the "Estudio preliminar" I discuss here (all published in 1940). See López Domínguez and Aparicio (225–249).

3 See the list of works published in the series in the entry on the collection in *Enciclopedia de la literatura en México*. The prologues Yáñez wrote for his contributions to the series, including his prologue to an anthology of the writings of Fray Bartolomé de las Casas, were collected and published by El Colegio de México in 1945. See *Fichas mexicanas*.

4 The conversation appears as follows: "Sacristán: Nuestra conversación no es de lo más limpio. . . . el Payo: Es verdad; pero ella se dirige a la limpieza." The more literal translation of Lizardi's text would be something closer to the following: "Our conversation isn't the purest. . . . It's true, but it aims to purify things." My translation in the main text seeks to give the sense in which Yáñez was glossing Lizardi's works in the anthology rather than being a translation of Lizardi in the context of the work. This also makes clearer the link I am drawing between Yáñez's PRI-ist aesthetic and political project and the dynamics of aesthetic and political form understood as an open-ended giving expression to the experience of formlessness that is understood as coterminous with poverty.

5 As just one example of this word play, we can consider the episode in volume 1 of *El periquillo sarniento* in which Pedro describes his early experiences with a schoolteacher, who, through punctuation and grammatical errors, seems to create a blasphemous play on words (operating as Lizardi's satirical critique of religious and educational institutions all at once through these linguistic displacements).

6 "Los paseos" is a text in which a writer, plagued by an insomnia-producing worry about debts and payments coming due, finally falls into a deep sleep and is guided in ghostlike form by a beautiful woman he recognizes as Truth. She guides him to serve as a witness to the crimes and corruption of the society in which he lives. She calls on him to write about them so that they can be corrected.

7 The phrase "our improper way of talking about things is aimed at giving them their proper form" is a paraphrased version of the passage Yáñez highlights from "Constitución política." It combines the two pieces of the idea shared by two characters into a single line. As noted earlier, the passage is: "Our way of talking about things certainly isn't proper . . . [but it] is aimed at giving things their proper form." For questions of style, I will use the paraphrased version interchangeably with the quoted version here.

8 "Plebeyos, indios, mulatos, negros, viciosos, tontos y majaderos" (Steinberg, "Originary" 54).

## Chapter 2 Icons of the Everyday

1 For an extended treatment of the satirization of Neruda and the international left from this period, see the important and excellent work by Salinas and others in Salinas C., *El Chile de Juan Verdejo*. For an account of how Peronism was processed and circulated in Chile through the political satire of *Topaze*, see Acuña.

2 As Fried has explained in his "trilogy *Absorption and Theatricality*, *Courbet's Realism*, and *Manet's Modernism*" there is a "current or tradition of antitheatrical

critical thought and pictorial practice" that emerged in France and "runs from Diderot and Jean-Baptiste Greuze in the 1750s and 1760s through David Géricault, Daumier, Courbet, Millet, Legros, and Fantin-Latour among others, along with a matching list of art critics, until it reaches a crisis of unsustainability in the art of Edouard Manet in the 1860s and 1870s. Thereafter it undergoes a fundamental change (of orientation, rather than purpose) that on the one hand indicates that the Diderotian project—of effectively denying the presence before the painting of the beholder—was no longer feasible in any of its classic forms but on the other suggests that the problem of the beholder—of acknowledging his presence while not addressing him in the wrong way—was now absolutely fundamental to advanced painting and sculpture" first in France and later the United States (*Why Photography* 99–100). Antitheatricality was premised on establishing the work of art as a mode of access to truth, and the "classic" pictorial strategies utilized to secure that status (e.g., absorption, the pastoral conception) were premised on compelling in the beholder the sense that "nothing in a [painting] . . . [is put] there *for him*" (100) to see or look at. That fiction (paintings are only painted to be looked at) was interrupted in its "classic forms" by things like "the too obvious use of contrast on the part of the artist" (100), which created a scenario of "falsity" or deliberate attempt to produce a reaction in (or manipulate) the beholder. As Fried explains, those "classic forms" enter into crisis in the 1860s and 1870s, but the fundamental issue for "advanced" art remained how the artwork could effectively establish a relationship with the beholder and achieve under a new historical sequence its status as a mode of access to truth about the world. Fried explains in *Art and Objecthood* that the operating premise of Minimalist or literalist art—"artworks" are simply objects in space that produce a situation of encounter—departs from a belief that art cannot or no longer will be able to achieve this status. The works Fried champions in that essay, however, are premised on the belief that achieving such a status is still possible. And the locus of that debate—is art something other than an object in the world—is the relationship between the artwork and the beholder. Neruda's central concern in his new poetic practice in the *Odas* is precisely the relationship between the poem and the reader as well as the related issue of the poet's labor and the labor of other workers in the world. Neruda's poetic practice in the *Odas* veers toward an embrace of "theatricality": what is in the poem is put there only for the workers who will "use" the poems to create a transformed world. While it's fairly clear why this union of aesthetics and politics would seem a viable path for a committed communist like Neruda, the goal of this chapter is to demonstrate that he did not fully reckon with the issues of theatricality-antitheatricality and, as a result, arrives at results that are insufficient for achieving the broader goals he has for the collection. For more on the political logic of theatricality and literalism, see Michaels, *Shape* and Di Stefano.

3 The historical sequencing of neoliberalism in Chile typically begins with Augusto Pinochet's 1973 coup and the economic plan of the "Chicago Boys," generally called El Ladrillo ("The Brick"). However, as some economic historians have demonstrated (and as I have tracked in cultural production in Chile), those neoliberal policies have an earlier provenance in Chile, starting in the 1950s with the hiring of the Washington, D.C.-based economic consulting firm Klein & Saks (which had previously been hired in Peru in the 1940s). See further explanation in my article "Cold War Caricatures."

4 This is perhaps confirmed by the fact that when the *Odas* were first published, they were praised by the conservative literary critic Alone while the left-wing poet Pablo de Rokha critiqued them. See Concha.

5 See Dawes's discussion of his agreements and disagreements with Sicard. See particularly chapter 3, note 92, where Dawes elaborates Sicard's thesis regarding "el Neruda diurno" (the Neruda of daylight) and "el Neruda nocturno" (the nocturnal Neruda), or, more broadly, the Neruda of light and shadow.

## Chapter 3 The Afterlife of Mexico, 1968

1 The legacy of 1968 is often pursued along national history lines. More recent scholarship has sought to track the interactions and interconnections between these seemingly disparate movements (the "global 68"). See Hawkins and Roskos, *Wounded Galaxies*. In that volume, I published an alternative version of the present chapter, focusing on different films and a different (though related) set of arguments and issues.

## Chapter 4 Photography and Borges's Landscapes of Poverty

1 For more on the use of the "public image" of writers, artists, musicians, and film stars in Latin America, see Niebylski and O'Connor's edited volume.
2 See Fried, *Why Photography Matters* and Michaels, *Beauty*.
3 Similarly, notes Salvesen, these photographers were turning away from a second tradition of commodification in landscape photography in their era: real estate photographs. Both Ansel Adams's "monumental" and commodified landscape photographs and real estate photographs focus on making "the subject itself attractive" ("'Real Estate'" 82) to a viewer. While the former wanted viewers to *conserve* the special places seen in the image (i.e., leave undeveloped), the latter wanted viewers to *buy* the special places seen in the image (i.e., develop). New Topographics photographers reacted against both tendencies in order to achieve for their photographs their status as pictures (as art). See Salvesen, "'Real Estate.'"
4 On this point, see Michaels, *Beauty*.
5 For more on Borges and history, see Balderston's *Out of Context*.

## Conclusion

1 See Jensen for reporting on this issue. For more on literature and the Anaconda Copper Company, see Siraganian, "Stateless Regionalism."

# Works Cited


Acosta, Abraham. "(De)Colonial Sources: The Coloniality of Power, Reoriginalization, and the Critique of Imperialism." *FORMA* 1.1 (2019): 17–36. https://formajournal.org.

———. "The Posthegemonic Turn." *New Approaches to Latin American Studies: Culture and Power*. Ed. Juan Poblete. London: Routledge, 2017. 255–271.

———. *Thresholds of Illiteracy: Theory, Latin America, and the Crisis of Resistance.* New York: Fordham University Press, 2014.

Acuña, Pedro. "Transnational Visual Parodies: Political Cartoons of Perón in the Chilean Satirical Magazine *Topaze*, 1943–1958." *Latin American Research Review* 59 (2024): 610–635.

Adams, Robert, et al. *New Topographics*. 3rd ed. Center for Creative Photography, University of Arizona, 2013.

Adorno, Theodor W. *Aesthetic Theory*. Trans. Robert Hullot-Kentor. Minneapolis: University of Minnesota Press, 1997.

*Ahí está el detalle*. Dir. Juan Bustillo Oro. Grovas-Oro Films, Cozumel Films, 2003.

Alonso, Carlos J. "Borges y la teoría." *MLN* 120.2 (2005): 437–56.

———. *The Spanish American Regional Novel: Modernity and Autochthony*. Cambridge: Cambridge University Press, 1990.

Balderston, Daniel. "Evocation and Provocation in Borges: The Figure of Juan Muraña." *Borges the Poet*. Ed. Carlos Cortínez. Fayetteville: University of Arkansas Press, 1986. 325–332.

———. *Out of Context: Historical Reference and the Representation of Reality in Borges*. Durham, NC: Duke University Press, 1993.

Barr-Melej, Patrick. *Reforming Chile: Politics, Nationalism and the Rise of the Middle Class*. Chapel Hill: University of North Carolina Press, 2001.

Bartra, Roger. *The Cage of Melancholy: Identity and Metamorphosis in the Mexican Character*. New Brunswick, NJ: Rutgers University Press, 1992.

———. *La jaula de la melancolía: Identidad y metamorfosis del mexicano*. México: Grijalbo, 1996.

Bauman, Zygmunt. *Liquid Times: Living in an Age of Uncertainty*. Cambridge: Polity, 2011.

———. *Wasted Lives: Modernity and Its Outcasts*. Cambridge: Polity, 2017.

Beasley-Murray, Jon. *Posthegemony: Political Theory and Latin America*. Minneapolis: University of Minnesota Press, 2010.
Beckman, Ericka. *Capital Fictions: The Literature of Latin America's Export Age*. Minneapolis: University of Minnesota Press, 2013.
Beverley, John. *Latinamericanism after 9/11*. Durham, NC: Duke University Press, 2011.
Borges, Jorge Luis. *Obras completas*. Vols. 1–4. Buenos Aires: Emecé, 2002.
———. "Post-Lecture Discussion of His Own Writing." *Critical Inquiry* 1.4 (1975): 719–722.
———. "Walt Whitman: Man and Myth." *Critical Inquiry* 1.4 (1975): 707–718.
Bosteels, Bruno. *La comuna mexicana*. Trans. Simone Pinet. Mexico: Akal, 2021.
———. *Marx and Freud in Latin America: Politics, Psychoanalysis, and Religion in Times of Terror*. London: Verso, 2012.
———. "The Mexican Commune." https://columbia.academia.edu/BrunoBosteels.
Boterbloem, Kees. *The Life and Times of Andrei Zhdanov, 1896–1948*. Montreal: McGill-Queen's University Press, 2004.
Bourdieu, Pierre. *The Social Structures of the Economy*. Trans. Chris Turner. Cambridge: Polity, 2016.
Bourdieu, Pierre, and Alain Accardo. *The Weight of the World: Social Suffering in Contemporary Society*. Trans. Priscilla Parkhurst Ferguson. Cambridge: Polity, 2019.
Bowman, Paul. *Post-Marxism versus Cultural Studies: Theory, Politics and Intervention*. Edinburgh: Edinburgh University Press, 2007.
Bravo Vargas, Viviana, and Mariana Mastrángelo, eds. *La izquierda en movimiento: Clase trabajadora y luchas populares en América Latina (Siglos XX y XXI)*. Buenos Aires: CLACSO, 2022. https://doi.org/10.2307/j.ctv3142tt6.
Brennan, James P., and Marcelo Rougier, eds. *Peronism and Argentina*. Wilmington, DE: Scholarly Resources, 1998.
———. *The Politics of National Capitalism Peronism and the Argentine Bourgeoisie, 1946–1976*. University Park: Pennsylvania State University Press, 2009.
Brown, Nicholas. *Autonomy: The Social Ontology of Art under Capitalism*. Durham, NC: Duke University Press, 2019. Kindle ed.
Bulmer-Thomas, Victor. *The Economic History of Latin America since Independence*. 3rd ed. New York: Cambridge University Press, 2014.
Buttes, Stephen. "Autogestión and Autonomy: Mexicanism, Cinematic Form and the Legacy of 1968." *Wounded Galaxies, 1968*. Vol. 1: *Geopolitics and Culture Wars*. Ed. Joan C. Hawkins and Joseph Roskos. Bloomington: Indiana University Press, forthcoming.
———. "Cold War Caricatures: *Topaze*, Hunger and the Politics of Poverty in 1960s Chile." *Chasqui* 46.1 (2017): 244–260.
———. "The Failure of Consuelo's Designs: Carlos Fuentes and Trompe l'Oeil Modernity." *Revista Canadiense de Estudios Hispánicos* 41.2 (2017): 437–464.
———. "The Partition of the Pelado: Poverty, Art, and the Making of the PRI." *FORMA* 1.1 (2019): 37–61.
———. "Re-fictionalizing the Argentine Dream: Poverty and the Return to Literature in *La virgen cabeza*." *A contracorriente* 14.3 (2017): 200–219.
———. "Shantytown Vistas and Immigrant Voices: Bernardo Verbitsky, Kenneth Kemble and the Art of Overcoming Peronism." *Revista de Estudios Hispánicos* 47 (2013): 267–290.
Buttes, Stephen, and Dianna C. Niebylski, eds. *Pobreza y precariedad en el imaginario latinoamericano del siglo XXI*. Santiago: Cuarto Propio, 2016.
Caillebotte, Gustave. *Le Pont de l'Europe*. 1876. Oil on canvas. Musée du Petit-Palais, Geneva, Switzerland.

———. *On the Pont de l'Europe*. 1876–1877. Oil on canvas. Kimbell Art Museum, Fort Worth, TX.

———. *Paris Street, Rainy Day*. 1877. Oil on canvas. Charles H. and Mary F. S. Worcester Collection. Art Institute of Chicago.

*Cananea*. Dir. Marcela Fernández Violante; Cinematography by Gabriel Figueroa. Mexican Film Institute (IMCINE), 1976.

Carballo, Emmanuel. *Protagonistas de la literatura mexicana*. 4th ed. Mexico City: Porrúa, 1994.

Chardin, Jean-Baptiste-Siméon. *The Game of Knucklebones*. Ca. 1734. Oil on canvas. Mary Frick Jacobs Collection. Baltimore Museum of Art.

———. *Soap Bubbles*. Ca. 1733–1734. Oil on canvas. Wentworth Fund, 1949. Metropolitan Museum of Art, New York.

Clark, Katerina. "Socialist Realism in Soviet Literature." *From Symbolism to Socialist Realism: A Reader*. Ed. Irene Masing-Delic. Newton, MA: Academic Studies Press, 2012. 419–432.

Concha, Jaime. "Estudio introductorio." *Odas elementales*. Ed. Jaime Concha. Madrid: Ediciones Cátedra, 1985.

Dalton, David S. *Mestizo Modernity: Race, Technology, and the Body in Post-Revolutionary Mexico*. Gainesville: University Press of Florida, 2021.

Dawes, Greg. *Multiforme y comprometido: Pablo Neruda después de 1956*. Santiago de Chile: RIL editores, 2014. eBook.

———. *Verses Against the Darkness: Pablo Neruda's Poetry and Politics*. Lewisburg, PA: Bucknell University Press, 2006.

*De todos modos Juan te llamas*. Dir. Marcela Fernández Violante. 1974. FilmotecaUNAM on YouTube. https://youtu.be/KV9CkcVEQoM.

Di Stefano, Eugenio Claudio. *The Vanishing Frame: Latin American Culture and Theory in the Postdictatorial Era*. Austin: University of Texas Press, 2018.

Di Stefano, Eugenio Claudio, and Emilio Sauri. "Making It Visible: Latin Americanist Criticism, Literature, and the Question of Exploitation Today." *Nonsite.org*, no. 13 (October 13, 2014). https://nonsite.org/making-it-visible.

Di Tella, Torcuato S. *History of Political Parties in Twentieth-Century Latin America*. London: Routledge, 2004.

Dove, Patrick. *Literature and Interregnum*. Albany: State University of New York Press, 2016.

Draper, Susana. *1968 Mexico: Constellations of Freedom and Democracy*. Durham, NC: Duke University Press, 2018.

*Enciclopedia de la literatura en México*. http://www.elem.mx/obra/coleccion/21.

Fernández Violante, Marcela. "'We Are Losing Our Identity': An Interview with Mexican Director Marcela Fernández Violante." Interview by Andrew Horton. *Literature/Film Quarterly* 15.1 (1987): 2–7.

*Fichas mexicanas*. Mexico City: Colegio de México, 1945. https://doi.org/10.2307/j.ctv8pzbnt.

Fierro, Alfonso. "The Proletarian Commune in Veracruz: José Manscidor's *La ciudad roja*." *Hispanic Review* 90.1 (2022): 83–105.

Foster-Rice, Greg, and John Rohrbach, eds. *Reframing the New Topographics*. Chicago: Center for American Places at Columbia College Chicago, 2010.

———. "'Systems Everywhere': New Topographics, and Art of the 1970s." *Reframing the New Topographics*. Ed. Greg Foster-Rice and John Rohrbach. Chicago: Center for American Places at Columbia College Chicago, 2010.

Frazier, Lessie Jo. *Salt in the Sand: Memory, Violence, and the Nation-State in Chile, 1890 to the Present*. Durham, NC: Duke University Press, 2007.

*Frida Kahlo: Pintura Mexicana*. Dir. Marcela Fernández Violante. 1971. FilmotecaUNAM on YouTube. https://youtu.be/IeiohNzT1yE.

Fried, Michael. *Absorption and Theatricality: Painting and Beholder in the Age of Diderot*. Berkeley: University of California Press, 1980.

———. *Another Light: Jacques-Louis David to Thomas Demand*. New Haven, CT: Yale University Press, 2014.

———. *Art and Objecthood: Essays and Reviews*. Chicago: University of Chicago Press, 1998.

———. *Courbet's Realism*. Chicago: University of Chicago Press, 1990.

———. "Density of Decision: Greenberg with Robert Adams." *Nonsite.org*, no. 19 (May 3, 2016). https://nonsite.org/density-of-decision.

———. *Manet's Modernism; or, The Face of Painting in the 1860s*. Chicago: University of Chicago Press, 1996.

———. *The Moment of Caravaggio*. Princeton, NJ: Princeton University Press, 2010.

———. *Why Photography Matters as Art as Never Before*. New Haven, CT: Yale University Press, 2008.

Garcíadiego Dantán, Javier, ed. *México (Moderno): A través de sus décadas*. Mexico City: El Colegio Nacional, 2019.

Gauss, Susan M. 2011. *Made in Mexico: Regions, Nation, and the State in the Rise of Mexican Industrialism, 1920s–1940s*. University Park: Pennsylvania State University Press.

Giblett, Rod, and Juha Tolonen. *Photography and Landscape*. Chicago: University of Chicago Press, 2012.

Gilly, Adolfo. *La revolución interrumpida*. 1971. Mexico City: Ediciones ERA, 2014.

Hatfield, Charles. *The Limits of Identity: Politics and Poetics in Latin America*. Austin: University of Texas Press, 2015.

Hawkins, Joan C., and Joseph Roskos, eds. *Wounded Galaxies, 1968*. Vol. 1: *Geopolitics and Culture Wars*. Bloomington: Indiana University Press, forthcoming.

*Histoire d'un Document: Historia de un documento*. Dir. Oscar Menéndez. Editorial La Rana Del Sur, 2004.

Jäger, Anton, and Daniel Zamora. *Welfare for Markets: A Global History of Basic Income*. Chicago: University of Chicago Press, 2023.

James, Daniel. *Resistance and Integration: Peronism and the Argentine Working Class, 1946–1976*. Cambridge: Cambridge University Press, 2001.

Jenkins, William, Nancy Hall-Duncan, and International Museum of Photography at George Eastman House. *New Topographics: Photographs of a Man-Altered Landscape; Robert Adams, Lewis Baltz, Bernd and Hilla Becher, Joe Deal, Frank Gohlke, Nicholas Nixon, John Schott, Stephen Shore, Henry Wessel, Jr.* Rochester, NY: International Museum of Photography at George Eastman House, 1975.

Jensen, Michael C. "Anaconda to Sell Mexico 51% of Its Cananea Mine." *New York Times*, August 28, 1971, 31.

Jurovics, Toby. "Same as It Ever Was: Re-reading New Topographics." *Reframing the New Topographics*. Ed. Greg Foster-Rice and John Rohrbach. Chicago: Center for American Places at Columbia College Chicago, 2010. 1–12.

Khan, Zoya. "*El Mapa de Luto* and the Chimera of a Kharisiri State: Subjectivity, Territoriality and Literature in *La Senda de Kharisiri*." *Bulletin of Spanish Studies* 99.2 (2022): 323–347.

Kite, Ralph. "Socialist Realism and the Spanish American Novel." PhD thesis, University of New Mexico, 1967.

Knight, Alan. *La Revolución Mexicana: Del Porfiriato al nuevo régimen constitucional.* Trans. Luis Cortés Bargalló and Argelia Castillo. Mexico City: Fondo de Cultura Económica, 2012.

Knight, Alan, and W. G. Pansters, eds. *Caciquismo in Twentieth-Century Mexico.* London: Institute for the Study of the Americas, 2005.

Knight, Alan, and Jaime Rodriguez. "The Mexican Revolution, 1910–1940." *Oxford Bibliographies in Latin American Studies.* https://www.oxfordbibliographies.com/view/document/obo-9780199766581/obo-9780199766581-0033.xml.

Laclau, Ernesto. "The Impossibility of Society." *New Reflections on the Revolution of Our Time.* London: Verso, 2010. 89–92.

———. *On Populist Reason.* London: Verso, 2005.

Laclau, Ernesto, and Chantal Mouffe. *Hegemony and Socialist Strategy: Towards a Radical Democratic Politics.* 2nd ed. London: Verso, 2014.

Larsen, Neil. *Determinations: Essays on Theory, Narrative, and Nation in the Americas.* London: Verso, 2001.

———. *Modernism and Hegemony: A Materialist Critique of Aesthetic Agencies.* Minneapolis: University of Minnesota Press, 1990.

———. *Reading North by South: On Latin American Literature, Culture, and Politics.* Minneapolis: University of Minnesota Press, 1995.

Lash, Scott. *Sociology of Postmodernism.* London: Routledge, 1990.

Lewin, Josefina. "La plástica comunista chilena ante el Realismo Socialista durante el preámbulo de la Guerra Fría (1948–1952)." *Arte, Individuo y Sociedad* 36.2 (2024): 353–367. https://dx.doi.org/10.5209/aris.91179.

Lewis, Oscar. *Five Families: Mexican Case Studies in the Culture of Poverty.* New York: Basic Books, 1959.

Leys, Ruth. *The Ascent of Affect: Genealogy and Critique.* Chicago: University of Chicago Press, 2017.

Lizardi, José Joaquí Fernández de. *El periquillo sarniento.* Ed. Carmen Ruiz Barrionuevo. 2nd ed. Madrid: Cátedra, 2008.

Loaeza, Soledad. *A La Sombra de La Superpotencia Tres Presidentes Mexicanos En La Guerra Fría, 1945–1958.* Mexico City: El Colegio de México, Centro de Estudios Internacionales, 2022.

López Domínguez, Héctor, and Héctor Aparicio. "Dos ensayos sobre Heidegger de Agustín Yáñez." *Theoría. Revista del Colegio de Filosofía* 38 (June 2020): 225–249. https://doi.org/10.22201/ffyl.16656415p.2020.38.1355.

Louis, Annick. "El testamento. Formas de realismp en *El informe de Brodie.*" *Jorge Luis Borges: Políticas de la literatura.* Ed. Juan Pablo Dabove. Pittsburgh: IILI, 2008. 331–354.

Loyola, Hernán. Estudio. *Obras completas de Pablo Neruda.* Vol 2. Ed. Hernán Loyola. Barcelona: RBA, 2005.

Michaels, Walter Benn. *The Beauty of a Social Problem: Photography, Autonomy, Economy.* Chicago: University of Chicago Press, 2015.

———. *The Gold Standard and the Logic of Naturalism: American Literature at the Turn of the Century.* Berkeley: University of California Press, 1987.

———. *Our America: Nativism, Modernism, and Pluralism.* Durham, NC: Duke University Press, 1995.

———. *The Shape of the Signifier: 1967 to the End of History.* Princeton, NJ: Princeton University Press, 2004.

*Misterio.* Dir. Marcela Fernández Violante. 1979. Alexander Street Academic Video Online.

Monsiváis, Carlos. *Escenas de pudor y liviandad*. Mexico City: Grijalbo, 1988.
———. *Mexican Postcards*. Trans. John Kraniauskas. London: Verso, 1997.
Monterde, Francisco, ed. *El libro del Consejo*. Mexico City: UNAM, 1939.
Moraña, Mabel, and Ignacio M. Sánchez Prado, eds. *El lenguaje de las emociones: Afecto y cultura en América Latina*. Madrid: Iberoamericana-Vervuert, 2012.
Moreiras, Alberto. *The Exhaustion of Difference: The Politics of Latin American Cultural Studies*. Durham, NC: Duke University Press, 2001.
Mosler, John, and Alexis González. "Marcela Fernández Violante: A Filmmaker Apart." *Américas* (January–February 1983): 14–19.
Mualem, Shlomy. "The Imminence of Revelation: Aesthetics and Poetics Expression in Early Wittgenstein and Borges." *Variaciones Borges* 18 (2004): 197–217.
Museum of Modern Art. "New Mexican Films to Be Presented Here." Press release, January 1977. https://moma.org.
———. "Recent Mexican Films at Museum." Press release, June 1974. https://moma.org.
Neruda, Pablo. "Hacia la ciudad espléndida." Nobel lecture, December 13, 1971. https://www.nobelprize.org/prizes/literature/1971/neruda/25206-pablo-neruda-nobel-lecture-1971/.
———. *Obras completas*. Ed. Hernán Loyola. Barcelona: RBA, 2005.
Newman, Elizabeth Terese. *Biography of a Hacienda: Work and Revolution in Rural Mexico*. Tucson: University of Arizona Press, 2014. http://site.ebrary.com/id/10843927.
Niebylski, Dianna C. "Gramáticas capitalistas, retóricas contrahegemónicas y la prensa obrera chilena: *Mano de Obra* de Diamela Eltit." *Pobreza y precariedad en el imaginario latinoamericano del siglo XXI*. Ed. Stephen Buttes and Dianna Niebylski. Santiago: Cuarto Propio, 2016. 415–457.
———. *Humoring Resistance: Laughter and the Excessive Body in Contemporary Latin American Women's Fiction*. Albany: State University of New York Press, 2004.
Niebylski, Dianna C., and Patrick O'Connor. *Latin American Icons: Fame across Borders*. Nashville: Vanderbilt University Press, 2014.
*Noticiario panamericano, no. 562: Actualidades argentinas*. Dir. Adolfo Rossi. Biblioteca Nacional Mariano Moreno, 1951–1952. https://catalogo.bn.gov.ar/F/?func=direct&doc_number=001166295&local_base=GENER.
"Omar Torrijos." *Encyclopedia of World Biography*, 2nd ed., vol. 15. Gale, 2004. 269–270. https://link.gale.com/apps/doc/CX3404706431/GVRL?u=iulib_fw&sid=bookmark-GVRL&xid=78af63ce.
Páez Varela, Alejandro, and Álvaro Delgado. *Izquierda (1923–2023): La Terca Travesía*. Mexico City: Grijalbo, 2023.
Pereira, Armando, Claudia Albarrán, Juan Antonio Rosado, and Angélica Tornero. *Diccionario de la literatura mexicana, siglo XX*. Mexico City: UNAM, Ediciones Coyoacán, 2004.
Perón, Juan Domingo. *La fuerza es el derecho de las bestias*. 1956. https://elortiba.org.
Pilcher, Jeffrey M. *Cantinflas and the Chaos of Mexican Modernity*. Wilmington, DE: Scholarly Resources, 2001.
Pippin, Robert B. *The Persistence of Subjectivity: On the Kantian Aftermath*. Cambridge: Cambridge University Press, 2005.
Pizzorno, Pablo. "Orígenes, trayectorias y radicalización de la identidad antiperonista durante el primer peronismo (1943–1955) (Un volumen)." PhD thesis, Universidad de Buenos Aires, 2018.
Poblete, Juan, ed. *New Approaches to Latin American Studies: Culture and Power*. London: Routledge, 2017.

Pozzi, Pablo A. *¡Usted es comunista! Clase, cultura y política en la Argentina contemporánea*. Prometeo Editorial, 2021. https://doi.org/10.2307/jj.12865288.

Pring-Mill, Robert. "El Neruda de las *Odas elementales*." *Coloquio Internacional sobre Pablo Neruda*. 1979.

Ramírez, Emma. "Ilustración y dominación: El Periquillo Sarniento bajo el Siglo de las Luces." *Revista de Humanidades: Tecnológico de Monterrey*, no. 21 (2006): 65–103.

Ramos, Julio. *Divergent Modernities: Culture and Politics in 19th Century Latin America*. Durham, NC: Duke University Press, 2001.

Rancière, Jacques. *Disagreement: Politics and Philosophy*. Minneapolis: University of Minnesota Press, 1999.

———. *The Emancipated Spectator*. Trans. Gregory Elliott. New York: Verso, 2009.

Rashkin, Elissa. *Women Filmmakers in Mexico: The Country of Which We Dream*. Austin: University of Texas Press, 2001.

Ravallion, Martin. *The Economics of Poverty: History, Measurement, and Policy*. Oxford: Oxford University Press, 2016.

Reber, Dierdra. *Coming to Our Senses: Affect and an Order of Things for Global Culture*. New York: Columbia University Press, 2016.

Reyes, Alfonso. "El Periquillo Sarnierto y la crítica mexicana." *Simpatías y Diferencias: Tercera Serie. Obras completas*, vol. 4. Mexico City: Fondo de Cultura Económica, 1956. 169–178.

Rivera, Diego. *Mural del Teatro de los Insurgentes*. 1953. Mexico City.

Rodríguez, Ileana, ed. *The Latin American Subaltern Studies Reader*. Durham, NC: Duke University Press, 2001.

Rohrbach, John. "Introduction." *Reframing the New Topographics*. Ed. Greg Foster-Rice and John Rohrbach. Chicago: Center for American Places at Columbia College Chicago, 2010. xiii–xxv.

*Rojo amanecer*. Dir. Jorge Fons. Edición limitada, Quality Films, 2000.

Romero, Luis Alberto. *Breve Historia Contemporánea de la Argentina*. 2nd ed. Fondo De Cultura Económica, 2005.

———. *A History of Argentina in the Twentieth Century*. Trans. James. P. Brennan. University Park: Pennsylvania State University Press, 2013.

Rulfo, Juan. *El llano en llamas*. Madrid: Cátedra, 1985.

Salinas C., Maximiliano. *El Chile de Juan Verdejo: El humor politico de* Topaze *1931–70*. Santiago de Chile: Editorial Universidad de Santiago de Chile, 2011.

Salvesen, Britt. "New Topographics." *New Topographics*. Robert Adams et al. 3rd ed. Center for Creative Photography, University of Arizona, 2013.

———. "'Real Estate Opportunities': Commercial Photography as Conceptual Source in New Topographics." *Reframing the New Topographics*. Ed. Greg Foster-Rice and John Rohrbach. Chicago: Center for American Places at Columbia College Chicago, 2010. 71–86.

Sánchez-Prado, Ignacio M. *Screening Neoliberalism: Transforming Mexican Cinema, 1988–2012*. Nashville: Vanderbilt University Press, 2014.

Sarlo, Beatriz, and Carlos Altamirano. *La batalla de las ideas (1943–1973)*. Buenos Aires: Ariel, 2001.

Sassen, Saskia. *Expulsions: Brutality and Complexity in the Global Economy*. Cambridge, MA: Belknap, 2018.

Sater, William F., and Simon Collier. *A History of Chile 1808–2018*. 3rd ed. Cambridge: Cambridge University Press, 2023.

Sauri, Emilio. "'A la pinche modernidad': Literary Form and the End of History in Roberto Bolaño's *Los detectives salvajes*." *MLN* 125.2 (2010): 406–432.
———. "Autonomy after Autonomy, or, The Novel beyond Nation: Roberto Bolaño's *2666*." *Canadian Review of Comparative Literature / Revue Canadienne de Littérature Comparée* 42.4 (2015): 396–409.
———. "'Dickens + MP3 ÷ Balzac + JPEG' or, Art and the Value of Innovation in the Contemporary Mexican Novel." *Mexican Literature in Theory*. Ed. Ignacio M. Sánchez-Prado. New York: Bloomsbury, 2018. 279–294.
———. "Faulkner and His Brothers." *Studies in American Fiction* 40.2 (2013): 259–283.
Sayers Peden, Margaret. *Selected Odes of Pablo Neruda*. Berkeley: University of California Press, 1990.
Sen, Amartya. *Collective Choice and Social Welfare*. Expanded ed. Cambridge, MA: Harvard University Press, 2017.
———. *Development as Freedom*. New York: Knopf, 1999.
———. "The Political Economy of Hunger: On Reasoning and Participation." *Common Knowledge* 25.1 (2019): 348–356. https://muse.jhu.edu/article/727152.
———. *Poverty and Famines: An Essay on Entitlement and Deprivation*. 1981. New York: Oxford University Press, 1982.
Sicard, Alain. *El pensamiento poético de Pablo Neruda*. Madrid: Editorial Greidos, 1981.
Siraganian, Lisa. *Modernism and the Meaning of Corporate Persons*. New York: Oxford University Press, 2022.
———. *Modernism's Other Work: The Art Object's Political Life*. New York: Oxford University Press, 2015.
———. "Stateless Regionalism and Corporate Power: Willa Cather's Public Relations Novel." *American Literary History* 35.1 (2023): 126–142. https://doi.org/10.1093/alh/ajac180.
Stavans, Ilan. *The Riddle of Cantinflas: Essays on Hispanic Popular Culture*. Rev. ed. Albuquerque: University of New Mexico Press, 2012.
Steinberg, Samuel. "Originary Debt (1816)." *Revista Hispánica Moderna* 66.1 (2013): 43–56.
———. *Photopoetics at Tlatelolco: Afterimages of Mexico, 1968*. Austin: University of Texas Press, 2016.
Tcach, César. "El parto de un desencuentro: El duelo peronismo-comunismo en Argentina (1943–1955)." *Nuevo Mundo/Mundos Nuevos* (2020). https://doi.org/10.4000/nuevomundo.82039.
Thornton, Niamh. "Re-framing Mexican Women's Filmmaking: The Case of Marcela Fernández Violante." *Latin American Women Filmmakers: Production, Politics, Poetics*. Ed. Deborah Martin and Deborah Shaw. New York: Bloomsbury, 2019. 197–216. https://doi.org/10.5040/9781350987012.ch-008.
Torres Estrada, Andrés Camilo. "A pesar de la muralla y los libros." *Hallazgos* 12.24 (2015): 125–137.
Wacquant, Loïc. "Bourdieu, Foucault, and the Penal State in the Neoliberal Era." *Foucault and Neoliberalism*. Ed. Daniel Zamora and Michael C. Behrent. Cambridge: Polity, 2016. 114–133.
———. *Punishing the Poor: The Neoliberal Government of Social Insecurity*. Durham, NC: Duke University Press, 2009.
———. "The Rise of Advanced Marginality: Notes on Its Nature and Implications." *Acta Sociologica* 39.2 (1996): 121–139.
———. *Urban Outcasts: A Comparative Sociology of Advanced Marginality*. Cambridge: Polity, 2008.

Wheelock, Carter. "Borges and the 'Death' of the Text." *Hispanic Review* 53.2 (1985): 151–161.
Williams, Gareth. *The Mexican Exception: Sovereignty, Police, and Democracy*. London: Palgrave Macmillan, 2011.
———. *The Other Side of the Popular: Neoliberalism and Subalternity in Latin America*. Durham, NC: Duke University Press, 2002. Kindle ed.
Williams, Raymond. *Marxism and Literature*. Oxford: Oxford University Press, 1977.
"Ya no le canta al pueblo." *Topaze* 22.1113 (February 12, 1954): 4.
Yáñez, Agustín, ed. *Crónicas de la Conquista*. Mexico City: UNAM, 1939.
———. *El Pensador Mexicano*. Mexico City: UNAM, 1962.
Yurkievich, Saúl. "Prólogo." *Obras completas*. Ed. Hernán Loyola. Barcelona: RBA, 2005. 9–79.
Zamora, Daniel, and Michael C. Behrent. *Foucault and Neoliberalism*. Cambridge: Polity, 2016.
Zelson, Louis G. "Francisco Monterde (1894–)." *The Americas* 10.2 (October 1953): 159–178.

# Index


Acosta, Abraham, 171n19, 171n21
Adorno, Theodor W., 24
aesthetic transparency, 71–72, 74–77, 79–84, 86–88, 92
affect, 17–20, 100, 112, 171n23
*¡Ahí está el detalle!*, 33, 48–56, 63
Amado, Jorge, 7–8
antitheatricality: in Borges, 122–123, 128–147; in *Cananea*, 151–159; contrasted with formlessness in Lizardi and Cantinflas, 64–68; contrasted with Neruda's aesthetic transparency, 72–88; defined, 26–29, 171–172n2; and *History of a Document*, 104–108; in *Rojo amanecer*, 93, 97, 108–117. *See also* Caillebotte, Gustave; *Cananea*; Chardin, Jean-Baptiste-Siméon; Fried, Michael; Michaels, Walter Benn; New Topographics photographers; poverty; *Rojo amanecer*; theory of the apartment
articulation, 13–15, 17–20, 94–95, 102, 148–149; and the balcony effect, 18; contrasted with posthegemony and modulation, 22; defined, 13, 17, 170n18; and the empty signifier, 15; and hegemony, 22–23, 171n19
*Así es mi tierra*, 56
autogestión, 89, 91–92, 102–107, 110; defined, 89

balcony effect: and the Boom, 22–23; defined as movement from formlessness to form, 18; and la mexicanidad, 48, 52–53, 96, 114, 152, 154–155; and Peronism, 9, 11–12, 14, 17–19, 122, 128, 147; and shot-reverse-shot structure, 18, 51–54, 156–157. *See also* antitheatricality; articulation; formlessness; hegemony; Peronism; posthegemony; theatricality
Balderston, Daniel, 136, 174n5 (chap. 4)
Bartra, Roger, 54, 61, 168n4; and the "Mexican Office," 49, 96, 99
Bauman, Zygmunt, 167n1
Beasley-Murray, Jon: and the balcony effect, 52–53; and the critique of cultural studies, 170n18; and the multitude, 171n24; and posthegemony theory, 17–23, 95–96, 148, 170n19
Becher, Bernd and Hilla, 127, 145–146
Beckman, Ericka, 6, 15, 21, 169n13. *See also* capital fictions
Boom, Latin American, 7–9, 14, 19, 22–23. *See also* balcony effect
Borges, Jorge Luis: and balcony effect, 122, 128, 147; and Evaristo Carriego, 129, 134, 136, 144; and *malevos*, 129; contrasted with Neruda, 119–122; and Perón, 119, 122, 126, 131–133, 136–137, 139, 142–143, 147; view of poverty as historical social relation, 130–133
Borges, Jorge Luis, individual works: "Borges and I," 118–122, 124, 127, 129, 131, 133, 143; *El informe de Brodie*, 122–124, 134; "El otro duelo," 132–136; "Juan Muraña," 129, 134–137, 146; "La muralla y los libros,"

Borges, Jorge Luis, individual works (cont.) 140–145; "La señora mayor," 130–131, 133–134, 137, 139, 143; "Mutations," 121–122, 128–129, 131, 136; "Pierre Menard, Author of the *Quixote*," 119–121, 127, 130, 133, 138, 143. *See also* crisis in representation; indexicality; New Topographics photographers; photography
Bosteels, Bruno, 102–103, 109, 116
Bourdieu, Pierre, 167n1
Brown, Nicholas, 64–68, 76

Caillebotte, Gustave, 110–112, 116
*Cananea*, 150–159
Cantinflas, 33–34, 48–58, 60–64, 66, 90
capital fictions, 6, 8, 10, 12–13, 16, 21, 158. *See also* Beckman, Ericka
capitalism, 5–16, 18, 21–22, 29, 126, 169n13; and Argentina, 123, 141–142, 146; and Cantinflas, 54, 58, 61, 64, 67; and Neruda, 69–73, 75–79, 82, 85, 87; and the PRI, 33–34, 44, 46, 92, 95, 97, 100–101, 103, 116; and Fernández Violante, 148, 150–152, 154–155, 157–158. *See also* commodity
Castro, Fidel, 9, 14, 169nn12–13
Chardin, Jean-Baptiste-Siméon, 28
climatological metaphors, 20–21, 111
commodity, 6, 8, 10, 26, 28, 125–126; and cinema, 48–49, 55–56; defined, 64–65; and Neruda, 71, 75–79, 83, 85, 87–88
Concha, Jaime, 173n4
"Constitución política de una república imaginaria," 32, 36, 37, 172n7
crisis in representation, 9, 20–24, 26–27, 29; and Borges, 123, 128; defined, 16, 21–22; and Neruda, 79; and the PRI, 61, 116–117; and Fernández Violante, 159
crisis of 1956, 7–8, 83, 87, 169n11
crisis of representation, 23, 108

Dawes, Greg, 70–71, 74–75, 81–83, 87–88, 169n11, 174n5 (chap. 2); and Sicard, 76–79. See also *Multiforme y comprometido*; *Verses Against the Darkness*
dedifferentiation, 64, 67, 72, 76–77, 79, 86; as related to poverty, 40–49; as related to the commodity, 52–60. *See also* formlessness
dialectic, the, 71, 76, 78, 83
*Disagreement*, 90–91, 99
Di Stefano, Eugenio, 149, 171n19, 171n21, 171n23, 173n3
Dove, Patrick, 141–142, 146
Draper, Susana, 104–109, 112–113

*El grito*, 149
*El llano en llamas*, 25–26
*El periquillo sarniento*, 32–48, 57–68; in comparison with *¡Ahí está el detalle!*, 48–56; and formlessness without form, 44–46, 53–55
*El señor fotógrafo*, 63
*Emancipated Specator, The*, 90–91, 106, 116
empty signifier, 13, 15, 23

Fernández Violante, Marcela, 149–159. See also *Cananea*
Fons, Jorge, 93, 96–98, 100–02, 108–110, 112–117. See also *Rojo amanecer*
form, 11, 13, 15–16, 18–19, 58; in Borges, 118–123, 139–147; defined, 4, 5–9, 22–27; in Fons, 97, 100–117; in Lizardi, 32–33, 35, 44–45, 47, 62–68; in Fernández-Violante, 151–159. *See also* Fried, Michael; Larsen, Neil; Michaels, Walter Benn; New Topographics photographers; theory of the apartment
formlessness: and Beasley-Murray, 17–21; in Cantinflas, 48–56; defined, 2, 4, 5–9, 22, 27; and Laclau and Mouffe, 13–17, 19–20; in Lizardi, 33–35, 37–38, 42–43, 45–46; in Mexico, 1968, 89–96; in Neruda, 72–88, 119, 121; and populism, 10–13; without form defined, 44–45, 55. *See also* aesthetic transparency; la mexicanidad (Mexicanism); posthegemony; poverty: defined as experience of formlessness; ways of seeing, being, doing, saying, and knowing
Fourth Cinema, 104
Fried, Michael: definition of antitheatricality, 27–29, 97, 149, 172–173n2; and objecthood, 65, 68, 76, 83, 92, 119–120; and photography, 125, 145–146; and the theory of the apartment, 110–113, 116

Gilly, Adolfo, 109

Hardt, Michael and Antonio Negri, 171n24
Hatfield, Charles, 121, 171n21, 171n23

hegemony, 13–14, 22; contrasted with posthegemony, 16–20, 94–96; defined, 170–171n19
*History of a Document*, 106–109, 112–113

indexicality, 127–128
infrapolitics, 93

Jäger, Anton, 168n2, 168n7, 169n9
Jusiticialism, 10–11, 13, 16, 18–19, 169n12, 169n14. *See also* Peronism

Laclau, Ernesto, 170nn18–19, 171n22; and articulation, 67, 95, 148–149; critique of, 13–23
la mexicanidad (Mexicanism), 2, 32–34, 38, 100, 155; defined, 31; as the "Mexican Office," 48, 55, 99. *See also* Bartra, Roger; pelado; PRI (Partido Revolucionario Institucional); Steinberg, Samuel; ways of seeing, being, doing, saying, and knowing; Yáñez, Agustín
Larsen, Neil: *Determinations*, 25–26; *Modernism and Hegemony*, 13–17, 23–25, 27–28, 61, 116, 148, 168n5, 170n19; *Reading North by South*, 7–9, 14, 22. *See also* crisis in representation
Lash, Scott, 76, 171n19
Lewis, Oscar, 169n9
Leys, Ruth, 171n23
Lizardi, José Joaquín Fernández de, 30–49, 54–68, 109, 172nn4–5. *See also* "Constitución política de una república imaginaria"; *El periquillo sarniento*; "Los paseos de la Verdad"; Yáñez, Agustín
"Los paseos de la Verdad," 32, 172n6
Louis, Annick, 127, 134, 136

meteorological metaphors, 20–21, 111
Michaels, Walter Benn, 76, 149; on antitheatricality, 173n2; on modernism, 169n8, 169n13; on photography, 174n2, 174n4
modernism: approaches to, 169n8; and autonomy, 97, 106; defined, 5, 7–9, 14, 19, 24–28; and Neruda, 71, 74, 77; relation to hegemony and postmodernism, 170n19. *See also* Fried, Michael; Larsen, Neil; Michaels, Walter Benn; Pippin, Robert; Siraganian, Lisa
Monsiváis, Carlos, 53–57, 60
Monterde, Francisco, 30–31, 38, 43, 62–63, 171n1, 172n2 (chap. 1)
Moreiras, Alberto, 171n21
*Multiforme y comprometido*, 81, 87, 169n11
multitude, 18, 20–21, 52, 93, 95, 171n24

Neruda, Pablo: and "Discurso de Estocolmo" (Nobel speech), 75; and *Geografía infructuosa*, 87–88; and *Las manos del día*, 78; and view of poverty as transhistorical experience, 79–80, 85–88. *See also* aesthetic transparency; *Odas elementales*
New Topographics photographers, 123–128, 145, 147, 174n3
Niebylski, Dianna C., 48, 167n1, 168n6, 174n1 (chap. 4)

objecthood, 65, 76, 83–84, 88, 92, 122, 127–128, 131; defined, 172–173n2
O'Connor, Patrick, 174n1 (chap. 4)
*Odas elementales*: "The Invisible Man," 71–74, 77–78, 80–82, 84–86, 88, 120; "Ode to Bread," 73, 75; "Ode to Clarity," 74; "Ode to Numbers," 84–85, 88; "Ode to Poverty," 85–86, 88; "Ode to the Simple Man," 80, 82–83, 85

partition of the perceptible, 90. *See also* ways of seeing, being, doing, saying, and knowing
"Paso del Norte" (*El llano en llamas*), 25–26
pelado, 33, 42–50, 52, 54–58, 61, 65, 67, 168n4; contrasted with peladito, 33, 48, 52, 54; and the PRI; and 1968 student-popular movement, 90, 92, 96, 99, 103. *See also* Bartra, Roger; Monsiváis, Carlos; Williams, Gareth; Yáñez, Agustín
Perón, Eva (Evita), 11–14, 17–18
Perón, Juan Domingo, 9–14, 17, 143, 169n12, 170n15, 170n17
Peronism: and the balcony effect, 18–19; and Borges, 119, 122, 126, 132–133, 136, 143, 147, 148; in comparison with the PRI, 52–55, 60; defined, 2, 10–13, 168n4, 169n14; as related to Neruda, 172n1. *See also* Jusiticialism
photography, 118, 121, 123–128, 145–147
Pilcher, Jeffrey, 48–49, 55
Pippin, Robert, 169n8

populism, 150–152, 154–156; and aesthetic transparency (Neruda), 71–80, 88; defined as "balcony effect," 52–53, 96; and empty signifier/articulation (Laclau), 13–20, 22–23, 67, 91, 94–95, 102, 105, 99, 148; and la mexicanidad (PRI), 34, 48, 59, 66; and Peronism, 8, 19, 21, 55, 139; poverty (formlessness) and the "third position" (alternative modernity), 29, 46, 55. *See also* formlessness
Posa Films, 54–55, 63–64
posthegemony, 17–22, 52, 89–100, 104, 148–149, 170n19
poverty: defined as experience of formlessness, 2–4, 8–10, 16–17, 19–23, 33–34, 36–39, 80–87, 91–93, 100, 103–104, 106–107, 118, 120–122, 144, 148, 172n4; defined as objective historical social relation, 1, 4, 7, 21, 24, 29, 33, 60, 65, 92, 100, 117, 128, 159; economic approaches to, 167n2, 168n3; sociological approaches to, 167n1; and subaltern studies, 170n19, 171n21. *See also* Sen, Amartya; Jäger, Anton; multitude; Wacquant, Loïc; Zamora, Daniel
PRI (Partido Revolucionario Institucional): and relation to mexicanidad defined, 2, 33–34; structures in the 1960s, 89–91, 93, 96, 98; utilization of the experience of formlessness (1940s and 1950s), 38, 43, 48–49, 55, 60–61, 65; and Fernández Violante's cinematic response (1970s), 149–151. *See also* la mexicanidad (Mexicanism); Peronism

Rancière, Jacques, 90–92, 95, 99, 105–106, 116, 141. See also *Disagreement*; *Emancipated Specator*; ways of seeing, being, doing, saying, and knowing
Rashkin, Elissa, 149–150
Ravallion, Martin, 168nn2–3
Revueltas, José, 102, 106
Reyes, Alfonso, 34, 62–65, 67–68
Rivera, Diego, 53, 63
*Rojo amanecer*, 93, 96–101, 104, 107–117
Rulfo, Juan, 25–26

Sánchez-Prado, Ignacio M., 101–102
Sassen, Saskia, 167n1
Sauri, Emilio, 149, 162, 171n19, 171n23
Sen, Amartya, 168n7
Sicard, Alain, 76–79, 82–84, 87, 174n5 (chap. 2)
Siraganian, Lisa, 169n8, 174n1 (concl.)
socialism, 1, 5–14, 21–22, 29, 44–46, 58, 170n19. *See also* crisis of 1956
socialist realism, 6–8, 10, 12, 169n11
Stavans, Ilan, 54
Steinberg, Samuel: and Lizardi, 34, 49; and the post-Mexicanism of the student-popular movement of 1968, 89–102, 112–114
Struth, Thomas, 145–146

theatricality, 92, 97, 110, 119–122, 124, 126–127, 130, 133–134, 141–142, 144; defined, 27–29; related to poverty, 72, 76, 80–89; related to the commodity, 61–68. *See also* objecthood
theory of the apartment, 112, 156
Third Cinema, 101, 104, 150–151, 155
Thornton, Niamh, 150
Tlatelolco Massacre, 89–94, 97–104, 109, 113–117
*Topaze*, 69–70, 172n1
Torrijos, Omar, 9, 14, 169n12

*Verses Against the Darkness*, 70–71, 74–77

Wacquant, Loïc, 167n1, 168n5, 168n7
ways of seeing, being, doing, saying, and knowing: and Cantinflas, 52; and la mexicanidad, 49, 55, 96; and Rancière, 90; and relation to poverty, 3; and Yáñez, 32, 36–37, 39–42, 45, 58, 60. *See also* form; formlessness
Williams, Gareth, 33, 54, 94–96, 148, 171n21

Yáñez, Agustín, 90, 93, 100, 171n2, 172nn3–4, 172n7; and formlessness, 33–39, 41–48, 58–61, 65; on the Lizardi and the pelado, 30–52, 54, 56–62, 64–68. *See also* poverty: defined as an experience of formlessness; PRI (Partido Revolucionario Institucional)
Yurkievich, Saúl, 74–75

Zamora, Daniel, 168n2, 168n7, 169n9
Zhdanovism, 6. *See also* socialist realism

## About the Author

STEPHEN BUTTES is associate professor of Spanish at Purdue University Fort Wayne. He writes about aesthetics and politics in Latin America. He is co-editor (with Dianna Niebylski) of *Pobreza y precariedad en el imaginario latinoamericano del siglo XXI*. His writing about teaching has appeared in various venues, including most recently in the volume *Approaches to Teaching the Work of Jorge Luis Borges*. He is editor-in-chief and a founding editor of the peer-reviewed journal *FORMA: A Journal of Latin American Criticism & Theory* (formajournal.org).